DATE DUE

MY 21 '97			
AP 1 '98			
DE 9 '98			
MR 18 '99			
DE 11 '99			
DE 18 '00			
DE 20 '00			
MY 30 '01			
NO 01			
DE 18 '03			

Americans View Crime and Justice

Americans View Crime and Justice

A National Public Opinion Survey

Timothy J. Flanagan
Dennis R. Longmire
editors

SAGE Publications
International Educational and Professional Publisher
Thousand Oaks   London   New Delhi

2455 Teller Road
Thousand Oaks, California 91320
E-mail: order@sagepub.com

SAGE Publications Ltd.
6 Bonhill Street
London EC2A 4PU
United Kingdom

SAGE Publications India Pvt. Ltd.
M-32 Market
Greater Kailash I
New Delhi 110 048 India

Printed in the United States of America

Library of Congress Cataloging-in-Publication Data

Flanagan, Timothy J.
    Americans view crime and justice: A national public opinion
survey /editors, Timothy J. Flanagan, Dennis R. Longmire.
      p. cm.
    Includes bibliographical references.
    ISBN 0-7619-0340-2 (alk. paper). — ISBN 0-7619-0341-0 (pbk.: alk. paper)
    1. Criminal justice, Administration of—United States—Public opinion.
    2. Crime—United States—Public opinion. 3. United States—Public
opinion. I. Flanagan, Timothy J. II. Longmire, Dennis R.
    HV9950.A495 1996
                                                            96-4513

This book is printed on acid-free paper.

96 97 98 99 10 9 8 7 6 5 4 3 2 1

Production Editor: Gillian Dickens   Typesetter: Marion S. Warren

Contents

Preface

 Virtually everyone who studies the scholarship on public attitudes about crime and criminal justice develops a keen sense of
the shortcomings of that knowledge base. These limitations are the
product of at least two independent forces. First, the opinion survey
"business" in the United States is fueled primarily by the interests (and
dollars) of the business and political sectors. The largest single component of the survey research industry in the United States is the market
research sector. Perhaps the fastest *growing* segment of the industry is
political polling, as candidates ranging from presidential contenders to
local school board aspirants rush to tailor their message to the presumed
interests of the electorate. It is not surprising that the subjects of these
client-driven surveys often do not include crime and justice issues in
any meaningful way.

Second, criminologists themselves have given insufficient attention
to public opinion as a critical element of the study of crime and justice.
Too often the views of the public are dismissed as uninformed, mercu-
rial, and reactionary. Crime scholars, program developers, and justice
agency administrators are only beginning to appreciate the relevance
and importance of public attitudes, beliefs, and opinions in discussions

of crime control policy. The President's Commission on Law Enforcement and Administration of Justice (1967) understood the relationship of public opinion and public policy more than a quarter century ago. The commission concluded that "what America does about crime depends ultimately upon how Americans see crime" (p. 49). We undertook this project in the hope of providing a clearer picture of "how Americans see crime" and criminal justice.

This book originated in our individual work on public opinion about crime and justice issues. Dennis Longmire has directed the Survey Research Center in the College of Criminal Justice at Sam Houston State University for many years. Since 1977, the Survey Research Center has conducted the Texas Crime Poll, an annual statewide survey of citizen attitudes toward criminal justice policies and agencies, fear of crime, victimization experience, and related topics. Timothy Flanagan participated in the development of the *Sourcebook of Criminal Justice Statistics* for more than 17 years and focused on Section 2 of that volume, "Public Attitudes Toward Crime and Criminal Justice-Related Topics" for most of that period. The occasion to join these separate experiences with the chance to design, conduct, and analyze a national survey was a real opportunity. The National Opinion Survey on Crime and Justice—1995 (NOSCJ) enabled us to capitalize on our previous work and indulge ourselves in asking questions that we have always wanted to ask.

From its inception, the NOSCJ was a collaborative effort. Barbara Sims and Vincent West, doctoral students in the College of Criminal Justice and staff members of the Survey Research Center, contributed to the development of the NOSCJ questionnaire and helped select the survey contractor. The staff of the Public Policy Research Institute (PPRI) at Texas A&M University were professional and constructive partners in finalizing the survey questionnaire and collecting the data. We are especially grateful to James Dyer, Clay Hanks, and Rickie Fletcher of PPRI for their vast experience and expertise in survey methods. We appreciate the help of Doris Ulrich, Rosa Coss, Jim Sessions, and David Epps of Sam Houston State University.

Of course, we owe our largest debt to the colleagues who agreed to analyze the NOSCJ data and contribute chapters to this volume. These scholars, most of whom are associated in some way with the College of Criminal Justice at Sam Houston State University, signed on when the NOSCJ was in the "idea" stage, and they devoted many hours to the project. Most of them wish they had twice as many questions in the final questionnaire, twice as many pages allotted to their chapters, and half as many revisions and suggestions from the editors. The halls of the

Criminal Justice Center have been enlivened in recent months with animated discussions about the project, analytic methods, and findings. The volume benefited tremendously from the collegial discussion of draft materials held at a daylong authors' conference in late September, 1995. We each left the conference with a long list of suggestions and comments that improved the final product.

Finally, we deeply appreciate the financial support of this and other projects at the Criminal Justice Center by the Legislature of the State of Texas. Additional financial support for the NOSCJ was provided by the Houston Endowment Inc., a long-term supporter of the academic and professional education programs of the Criminal Justice Center.

Points of view or opinions expressed in this volume are the contributors' and do not represent the official policy or positions of the state of Texas or of the Houston Endowment, Inc. We have shared the findings of the NOSCJ and a companion survey of Texas citizens with criminal justice administrators and policymakers in several forums and have integrated the project into the center's continuing professional education programs. We hope that presentation and discussion of the findings assist decision makers in understanding the public perspective on the important criminal justice issues and decisions that face Texas and the nation.

We also hope that our work generates more interest in survey research on citizen perspectives on crime and justice concerns. In our view, discussions of alternative crime control policies and programs would benefit from periodic close *listening* to the views of Americans. We need more frequent, comprehensive, and nonpartisan assessments of public opinion on this critical domestic policy issue. Scholars who bemoan the direction and philosophy of recent crime control efforts often assume, as do political leaders, that these initiatives and statutes are responsive to what the public "wants," or even "demands." Too often, these assumptions are made without serious consideration of the range and diversity of public opinion on crime and criminal justice. We hope that *Americans View Crime and Justice* contributes to a better understanding of public sentiment on these issues and to a fuller discussion of the policy options available to address the challenge of crime in the years ahead.

Timothy J. Flanagan
Dennis R. Longmire

Public Opinion
on Crime and Justice
History, Development, and Trends

TIMOTHY J. FLANAGAN

The idea that public sentiment about political, social, and economic issues should be taken into account by governing officials has been a mainstay of citizen expectations in democracies for centuries. This view is summarized in the observation that

> the general public is especially competent, probably more competent than any other group—elitist, expert or otherwise—to determine the basic ends of public policy, to choose top policy makers, to appraise the results of public policy, and to say what, in the final analysis, is fair, just, and moral. (Childs, 1965, p. 350)

This faith in the judgment and temperament of the people assumes that political, social, economic, and moral issues are "common concerns" of the citizenry and therefore that a concept of *public opinion*, defined as "the shared opinions of a collection of individuals on a common concern" (Yeric & Todd, 1983, p. 4) exists, can be identified, and can be communicated to decision makers. In America in the late 1990s, the fact that issues of crime, delinquency, and criminal justice are among the

1

most salient common concerns of the citizenry can be easily established. Understanding the dimensions and form of public opinion on these concerns and the implications of these views for the development of rational and effective public policy in relation to crime and justice is the concern of this volume.

The Voice of the People

In *Numbered Voices: How Opinion Polling Has Shaped American Politics*, Susan Herbst (1993) observed that numbers obtained from surveys of the public are powerful "democratic symbols" in contemporary America. She argued that

> the reason that polls are so pervasive is that they work symbolically on two levels at once: They are scientifically derived data, *and* they are representative of general public sentiment. Sampling itself is a democratic notion. So while there are (and no doubt, will always be) complaints about and assaults on polls in public discourse, these data are omnipresent symbols nonetheless. (p. 38)

Herbst (1993, p. 49) reminds us that sample surveys of the public are the most recent in a long line of mechanisms through which the public makes its will, preferences, concerns, and reactions known to those who govern. Earlier methods of expressing the public view included oratory and rhetoric (since at least the 5th century B.C.), petitions (dating from the late 17th century), revolutionary movements, strikes, general elections, and letters to the editor.

The citizenry's desire to make its will known and its leaders' desire to understand the will of the people should be reciprocal, for, as political scientist V. O. Key, Jr. (1961) wrote, "Unless mass views have some place in the shaping of policy, all the talk about democracy is nonsense" (p. 7). George Washington worried about how best to determine the public will on matters confronting the new democracy, and he recognized that "it is on great occasions only and after time has been given for cool and deliberate reflection that the real voice of the people can be known" (1796, cited in Roll & Cantril, 1972, p. 118). Abraham Lincoln wrestled with what Tocqueville called the "tyranny of democracy" and concluded that while acting as their [the people's] representative, I shall be governed by their will on all subjects upon which I have the means of knowing what their will is; and upon all others, I shall do what my own judgment teaches me will best advance their interests. (1836, cited in Roll & Cantril, 1972, p. 140)

Development of Modern Opinion Polls

The modern sample survey is a direct descendant of "straw polls," which were a fixture of American political life in the 1820s. Moore (1992) describes straw polls and other forms of preelection polling as a "time honored sport" in America (p. 33). He reported that the first published presidential poll was a straw vote taken in Delaware and published in *The Harrisburg Pennsylvanian* on July 24, 1824 (Andrew Jackson defeated John Quincy Adams, 335-169). Straw polls became standard fare in newspaper coverage of elections throughout the latter half of the 19th century and into the 20th, until the *Literary Digest* fiasco of 1936.

The *Literary Digest* distributed ballots concerning public attitudes toward prohibition in the 1920s. By 1936, the huge *Digest* poll had correctly predicted each presidential election winner since 1920. As Bradburn and Sudman (1988) recount,

> Using methods that it had used earlier, the *Literary Digest* mailed ten million ballots to households listed in telephone directories or state auto registrations. Of course, there were very large biases in favor of upper-income households, since in 1936 lower-income households did not have telephones or cars. Of the mailed ballots, 2.4 million were returned, an impressively large number but only a quarter of all mailed. Again, non-response biases strongly favored those who were the most committed Republicans. The *Literary Digest* predicted that Alfred Landon, the Republican candidate, would get 57 percent of the major party vote. In fact he received only 38.5 percent. (p. 19)

The failure of the *Digest's* massive mail survey to accurately predict the 1936 presidential election outcome was exacerbated by the fact that each of the "founding fathers" of modern public opinion polling, George H. Gallup, Elmo Roper, and Archibald Crossley, correctly predicted Franklin D. Roosevelt's reelection. Indeed, Gallup had publicly predicted the failure of the *Literary Digest* poll in advance and explained why the biases inherent in its methods would lead to inaccurate predictions (Roll & Cantril, 1972, p. 10).

The years leading to World War II witnessed a great expansion in the development and use of survey research by political leaders, government agencies, the media, and others. Sudman and Bradburn (1987) recounted this history on the occasion of the 50th anniversary of the journal *Public Opinion Quarterly* in 1987. They observed that the U.S. Department of Agriculture, the Bureau of Labor Statistics, and the Census Bureau were the early leaders in the development of survey methods. During the war, the Research Branch of the U.S. Army, under the direction of University of Chicago professor Samuel Stouffer, produced more than 300 reports on attitudes of military personnel. This research program yielded important studies of mental health, stress, morale, and other issues of central concern to social scientists during and after the war.

University-based polling organizations such as the Bureau of Applied Social Research at Columbia University (1940), the National Opinion Research Center at the University of Chicago (1941), and the Survey Research Center of the University of Michigan (1946) provided a critical mass of scholars for the development of survey methodology. These centers were complemented by the proliferation of state-level polls such as the Texas Poll (1940), the Iowa Poll (1943), the Minnesota Poll (1944), and the California Poll (1946) in conjunction with major newspapers. The leading professional organization of survey researchers, the American Association for Public Opinion Research, was established in 1946 (Sudman & Bradburn, 1987).

The infant polling industry received an embarrassing setback in 1948, when all three national polling organizations (Gallup, Roper, and Crossley) predicted Thomas E. Dewey's victory over Harry Truman. Truman received 49.5% of the total presidential vote to Dewey's 45.1%. The postmortem analyses of "what went wrong" identified several major problems, including stopping interviewing too soon prior to election day and failure to detect the leanings of undecided respondents. Improvements to election polling designed to counter these problems include the ubiquitous "tracking polls" that monitor shifts in public perceptions and sentiments about candidates, more sophisticated area sampling methods, and others.

Much wider use of surveys and polls inside and outside of electoral politics has characterized the period from 1960 to the present. These include regular surveys that monitor employment and other economic indicators, health care use patterns, self-reported drug use, and the National Criminal Victimization Survey (formerly called the National Crime Survey), conducted annually by the Census Bureau on behalf of the Department of Justice. In criminal justice matters, survey data collected from offenders, victims, and citizens are now used to enhance and supplement the "official" portrait of the nature and extent of crime and the characteristics of criminals drawn from police arrest statistics. For example, one of the central tenets of the movement toward community policing strategies in law enforcement is that the public's fear of crime, derived from sample surveys of community residents, is as important an indicator of the quality of life as are official crime statistics.

Value of Survey Data on Crime and Justice

Periodic assays of public sentiment about crime and justice serve important purposes. First, Hindelang (1974) observed that they are a "running historical record of changes in the stance of the public regarding matters central to criminal justice" (p. 101). For example, examination of trends in public attribution of crime causation—the laypersons' etiological theory of crime causation—shows that Americans have undergone conspicuous shifts in thinking about the causes and correlates of crime and delinquency. Where economic and social conditions were once primary in lay explanations of deviance, contemporary Americans focus on criminal behavior as willful, rationally motivated behavior by predatory offenders (Flanagan, 1987).

Second, Hindelang (1974) noted that public opinion research "may also foreshadow impending popular pressure for legislative changes in criminal justice" (p. 101). In the study of public attributions of crime causation described above, clear linkages could be drawn between the public's view of what *causes* crime and notions about effective *crime control*. Stinchcombe and his colleagues (1980) commented that "if the perception of the average criminal changes over time from a too highly spirited boy down the block to a dangerous young black man with a gun, the appropriateness of harsher punishments might increase" (p. 143). Rennie (1978) argued that interaction between beliefs about crime causation and control has been a central feature of social control policy for centuries. Thus, public opinion data on crime and the operations of the criminal justice system may be a social barometer to measure satisfaction with important government services and may illuminate the public's mood and priorities for criminal justice reform.

In addition to identifying issues and priorities, public opinion data can function as "a system of dikes which channel public action or which fix a range of discretion within which government may act or within which debate at official levels may proceed" (Key, 1961, p. 552). Key argued that these opinion dikes "define areas within which the day-to-day debate about the specific course of action may occur" (p. 552). For example, periodic surveys that probe citizens' willingness to relinquish constitutional protections in the name of fighting crime help to establish limits on the crime control debate. Among the findings of these surveys is that Americans have always been reluctant to approve government-authorized interception of wire and oral communications as means to investigate crime (Flanagan, 1993). We will return to this function of public opinion—its relation to the development and implementation of public policy in criminal justice—in Chapter 12.

These uses of public opinion survey data coincide with basic populist notions that the government *ought* to be interested in, seek out, endeavor to understand, and implement government policies that flow from the will of the people. As Bradburn and Sudman (1988) observed, it may not be coincidental that two of the persons most closely associated with the development of opinion polling in America, George Gallup and Elmo Roper, shared roots that were "clearly in Midwestern populism" of the turn of the 20th century (p. 18). These scholars assessed the strengths and limitation of polls in advancing democratic ideals and concluded that "the polls have been and will continue to be the best way of measuring the voice of the people" (p. 230).

Characteristics and Limitations of Public Opinion Survey Data

Despite their value and importance in gauging public sentiment in an increasingly diverse nation, polls and poll data have inherent features and limitations that must be considered. First, it is essential to remember that public opinion on issues such as crime and justice is dynamic. Attitudes and opinions on crime and justice issues are subject to both long-term shifts and to seismic changes due to catastrophic events. On matters concerning crime and justice, one finds issues on which the public has clearly changed its mind over a long period of time, and issues on which sudden spikes of sentiment are short-lived and return to previous levels after a short period of time. Some examples of these basic trends are discussed below.

Second, it is critical to keep in mind that the results of a single survey of the public represents a "snapshot" of public opinion taken at a specific time. There are considerable dangers in drawing inferences about long-term change in the public mood on the basis of cross-sectional single snapshot data. Third, any single snapshot represents only one "pose"—for example, the percentage of respondents who favor the death penalty "for persons convicted of murder"—and there are numerous ways to pose the question. Research indicates that methodological details like question wording, response alternatives, question ordering, and many others are consequential in public opinion research (see Dyer, Chapter 12 in this volume). Critics of public opinion polls seize on these methodological nuances as evidence that poll data are idiosyncratic and thus untrustworthy (Dionne, 1992). Pragmatists realize, however, that no single poll is perfect and that a growing body of scientific research on survey technique is improving the quality of poll data (see Crespi, 1989; Dillman, 1978; Groves, 1987).

Fourth, it is important to remember that public opinion is rarely, if ever, monolithic. Philip Converse (1987) commented that

> the user hearing about results on an opinion item tends to think of the two camps, pro and con, as monolithic blocs of pure types, whereas the experienced analyst is painfully aware of such overpowering heterogeneity within camps that the "camp" metaphor is itself usually stronger than is appropriate. (p. S18)

In the criminal justice context, this observation cautions us to acknowledge that even in the face of 85% to 90% support for capital punishment, or a trend of 90% of adults responding that courts in their area do not deal with criminals "harshly enough," important pockets of discord exist within lopsided tallies. Just as important, disregarding the oppositional positions of the minority on these questions may disenfranchise specific subgroups of the American people.

Some Concerns About Public Opinion Surveys

As noted above, some have argued that public opinion survey data are too limited or conceptually flawed to be considered on issues as important as crime and justice. For example, TRB, writing in *The New Republic* under the headline "Vox Pop Crock," argued that "polls don't measure public opinion. They create it, often with building blocks of ignorance, prejudice, and simple muddle" (cited in Bradburn & Sudman, 1988, pp. 204-207). TRB went on to castigate pollsters for reporting "opinions about the unknowable," for asking questions that are "silly," and for failing to capture "reasoned views" in poll data.

John Doble of the Public Agenda Foundation examined several fallacies that characterize thinking among those who dismiss poll results. One of the most common criticisms is that the public is ignorant of the facts on many issues to which they readily offer opinions to survey interviewers. But Doble (1987a) argues that it is mistaken to assume that respondents with little detailed factual *knowledge* of an issue also fail to grasp underlying *concepts*. It may be true that most of the respondents who reply that courts in their area are "not harsh enough" in sentencing criminals have never been inside a courtroom and have not read official reports on criminal sentencing patterns. This ignorance does not mean, however, that survey respondents are incapable of forming meaningful perceptions of justice, just deserts, and leniency in judicial sentencing of convicted felons. Leslie Wilkins (1974) argued that "in criminal justice matters, the degree of confidence with which views are expressed tends to be inversely proportional to the quality of knowledge" (p. 247). A decade later, he added:

> There is a class of question where knowledge relating to the subject matter is of no importance. These are questions of moral values, attitudes and opinions. . . . Many, if not most of the meaningful questions about fairness, punishment and the products required of the social system (including the criminal justice system) do not require knowledge. (Wilkins, 1984, p. 84)

A second fallacy, according to Doble (1987a), is that persons with little substantive knowledge of an issue also have little interest in it. Although few survey respondents who favor capital punishment have read the scientific research on the deterrent effect of the death penalty, lack of knowledge does not prevent them from forming attitudes toward just punishment and opinions about capital punishment that are deeply held.

Third, Doble suggests that analysts and commentators often misinterpret the mood of the public as presented in poll data because they view the data through *ideological filters*. He provided an example of strong public opposition to a proposed march through Skokie, Illinois, by members of the Ku Klux Klan. Some commentators viewed the opposition by Skokie citizens, many of whom were survivors of German concentration camps, as evidence that the public was too eager to limit free speech. Doble argues that Skokie residents viewed the confrontation *in different terms*, as provocation by troublemakers. In this view, Doble argues, allowing the KKK to appear on the *Donahue* show is one thing, but allowing members of a group espousing concepts such as "ethnic purity" in the Skokie setting is clearly another.

Fourth, some argue that fluctuations in poll data demonstrate that the public is merely *reactive* and therefore not to be trusted. It is axiomatic that extraordinary events cause intensive attention to be focused on issues. For example, the attempted assassination of President Ronald Reagan in 1981 provoked a high level of attention to issues such as gun control policy and the insanity defense in criminal procedure. And these singular events can cause short-term changes in public attitudes about these issues. This does not mean, according to Doble, that the public is fickle or impetuous. Rather, it illustrates that people's initial reaction to a crisis may be different from their considered view. Doble argues that on some issues the public simply needs time and information so they can "work through" the drama of the event to the more considered view. For opinion researchers, this implies that overnight polls and their accompanying instantaneous analyses must be balanced with repeated soundings and trend analyses.

Finally, Doble observed that many critics assert that public opinion should be ignored because the public is *inconsistent* in their views. If poll results incorporate such whims, why are they to be trusted? Of course, some inconsistency is a product of human nature—we all want our taxes to be reduced while we demand more and better services from governments. But how do we reconcile the views of a public that supports punishment as the main goal of sentencing *criminals* but also strongly favors providing nonpunitive treatment, education, counseling, and training programs for *inmates*? Does this prove that Americans do not know what they want from the corrections system, or that their views on these matters is "mushy" (Converse, 1987)? As discussed in Chapter 6, Innes describes an overarching purpose of the criminal justice system that many Americans share and that provides a defensible explanation to this seeming paradox.

In addition to these concerns about the relevance and integrity of public opinion survey data, considerable debate exists about its use in the formulation of public policy. We will return to that debate in Chapter 11.

Themes and Trends in Opinions on Crime and Justice

In this brief overview preceding the detailed analyses of topics presented in Chapters 2-10, I wish to introduce three themes that characterize major aspects of public opinion about crime and justice issues over time. The first of these is the remarkable *temporal stability* in many aspects of public attitudes, including perceptions of crime, fear of crime, evaluations of the police, the role of government spending in fighting crime, gun control, and drug control policy. In examining these trends, I have relied on time series presented in the annual volumes of the *Sourcebook of Criminal Justice Statistics* (Flanagan, 1993) and on a recent review of trends published by Warr (1995).

Perceptions of "more crime in my own area" from year to year have been held by about 50% of Americans for two decades. At the same time, designation of crime as the "nation's most important problem" was consistently below 6% during the 1980s. Therefore, about half of adult Americans perceived that crime was increasing in their own area, but issues such as unemployment, cost of living, and international problems were viewed as the nation's top problems. Ironically, the time period that featured stability in respondents' perceptions about crime was characterized by increases and decreases in the official crime rate.

Similarly, Warr (1995) observed that the "most striking feature" of time series on *fear of crime* and the *violent crime victimization rate* during the past two decades has been "relative constancy." Moreover, "this stability stands in sharp contrast to recurring media accounts of 'skyrocketing' or 'epidemic' fear in the United States" (Warr, 1995, p. 297).

Another area in which attitudes have been steady is in citizens' assessments of the honesty and ethical standards of law enforcement personnel and in reactions to a vignette in which a police officer might use physical force against an adult male citizen. In the former series, 37% to 44% of respondents viewed the honesty and ethical standards of police officers as *very high* or *high* during the past 15 years. In the latter series, between two thirds and three quarters of Americans during the past two decades reported that they can imagine a situation "in which [they] would approve a policeman striking an adult male citizen." During the same period, however, less than one quarter of survey respondents have responded affirmatively to the question: "Everything considered, would you say that you approve or disapprove of wiretapping?"

One of the most unswerving time series in polls on crime and justice is on opinions about whether the government is spending sufficient

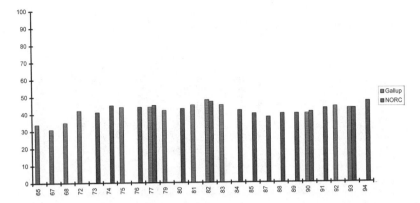

Figure 1.1. Americans' Fear of Walking Alone at Night Within a Mile of Home, Gallup Polls and National Opinion Research Center Surveys, Selected Years, 1965-1994

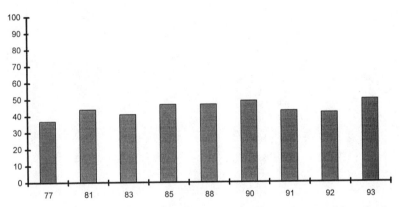

Figure 1.2. Americans Responding That the Honesty and Ethical Standards of Police Officers Are Very High or High, Gallup Polls, 1977-1993

resources to "halt the rising crime rate." Warr (1995) observed that "Americans have long believed that too little money is spent to control crime. Approximately two-thirds . . . think that increased funding is necessary, and very few think that too much is being spent" (p. 300). Similar temporal stability exists in public opinion on three specific crime control strategies: harsher sentencing of convicted criminals

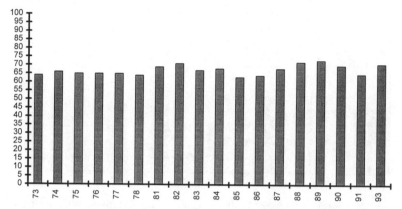

Figure 1.3. Americans Agreeing That Too Little Money Is Spent to Halt the Rising Crime Rate, National Opinion Research Center Surveys, 1973-1993

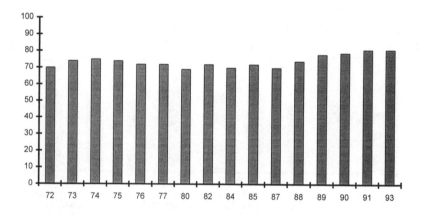

(79%-85% responded *not harshly enough* between 1976 and 1994), capital punishment of murderers (60%-75% support between 1974 and 1994), and gun control (70%-80% favor requiring a police permit to purchase a gun between 1973 and 1991). Not surprisingly, these strategies have been called the "75% solutions" in the mind of the public. In a different vein, support for reducing drug offenses by legalizing marijuana enjoyed precisely the level of support (18%) in 1991 as it did in 1973, and varied little in the interim years.

A second theme that characterizes public opinion on crime and justice is apparent logical inconsistency between views on related issues. As noted earlier, however, some of these presumptively contradictory beliefs are reconcilable. One example of this phenomenon is that a majority of Americans claim to support capital punishment for murder and that support is motivated primarily on *utilitarian* grounds such as deterrence. Yet, when queried about the effect on their views if the deterrent assumption were eliminated, most respondents maintain their views. Among death penalty supporters, a large majority remains in favor of capital punishment even when the deterrence premise is eliminated. Opposers remain opposed even if a deterrent effect is assumed. Either deterrence of crime is not as important in attitudes toward the death penalty as respondents think, or other motivations for their support lie just below the surface of their espoused deterrence-induced support, or attitudes toward the death penalty are much more complex than we think. Dennis Longmire attempts to disentangle this paradox in Chapter 7.

The presumed inconsistency in the public's view about criminal justice is also raised concerning gun control. Although the percentage of American households that report gun ownership has been stable at about 48% for nearly two decades, there have been very high levels of support for various restrictions on gun ownership during the same period. These measures include firearms registration, banning of assault-style weapons, and waiting periods for gun purchases. At the same time, there has been little support for outright government bans on gun ownership. These diverging views illustrate the fact that public opinion on an important topic such as gun control is a melting pot of views on various aspects of the larger issue. This complexity of views on crime and justice issues is also a feature of Americans' opinions about prisons and imprisonment, as discussed in Chapter 6.

Another theme that emerges as one studies public opinion about crime and justice is that Americans are essentially sensible and fundamentally pragmatic about most issues. For example, although the overblown rhetoric of politicians may invite the public to view the governments' efforts as a "war on drugs" and drug use, a large share of the public sees the highly publicized initiatives as having little if any effect on street-level drug use in American cities. And although the media and political leaders debate the merits of demand reduction and supply reduction approaches to stemming illegal drug use, the public recognizes that a balanced approach is needed. Cintrón and Johnson describe Americans' views on these issues in Chapter 9.

Another example of American pragmatism regarding crime and justice is in the public's opinions about prisons and prison life. The "film-ability quotient" of boot camp prisons, striped uniforms, and other correctional "reforms" leads politicians and the media to celebrate the return to breaking rocks and chain gangs as the solution to street crime, but Americans favor a balanced approach that includes work, training, and education in addition to secure confinement (American Correctional Association, 1995). Finally, the public's responses to National Crime Survey interviewers when asked why they failed to report victimization incidents to the police also reveal a pragmatic assessment. Given that "clearance rates" for property crimes have fallen below 20% in recent years, many Americans do not report known victimizations to the police because they conclude that the police cannot do much anyway, or that minor thefts would be considered trivial by the police. Research on reporting of crimes to the police reveals that victims make sensible assessments of the seriousness of the victimization and the likelihood of resolution of the matter by government agencies. As a result, victimizations involving weapon use, physical injury to the victim or the victim's property, and substantial loss are more likely to be reported than incidents that do not include these elements, and completed crimes are much more likely to be reported than unsuccessful attempts.

Conclusion

The existing knowledge about Americans' opinion concerning crime and justice is composed of numerous episodic soundings by survey researchers whose principal interests are in market research and political polling (more than 90% of the polling business in the United States is devoted to market research). Criminologists and policymakers interested in designing crime control policies and programs that are consonant with the views of the public on criminal justice have relied on the one or two questions that are included in annual omnibus polls, or in rare surveys devoted to criminal justice issue that appear sporadically. Because much of the work in this area is not based on the work of criminal justice scholars, criminologists often complain that surveys fail to address the timely and important issues, or do so in insufficient depth.

The National Opinion Survey on Crime and Justice—1995 and the analyses that follow were designed to address this paucity of detailed knowledge about public opinion on crime and justice. The chapters examine data derived from a questionnaire of more than 140 crime- and justice-related items that was completed by a nationally representative sample of American adults. The survey sought to cover a broad range of topics, but also to delve into these issues much more deeply than one or two general questions would permit. In each chapter, contributors not only provide a rigorous analysis of the data collected in the survey but also attempt to place the findings within the broader context of previous survey research on the topic. We hope the results provide new insights into the public mind on crime and justice issues and further our understanding of Americans' thinking on these critically important issues.

We believe that comprehensive periodic surveys of public opinion on crime and justice issues like the National Opinion Survey on Crime and Justice—1995 will lead to better-informed criminal justice policy and practice. Just as important, we believe that regular assessments of public opinion on crime and justice issues are at least as important to enlightened justice initiatives as consumer confidence surveys are in informing us of the health of the national economy. As criminal justice agencies strive to improve the collection, processing and analysis of official data on the crime problem, we urge that attention to surveys of the public on their concerns and reactions to crime and criminal justice receive attention.

2

America's Fear of Crime

BAHRAM HAGHIGHI

JON SORENSEN

During the past two decades, criminologists have devoted considerable attention to understanding the scope and intensity of fear of crime among citizens (Smith & Hill, 1991). No subject matter in criminology has gained more attention from researchers than citizens' concern for criminal victimization and their fear of becoming victims of crime. Even so, the authors of one recent study state that "fear of crime is a very important social problem about which we know very little" (Liska, Sanchirico, & Reed, 1988, pp. 835-836).

Several national polls also indicate that citizens are deeply concerned about becoming victims of crime. One recent survey found that respondents are more concerned about injuries caused by violent victimization than injury in motor vehicle accidents, despite the fact that the latter occurs in higher proportion (Bureau of Justice Statistics, 1988). Similarly, people are more concerned with violent victimization than cancer death, injury from fire, and heart disease death combined (Bureau of Justice Statistics, 1985). In two public attitude polls conducted by the

National Law Journal in 1989 and 1994, the concern for safety and fear of crime showed significant increases during that period. Whereas in 1989 approximately 34% of the public were "truly desperate" about crime, the percentage soared to 62% in 1994 (Sherman, 1994). In that survey, over three fourths of Americans showed a willingness "to give up basic civil liberties if doing so might enhance their personal safety" (Sherman, 1994).

Issues in Measuring Fear of Crime

Fear of crime is one of the most complex phenomena in criminology insofar as it cannot be measured precisely. In fact, as Warr (1984) describes, the term "fear of crime has acquired so many divergent meanings in the literature that it is in danger of losing any specificity" (p. 681). Recent investigations reveal that prevalence and intensity of fear among many groups (e.g., women, older persons) may have been overestimated and in some instances exaggerated (Ferraro & LaGrange, 1987; Jeffords, 1983; LaGrange & Ferraro, 1989). Three general methodological problems have been identified in measuring fear of crime: interpreting perceived crime risk as fear of crime, emphasizing fear of violent victimization while neglecting the more common nonviolent victimizations, and using ambiguous indicators of crime fear.

Ferraro and LaGrange (1987) assert that many researchers have failed to distinguish between *risk* of victimization and *crime fear*. In many instances, measures of perceived crime risk are mistakenly interpreted as measures of crime fear (LaGrange & Ferraro, 1989; Wiltz, 1982). Most opinion researchers ask questions regarding the respondents' crime concern rather than whether they are afraid of becoming victims of crime. For instance, the National Opinion Research Center (NORC) asks, "Is there any area near your home—that is, within a mile or so—where you would be afraid to walk alone at night?" Similarly, the National Crime Survey routinely asks, "How safe do you feel or would you feel being out alone in your neighborhood at night?" Although the above questions may reflect the respondents' concern for walking alone in the neighborhood, they failed to measure the persons' fear of crime (LaGrange & Ferraro, 1989; Lee, 1982; Taylor & Hale, 1986; Warr, 1984). Such questions are fear provoking because most people's "routine activities" do not include walking alone in the neighborhood at night, especially females and older persons (Cohen & Felson, 1979). Hence, the above-mentioned questions reflect a more general safety concern and are not true indicators of crime fear across race, gender, and location (Lee, 1982).

The second common source of error in assessing fear of crime is reflecting fear of "personal" victimization as an indication of citizens' fear of all criminal activities. According to Smith and Hill (1991), "Personal victimization may indeed represent the types of imagined experiences that the general public fears most, but the question wording fails to tap the types of criminal victimization experiences that, by a factor in excess of 10 to 1, people are more likely to have, namely property victimization" (p. 220). Most reported studies document people's fear of violent offenses without giving proper attention to their views on nonviolent property crimes.

How specifically one measures crime fear has also been the subject of criticism. Several studies measuring fear of crime have relied on analyzing data containing single-item indicators of crime fear. These questions are usually worded in a broad and generic sense. Questions such as "How fearful are you of being the victim of a serious crime?" will produce more ambiguous rather than specific results (LaGrange & Ferraro, 1989). LaGrange and Ferraro (1989) argue that such questions are inadequate, lacking specificity and being prone to error because one cannot determine which crimes one fears.

In sum, variation in the volume, depth, and intensity of fear of crime recorded by numerous researchers is often a function of the type of questions asked in various surveys, as opposed to true variance. Nevertheless, the concern for safety and criminal victimization can be assessed with a certain degree of accuracy by asking respondents how worried they are about becoming victims of a particular type of crime (Bureau of Justice Statistics, 1988). Although fear is a complex psychological phenomenon, its boundaries can be assessed, with some degree of accuracy, by asking people how much they worry about particular types of crime. In the National Opinion Survey on Crime and Justice—1995 (NOSCJ), respondents were asked to what extent they worried about various types of crimes. Findings from the NOSCJ will be discussed after a brief review of the literature.

Background

Fear of crime continues to be the subject of numerous criminological studies. The most common question posed by researchers is, "Who is fearful and why?" (Warr, 1990; Will & McGrath, 1995). Researchers in this area have focused on profiling the people who are fearful of criminal victimization. Many have reported substantial differences between male and female, young and old, and rich and poor. Others have assessed the effect of prior victimization on the formation of crime fear. Still others have looked into the mass media as the prime source of creating fear among many citizens.

Gender and Age

In light of accumulated research, the most consistent findings are that women and older persons are more fearful of crime than are men and younger people (Garofalo, 1981b; LaGrange & Ferraro, 1989; Parker, 1993; Parker & Ray, 1990; Warr, 1984), even though both groups are less likely to be victims of crime (Garofalo, 1981b; Yin, 1980). This paradox has led many researchers to conclude that no meaningful association exists between criminal victimization and fear of crime. Some researchers have interpreted the high degree of fear among women and older persons as a function of actually being, or feeling, vulnerable in criminal situations. Junger (1987), for instance, relates women's high fear of crime to their inability to handle dangerous situations, whereas Maxfield (1987) suggests that their higher level of fear is not due to actual vulnerability, but to feelings of vulnerability.

Race and Ethnicity

Race also plays a significant role in the analyses of crime fear. A growing body of literature suggests that African Americans are disproportionately more fearful of crime than are their white counterparts (Hindelang, Gottfredson, & Garofalo, 1978; Parker, 1993; Skogan & Maxfield, 1981). The relationship between ethnicity and fear of crime, however, suffers from lack of attention in the literature. Only a handful of studies have examined fear of crime in the Hispanic population. Parker (1993) compared African American and Hispanic survey respondents and found that Hispanics, who reported the greatest likelihood of victimization, also scored higher on the fear factor than did their African American counterparts. Considering the interaction between ethnicity and gender, Parker recorded the greatest concerns about victimization among Hispanic women.

Socioeconomic Status

Very little attention has been devoted to exploring the correlation between socioeconomic status and fear of crime. It is possible that many researchers have examined the effect of this variable on crime fear, but due to lack of statistical significance did not include it in their final outcome. Will and McGrath (1995), however, report that socioeconomic status "provides an important insight into understanding the overall problem of fear of crime" (p. 174). Their data showed that even when the effects of gender and age were controlled, the underclass reflected a higher degree of crime fear than the nonpoor, the reason for which may be their higher likelihood of actual victimization, particularly with regard to street crimes (Will & McGrath, 1995).

Victimization Experience

The relationship between victimization experience and fear of crime has been analyzed in many studies and has produced conflicting results. Some studies point out that crime fear is a function of experience with victimization (e.g., Skogan & Maxfield, 1981). Several studies have also recorded that people with knowledge of criminal incidents or those who have witnessed crime may reflect higher levels of crime fear (Belyea & Zingraff, 1988; Lawton & Yaffe, 1980; Lee, 1983; Stafford & Galle, 1984). Yet other studies report that crime fear tends to be only marginally related to victimization experience (Liska et al., 1988) or totally unrelated (Bishop & Klecka, 1978). Despite this disparity, there is a consensus among researchers that those who characteristically reflect the highest fear of crime are those who are least likely to be victimized.

The Media

The paradoxical nature of crime fear led Stafford and Galle (1984) to conclude that an individual's perceived fear of crime must originate from indirect sources. In Garofalo's (1981b) view, the mass media play an important role in the formation of crime fear among citizens. It appears that repeated references to crime, particularly violent offenses, in the media may affect people's sense of security and fear of crime. This element is particularly important because the media tend to distort the types of criminal victimization occurring and exaggerate true accounts of criminal victimization in the community. Priyadarsini (1984) suggests that many media crime reports are biased, being "highly graphic," involving "sensational portrayals," and including "embellished descriptions" (p. 320). Heath (1984), noting a high level of sensationalism in media presentations of crime and victimization, concluded that emphasis on random and sensational crimes by local media leads to an increased fear of crime among the community members. Finally, Williams (1993) reported that newspaper readership groups displayed average levels of crime fear, whereas broadcast watchers displayed the least, and low-market tabloid readers reflected the highest crime fear.

The Present Study

Our analysis of fear of crime and concern for safety was based on the NOSCJ. One of the sections of the survey includes seven questions designed to tap respondents' fear of crime. The seven questions cover a range of personal and property offenses. On each of the questions, respondents were asked how often they worry about various types of crime—*very frequently, somewhat frequently, seldom,* or *never.* For the purpose of analyses in this chapter, responses were dichotomized into worry (very frequently or somewhat frequently) or not worry (seldom or never). Table 2.1 shows the percentage of respondents who worried about the seven types of offenses.

The majority of respondents did not worry frequently about any of the various categories of crime. The type of crime that caused respondents the least worry was getting murdered. In fact, less than one fifth of Americans reported worrying frequently about being murdered. We found that only 6.7% of Americans worried very frequently about being murdered, whereas over half (54.5%) never worried about being murdered. Other categories of crime that elicited lower levels of fear among the public included being beaten up, knifed or shot, getting mugged, being burglarized while someone is at home, and being attacked while driving a car. The percentages of respondents reporting that they frequently worried about these offenses ranged from one quarter to less than one third. Between 39% and 45% of the respondents never worried about these offenses.

The category of crime that caused the most concern among respondents was the concern for being burglarized while no one is at home. Nearly one half (45.4%) of the respondents mentioned fear of being

Table 2.1 Americans' Worry About Selected Types of Victimization

Question: "Next, I want to ask you how much you worry about each of the following situations. Do you worry very frequently, somewhat frequently, seldom, or never about":

Type of Victimization	Worry[a]		Not Worry[b]	
	n	%	n	%
Yourself or someone in your family getting sexually assaulted	385	38.4	618	61.6
Being attacked while driving your car	308	30.8	692	69.2
Getting mugged	279	27.8	724	72.2
Getting beaten up, knifed, or shot	260	25.9	742	74.1
Getting murdered	187	18.6	816	81.4
Your home being burglarized while someone is at home	286	28.5	719	71.5
Your home being burglarized while no one is at home	456	45.4	548	54.6

a. Includes "very frequently" and somewhat "frequently."
b. Includes "seldom" and "never."

burglarized while away from home, whereas only about one quarter (25.7%) reported that they never worried about being burglarized while away. Another type of crime that tended to elicit fear more often than others was sexual assault. Well over one third of Americans worried about themselves or someone in their family being sexually assaulted. Nearly 12% indicated that they worried very frequently about sexual assault, whereas only 27.8% reported never having such worries.

The descriptive data on fear of crime in Table 2.1 presents a portrait that only partially corresponds to actual risk of victimization. Burglary while away from home (the type of crime included in the questionnaire that is most likely to be experienced by Americans) was also the type of crime about which they were most worried. Murder was the least worrisome crime and also one that is in reality the least prevalent. Although fear of crime appears to be somewhat rational when looking at the particular type of crime, much of the fear cannot be accounted for by risk of victimization. The level of fear of violent personal crime, although lower than that for property crime, was still disproportionately high. As mentioned in the literature review, the risk of victimization for property versus violent crime is a ratio of 10:1 (Smith & Hill, 1991), so that if actual risk were the only factor affecting fear of crime, we should expect fear of burglary while away from home (one form of property crime) to be 10 times higher than the level of fear of violent personal crimes. In fact, the only crime for which fear was elicited at a factor of over 2:1 for property versus personal crime was murder.

Some of the crimes that elicited higher levels of fear are independent of actual risk. The actual risk of being attacked while driving a car is lower than most of the other types of personal offenses, yet it provoked more fear than all but sexual assault. This disproportionate level fear of being attacked while driving a car may be due to recent media coverage of car-jackings.

The Media and Fear of Crime

The effect of media on fear of crime is presented in Table 2.2. Our analysis revealed that the degree of local media attention given to violent crime was significantly related to fear of sexual assault; getting mugged, beaten up, knifed, or shot; and being burglarized while at home. On the other hand, fear of car-jackings, being murdered, or being burglarized while not at home was not significantly related to violent crime coverage by the media.

Although the degree of violent crime coverage appeared to be a contributing factor in crime fear formation, the source of news did not affect respondents' views. Precisely, those receiving news about crime from the broadcast media (television and radio), newspapers, or another person displayed similar levels of fear. Despite the above finding, those who labeled themselves as "regular viewer(s) of television programs that deal with crime and criminal justice issues, such as *Cops, Real Stories of the Highway Patrol, Justice Files*, or *America's Most Wanted*," were more fearful of being sexually assaulted; getting beaten up, knifed, or shot; and getting killed (see Table 2.2). Fear of other crimes such as car-jacking, mugging, or burglary victimization was not affected by watching these television crime and justice programs. Considering the hours of television watched, heavy viewers of television reflected fear of property victimization but were no more likely to fear personal offenses.

In addition to the media, several other factors can also be expected to influence fear of crime beyond actual victimization. Many of the variables found to influence fear of crime in previous studies are included

Table 2.2 Relationship Between Media Exposure and Fear of Victimization (percentage worried)

Question: "Next, I want to ask you how much you worry about each of the following situations. Do you worry very frequently, somewhat frequently, seldom, or never about: W1, Yourself or someone in your family getting sexually assaulted; W2, Being attacked while driving your car; W3, Getting mugged; W4, Getting beaten up, knifed, or shot; W5, Getting murdered; W6, Your home being burglarized while someone is at home; W7, Your home being burglarized while no one is at home?"

| | Type of Victimization | | | | | | |
	W1	W2	W3	W4	W5	W6	W7
National	38.4	30.8	27.8	25.9	18.6	28.5	45.4
Local media attention to violent crime							
Too much	42.2*	33.1	32.8*	26.7*	19.5	34.9*	46.6
About right	33.3	27.0	23.6	22.6	16.9	23.6	44.8
Too little	46.9	33.8	29.3	34.9	21.3	26.0	42.6
Source of crime news							
Broadcast	39.0	30.1	29.3	27.2	19.3	29.0	44.5
Print	37.5	33.9	23.8	21.3	13.2	27.3	50.1
Other	37.3	30.7	25.2	27.0	27.4	25.0	42.8
TV crime show viewer							
Yes	43.9*	31.9	28.8	31.1*	24.1*	30.5	47.8
No	33.9	29.9	27.2	21.8	14.0	26.6	43.5
TV hours per week							
Less than 10	38.2	26.4	24.3	22.7	14.6	20.8*	40.7*
10 to 20	39.7	31.9	30.0	28.9	20.8	31.3	49.4
21 to 30	39.3	36.5	30.3	29.4	21.0	39.4	52.0
More than 30	36.1	37.6	32.0	21.8	22.2	23.2	28.1

*Differences between groups are significant at $p < .01$ level.

in the NOSCJ. To more fully understand the concept of crime fear, Table 2.3 presents data on the relationship between fear of particular types of crime and other variables available in the NOSCJ that have most often been found to be related to, or could reasonably be expected to be related to, fear of crime.

Table 2.3 Relationship Between Selected Independent Variables and Fear of Victimization (percentage worried)

Question: "Next, I want to ask you how much you worry about each of the following situations. Do you worry very frequently, somewhat frequently, seldom, or never about: W1, Yourself or someone in your family getting sexually assaulted; W2, Being attacked while driving your car; W3, Getting mugged; W4, Getting beaten up, knifed, or shot; W5, Getting murdered; W6, Your home being burglarized while someone is at home; W7, Your home being burglarized while no one is at home?"

	Type of Victimization						
	W1	W2	W3	W4	W5	W6	W7
National	38.4	30.8	27.8	25.9	18.6	28.5	45.4
Age							
18-29	34.0*	27.1	22.4	27.4	18.9	26.0*	46.7*
30-39	40.8	29.9	23.5	23.5	18.0	29.5	46.9
40-49	43.2	34.8	34.5	32.1	22.9	34.1	47.7
50-59	42.9	36.1	33.5	25.1	16.9	35.1	52.6
60-69	37.5	32.9	29.0	22.7	16.0	21.6	38.0
70 or older	26.3	25.5	30.5	19.3	13.9	18.1	32.6
Race/ethnicity							
White	38.5*	30.6	26.7	24.8	16.7*	27.5	45.1
Hispanic	52.8	37.6	43.2	37.4	27.0	34.8	51.0
Black	28.3	32.3	28.0	29.9	30.1	31.5	44.5
Other[a]	28.7	13.6	15.4	13.9	12.2	30.4	42.8
Gender							
Male	29.0*	22.2*	20.8*	19.8*	14.3*	26.2	43.8
Female	47.0	38.8	34.3	31.7	22.7	30.5	46.8
Education							
Less than high school	40.1	30.3*	30.2*	29.9	24.1	25.9	40.6
High school graduate	36.7	23.4	21.0	23.6	14.7	27.7	46.2
Some college	37.2	31.8	28.0	27.3	20.4	28.6	46.6
College graduate	40.3	37.3	33.5	25.1	18.6	29.2	43.3
Live alone							
Yes	25.6*	21.8	26.2	21.5	12.0	18.1*	35.0*
No	39.6	31.4	27.8	26.2	18.9	29.1	45.9
Community type							
Rural	33.5	31.4	25.8*	20.1*	15.4	25.5	40.2
Small town	39.4	28.2	19.6	18.3	16.3	22.4	40.0
Small city	46.0	28.4	30.6	30.1	17.1	31.6	47.4
Suburb	35.6	32.1	27.5	27.6	20.5	31.9	45.6
Urban	39.4	35.1	39.2	34.6	24.5	30.3	54.0

a. Category contains fewer than 50 cases.

*Differences between groups are significant at $p < .01$ level.

Gender and Age

As found in previous studies, females were more fearful of sexual assault and the other personal violent crimes than were males. Women, however, were not significantly more fearful having their homes burglarized. The findings on sexual assault are not surprising because women are at an increased risk of victimization. The higher level of fear on the part of females toward violent nonsexual offenses supports the vulnerability hypothesis. That is, females, although much less likely than males to be victims of such offenses, worry disproportionately about these types of offenses.

Age was not significantly correlated with the violent nonsexual offenses, as has been frequently noted in previous studies. Fear of sexual assault and burglary was related to age. Young respondents were more fearful than older persons. These findings contradict the literature on vulnerability and suggest that fear of crime is related to age in terms of risk. Older persons are less likely to be sexually assaulted or to have their homes burglarized. The routine activities of their everyday lives puts them at a lower risk for these types of victimizations.

Race and Ethnicity

Race/ethnicity was related to fear of crime in the predicted direction, nonwhites being more worried than whites and Hispanics being more worried than non-Hispanics. Race/ethnicity was significant, however, for only two of the seven measures. Hispanics were nearly twice as likely as non-Hispanics to worry about sexual assault of themselves or someone in their household. Race and ethnicity influenced fear of being murdered. Both African Americans and Hispanics were more than twice as likely as whites to worry about being murdered.

Urbanization

The relationship between urbanization and fear of crime supports that found in the literature for two of the seven measures. Fear of being beaten, knifed, or shot, and fear of getting mugged increased as level of urbanization increased. For example, approximately one fifth of those living in rural areas and small towns feared being beaten, knifed or shot, whereas approximately one fourth of those living in small cities and suburbs expressed such worries, compared to one third of those in urban areas. The relationship between urbanization and being mugged is similar, again, with the largest differences between those in urban versus all other locations.

Other Demographic Variables

The remaining demographic variables provide little explanation for fear of crime. Although education was significantly correlated with worries about being attacked while driving in the car or getting mugged, it did not produce a consistent relationship. Those with high school educations tended to be less worried than those with less education or more education (some college or college graduates). Similarly, our analysis failed to record meaningful relationships between marital status, income, and fear of crime.

Multivariate Analysis

The results from logistic regression are presented in Table 2.4 to assess whether specific independent variables influenced crime fear when simultaneously controlling for all of the predictor variables.[1] Of the three models presented in Table 2.4, the pseudo R^2 varies from .050 to .185.[2] The fear of sexual assault model was least successful, the predictor variables accounting for only 5% of the variance in fear of crime. The fear of personal crime model was most successful, with predictor variables accounting for 18.5% of the variance in fear of crime. Fear of property crime was in between, its independent variables accounting for 11.7% of the variance.

Within each model, the individual beta coefficients were consistently positive or negative across models, suggesting that the same factors were at work in explaining the fear of various types of crime; however, their magnitude varied across models. Of the significant coefficients predicting fear of sexual assault, older persons and males were both negatively related, suggesting that females and younger persons were more worried about this type of crime. Hispanics and those in households with multiple residents exhibited significantly higher fear of sexual assault than non-Hispanics and those dwelling alone. The significant coefficients in the model predicting fear of personal violent victimization indicated that females and residents of urban areas were more fearful of these criminal incidents. The only significant coefficient in the model predicting property crime indicated that younger persons were more fearful of being burglarized. These findings support the relationships presented in Table 2.3.

Table 2.4   Logistic Regression Models of Fear of Victimization

	Type of Victimization		
	Sexual Assault	Personal	Property
Older persons	−.453*	−.207	−.682*
Male	−.791*	−.786*	−.227
White	.405	.116	.443
Hispanic	1.027*	.517	.373
Urban	.006	.593*	.400
Multiple residents	.550*	.326	.311
Constant	−.979	−.396	−.589
Pseudo R^2	.050	.185	.117

*Coefficients are significant at $p < .01$ level.

Conclusion

This chapter has examined fear of crime by taking into consideration the three primary sources of error suggested by researchers. First, as was recommended in prior research, attempts were made to distinguish fear of property crime from fear of personal offenses. Further distinctions were made between sexual assault and other violent offenses. This distinction was based on the assumption that women will reflect different degrees of concern and fear in reference to sexual offenses than men will. Second, questions were designed to elicit directly respondents' fear of being victimized rather than measuring their perceived risk of victimization and interpreting the results as the respondents' probable fear of victimization. Third, unlike most previous research, this study did not rely on the analysis of single-item indicators of crime fear. Respondents were asked about their fear of crime in reference to specific types of crime (five personal offenses and two property offenses).

This analysis builds on recent research by confirming the position that people are not commonly worried about personal and property victimizations. In fact, the majority of respondents showed little worry in reference to becoming victims of violent and sexual offenses. Also, as Smith and Hill (1991) found, respondents showed more concern about property offenses than violent personal offenses.

In analyzing fear of violent offenses, we found conflicting results. It appears that respondents were more concerned about becoming victims of car-jacking than aggravated assault, robbery, or murder. Although car-jacking occurs far less frequently than other types of violent offenses, it has produced more concern among citizens than other traditional violent offenses. One could speculate that this fear of car-jacking might be a direct result of recent media coverage of such incidents in some major cities.

Women appeared to be more fearful of sexual assault and other personal offenses than were males, but they were less fearful of property offenses than men. This finding supports Junger's (1987) vulnerability hypothesis that although women are proportionately victimized less often than men, they reflect a higher degree of fear of personal offenses because they feel less able to defend themselves.

Findings from this study support the frequently examined correlations between race/ethnicity and fear of crime. Minorities are more fearful of criminal victimization than are white citizens. Among minorities, Hispanics are nearly twice as likely as African Americans to worry about sexual assault of themselves or someone in their household. Similarly, African Americans and Hispanics are more than twice as likely as whites to fear homicide victimization.

Finally, media exposure emerged as a significant factor in shaping citizens' fear of crime. The degree of local media crime coverage was a prime factor in shaping the viewers' perception of becoming victims of violent offenses. In fact, those who believed their local media had given "too much" attention to crime coverage scored high on fear of sexual assault, robbery, aggravated assault, and burglary. It was not, however, important whether the source of news was the broadcast news or print. It appears that the frequency of receiving the crime news rather than the source of crime news is a factor in generating fear among citizens. Likewise, regular viewers of television crime programs (e.g., *Cops, Real Stories of the Highway Patrol, America's Most Wanted*) showed higher degree of fear about probability of being sexually assaulted, beaten and knifed, and getting killed.

This study did not examine the effect of prior victimization experience on formation of crime fear. One may expect a higher degree of crime fear among those who have experienced personal, property, or sexual assault in the past. Likewise, those who experienced indirect victimization (i.e., victimization of friends or relative) may reflect a higher degree of fear than those who did not. Finally, future studies should include some contextual variables such as political, cultural, and community aspects in assessing fear of crime.

Notes

1. A number of modifications have been made to accommodate the logistic regression. The variables found to be insignificant or inconsistent in Table 2.3 were dropped. The remaining independent variables were dichotomized and coded 0 or 1, with 1 reflecting the presence of the attributes listed in Table 2.4. Finally, as evidenced by the findings in Table 2.3 and correlations between the fear questions (not reported), it was possible to combine some of the fear questions. Although fear of sexual assault stands alone as single category, fear of personal crime includes all personal victimizations with the exception of sexual offenses, and fear of property crime includes being the subject of household burglary.

2. The pseudo R^2 is based on the percentage correctly classified by the model over chance in a contingency table analysis.

3

Support and Confidence

Public Attitudes
Toward the Police

W. S. WILSON HUANG

MICHAEL S. VAUGHN

Law enforcement agencies need a cooperative citizenry to ensure effective police work because of the reciprocal nature of police-public interaction. This fact has been known since the time of Sir Robert Peel, who said that the "police are the public and the public are the police." Criminal justice researchers call this phenomenon the co-production of police services, meaning that there is a symbiotic relationship between the police and the public (Bayley & Skolnick, 1986; Reiss, 1971). Indeed, Reiss (1971) reported that 87% of police-citizen encounters involved police responding to citizen calls for service, and Black (1970) found that over three fourths of police activities were generated by citizen calls for service. Other researchers have pointed out that as community policing grows in scope, contacts between citizens and law enforcement agents become increasingly important (Smith, 1994). Thus, planning and implementing policing strategies require careful measurement and evaluation of citizen attitudes toward the police.

Favorable Attitudes Toward the Police

Starting with the 1967 President's Commission on Law Enforcement and Administration of Justice, numerous surveys have shown that the general public is pleased with the quality of police work (Decker, 1985; Walklate, 1992; White & Menke, 1978). For example, Reiss (1967) found that 70% of respondents in Boston and Chicago thought the police were doing a *very good* or *fairly good* job. More recently, Maxfield (1988) reported that 90% of residents in London thought the police were doing at least a *fairly good* job.

Numerous public opinion polls[1] confirm these empirical findings. In a 1993 national telephone poll of 2,004 Americans conducted by Family Circle, 73% of respondents rated the quality of police service as *excellent* or *good*; only 23% said police service was *only fair* or *poor*. In the same year, the American Bar Association's survey of 1,202 Americans found that 79% of respondents held *favorable* opinions toward police officers. In addition, a 1991 national telephone poll of 1,283 respondents conducted by CBS News/New York Times found that 55% of Americans had a *great deal* or *quite a lot* of confidence in their local police; 86% had at least *some* confidence in their local police. These results show that the general public possesses favorable attitudes toward the police.

Correlates of Attitudes Toward the Police

Support for the police has consistently been high, but positive attitudes are tempered by demographic, experiential, and other factors. These individual variables are presented below as the correlates of attitudes toward the police.

Race

Race is one of the strongest predictors of attitudes toward the police (Peek, Lowe, & Alston, 1981). Beginning with the Kerner Commission (National Advisory Commission, 1968) and the President's Commission on Law Enforcement and Administration of Justice (1967), it has been known that African Americans view the police more antagonistically than do whites (Garofalo, 1977). According to Jacob (1971), there is a "climate of distrust" between African Americans and law enforcement officials because of the involuntary negative contacts between the two groups. African Americans believe that whites receive preferential police treatment and that African Americans are the subjects of discrimination (Waddington & Braddock, 1991). For example, Hindelang (1974) reported that 67% of whites held favorable attitudes toward the police, whereas only 43% of African Americans did. More recently, a 1993 USA Today/CNN/Gallup national telephone poll of 840 American adults found that 74% of whites compared to 48% of African Americans rated the police as *good*.

Aberbach and Walker (1970) reported that African Americans compared to whites are generally less satisfied with all government services. The perception of police discrimination held by African Americans appears to be greater in ghetto areas, suggesting a socioeconomic status or class effect on attitudes toward the police. Because of the correlation between race and class, Albrecht and Green (1977) attempted to disentangle the effects of class from race; they found that low-income African Americans living in inner-city areas possess the least favorable attitudes toward the police.

Although earlier studies (Carter, 1985) argued that Hispanics' attitudes toward the police track that of other racial minorities, especially African Americans, Lasley (1994)[2] maintained that ethnic minorities do not share monolithic attitudes toward the police. According to Lasley, Hispanics take a "middle ground" between whites and African Americans in rating attitudes toward the police. The middle ground hypothesis has been supported by polling data. A 1988 telephone poll of 1,147 New York City residents conducted by the New York Times found that 69% of African Americans, 53% of Hispanics, and 37% of whites said the police favor one race over another. Of those who indicated one race was favored, 33% of whites believed that their own race received favorable police treatment, whereas 65% and 51% of African Americans and Hispanics, respectively, said that whites received preferential police treatment.

Gender

Some studies have suggested that females hold more positive attitudes toward the police than do males (Lasley, 1994), whereas at least one other study (Thomas & Hyman, 1977) has shown that males hold more positive attitudes toward the police than do females. Still other research has reported no clear distinction between the sexes in attitudes toward the police (Dunham & Alpert, 1988; Murty, Roebuck, & Smith, 1990). Lasley (1994) studied attitudes toward the police of residents in Los Angeles before and after the Rodney King incident, finding that both men and women held less favorable attitudes toward the police after the King incident than they did before. Lasley also reported that several months after the incident, attitudes toward the police among African American males continued to decline precipitously, whereas attitudes toward the police among African American females did not continue to decline.

Age

Age is one of the most studied predictors of attitudes toward the police (Sullivan, Dunham, & Alpert, 1987). Early research showed that young persons (e.g., 30 years or less in age) generally have more negative attitudes toward the police than do older adults (Garofalo, 1977; Hindelang, 1974; Thomas & Hyman, 1977). This phenomenon was attributed to the fact that youngsters, especially adolescents (Bouma, 1973), have more negative experiences with the police (Smith & Hawkins, 1973) and have a "low-level of attraction" with law enforcement officers (Singer & Jonas, 1985, p. 53). Today, however, some research shows a curvilinear relationship between age and attitudes toward the police. For example, Zevitz and Rettammel (1990) have found that elderly respondents hold less favorable attitudes toward the police than do middle-age or younger adults.

Education

Previous research on the subject has revealed that educated respondents were more likely to rate police officers positively than were those with less education (Murty et al., 1990). Hindelang (1974), however, showed no significant differences between education and attitudes toward the police, and Peek et al. (1981) reported that highly educated whites possess negative attitudes toward the police. These inconsistent results suggest the relationship between education and attitudes toward the police is uncertain.

Community Type

Some research has found that people who live in suburbs hold more positive attitudes toward the police (Center for Public Policy, 1988) than do inner city residents (Hindelang, 1974; Thomas & Hyman, 1977). Other research has indicated that persons living in smaller non-metropolitan areas hold more favorable attitudes toward the police than residents of large metropolitan areas (Zamble & Annesley, 1987). These findings suggest that rural and suburban residents are more likely to express favorable attitudes toward the police than their urban counterparts.

Political Ideology

One study found that among all predictive variables, conservatism was the strongest determinant of positive attitudes toward the police (Zamble & Annesley, 1987). Another researcher reported that Republicans hold more favorable attitudes toward the police than Democrats (Hindelang, 1974). Bouma (1973) also found that students who regularly attend church or Sunday School have more positive attitudes toward the police than those who do not. Hence, there appears to be a direct association between conservative values and attitudes toward the police.

Socioeconomic Status

Many studies have shown that low-income people hold less favorable attitudes toward the police (Jacob, 1971; Thomas & Hyman, 1977), but the relationship between attitudes toward the police and socioeconomic status is unclear (Winfree & Griffiths, 1977). Research has not clarified the confounded effects of race, class, and education on attitudes toward the police. Low-income individuals and whites with advanced schooling, for example, have negative attitudes toward the police (Peek et al., 1981), whereas middle-class whites show more positive attitudes toward the police than do working-class whites (Jacob, 1971). The effect of income on attitudes toward the police among African Americans is also unclear (Peek et al., 1981), although Murty et al. (1990) found that white-collar African Americans hold more positive attitudes toward the police than blue-collar African American workers. They also reported that employed African Americans hold more favorable images of the police than unemployed/underemployed African Americans.

Police Contacts

Although attitudes toward the police are influenced by a complex set of individual and environmental factors, contact and experience with the police appear to have a major effect on attitudes toward the police (Jacob, 1971; Smith & Hawkins, 1973; Zevitz & Rettammel, 1990). Positive police contacts are more likely to result from a call for help or an automobile accident, whereas negative/involuntary contacts are usually related to being arrested or stopped for a traffic violation (Jacob, 1971). Polls have indicated that when citizens characterize their contact with police officers as *positive*, "the department's performance is almost always rated positive" (Reno Police Department, 1992, p. 10). The conventional wisdom is that positive police contacts increase favorable attitudes toward the police, whereas negative police contacts generate suspicion and mistrust, which lead to unfavorable attitudes toward the police.

Scaglion and Condon (1980) argued that although race has a significant effect on citizens' attitudes toward the police, "personal contact with the police is [the most] significant determinant of general satisfaction [with police services] than all other variables combined" (p. 490). Others have reported that positive police contacts can also ameliorate or neutralize negative police contacts (Rusinko, Johnson, & Hornung, 1978). This suggests that the general perception created during the police-citizen encounter is far more important than race or the nature of the police contact in determining citizen attitudes toward the police.

Findings

Confidence and Support for Police

The National Opinion Survey on Crime and Justice—1995 (NOSCJ) included seven questions to probe citizens' opinions and attitudes regarding their confidence in and support for the police. The first three questions (P1 to P3) asked respondents how much confidence they possessed in the ability of the police to protect citizens, solve crimes, and prevent crimes. These questions provided an assessment of public confidence in the ability of the police to control crime (hereafter crime control). A favorable attitude toward the police meant that respondents said that they had *a great deal* or *some* confidence in the crime control abilities of the police. The fourth to the sixth questions (P4 to P6) asked respondents to rate police promptness to citizen calls for service, the friendliness of the police, and the fairness of the police in dealing with people. In these three attitudinal measures, a favorable attitude meant that respondents rated each measure as *very high, high,* or *average.* With the last question (P7), respondents were asked whether they thought use of excessive force by the police in their local community was a problem. A favorable attitude was defined by the category *not a problem at all*.

Figure 3.1 presents the percentages of respondents who rated the police positively. Consistent with prior national and local polling data, the NOSCJ showed that a majority of respondents possessed favorable attitudes toward the police. Seventy-four percent of respondents were confident that the police could protect them from crime and solve crime. Similarly, 65% of the interviewees had high or some confidence in the ability of the police to prevent crime. About 78% of the respondents thought the police were fair when dealing with people and said the police responded quickly to citizen calls for service. Police friendliness received the most favorable rating from citizens; 84% of respondents rated the police as friendly. On the other hand, respondents held the least favorable attitudes on the use-of-force measure. About 53% of citizens believed that excessive use of force by the police was not a problem at all.

Demographic Differences in Attitudes Toward the Police

The findings above describe the national results from the NOSCJ for public support for and confidence in the police. Table 3.1 presents the percentages of respondents who reported favorable attitudes toward the police by individual demographic factors. The following discussion focuses on the factors that produced statistically significant differences in citizen attitudes toward the police.

Crime Control

Several studies (Feagin, 1970; Hahn, 1971) have reported racial differences in perceptions of police protection. A 1991 national poll conducted by CBS News/New York Times found that 76% of whites were *generally satisfied* with police protection in contrast to 53% of African Americans. Table 3.1 shows similar percentages of satisfaction for these two racial groups: 77% of white respondents had favorable police protection ratings, compared to 60% of African American respondents. Attitudes about the ability of the police to control crime also varied by marital status. Widowed respondents consistently reported more favorable attitudes toward police crime control efforts than did individuals who were married, divorced/separated, or individuals who never married. Moreover, Table 3.1 shows that respondents 60 years old or more

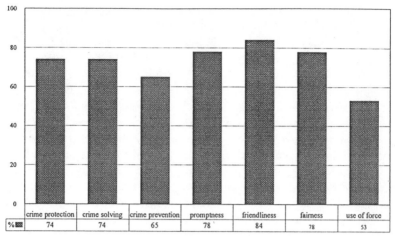

%▨	crime protection	crime solving	crime prevention	promptness	friendliness	fairness	use of force
	74	74	65	78	84	78	53

Percentages of respondents having favorable attitudes

Figure 3.1. Favorable Attitudes Toward the Police

possess more favorable attitudes toward police crime control efforts than did younger respondents.[3]

Results in Table 3.1 also indicate that attitudes toward the ability of the police to *prevent* crime had a greater variation across individual characteristics than the ability of the police to *protect* from or to *solve* crime. With crime prevention, respondents' favorable perceptions toward the police varied significantly across different groups on the basis of race, age, income, education, and marital background. Whereas race and marital status significantly influenced attitudes toward the ability of the police to solve crime, only marital status significantly influenced attitudes toward police crime protection. The results suggest that the American public's views toward the ability of the police to prevent crime are more diffuse than their views on the ability of the police to solve crime and protect them from crime.

Promptness

Research (Carter, 1985; Mirande, 1981) has found that ethnicity plays an important role in assessing police promptness. Hispanics, for example, believe that the police respond slowly to their calls for service. Consistent with this finding, Table 3.1 shows that Hispanics (83%) and

African Americans (75%) were slightly less likely compared to whites (86%) to report favorable attitudes toward police promptness. The NOSCJ also showed that older respondents (i.e., age 60 or above) and divorced/separated respondents possessed more positive perceptions of police promptness.

Friendliness

Research suggests that police temperament, politeness, and deportment are important contributors in citizen opinions of police friendliness (Brandl & Horvath, 1991). Race has been a significant predictor of attitudes toward police friendliness. A 1991 CBS News/New York Times poll found that 60% of whites considered the police as friends, whereas only 37% of African Americans did so. The NOSCJ findings presented in Table 3.1 show that 90% of white respondents perceived the police as friendly, compared to 74% of African Americans and 85% of Hispanics. Generally speaking, the NOSCJ showed a very high level of satisfaction with police friendliness within each racial group.

Table 3.1 also shows that younger Americans (18 to 29) had the least (76%) favorable views toward police friendliness. This result supports the empirical findings of prior research (Garofalo, 1977; Hindelang, 1974; Lasley, 1994; Murty et al., 1990). Table 3.1 also shows that widowed and married individuals also believed that the police were more friendly than individuals who never married.

Fairness

According to Biderman, Johnson, McIntyre, and Weir (1967), African Americans believe that the police treat them less fairly than police treat other racial groups. This finding has repeatedly been found in studies of attitudes toward the police (Smith & Hawkins, 1973; Sullivan et al., 1987). A 1992 Time/CNN national poll directly asked 1,102 respondents if they ever felt that they were "at risk of being treated unfairly" by the police. Overall, 68% said no, but only 23% of whites compared to 48% of African Americans believed they were at risk of unfair law enforcement treatment.

The NOSCJ results were consistent with those reported in prior research. As shown in Table 3.1, African American respondents had the lowest proportion of favorable views toward police fairness among the various racial groups. Younger, single, and low-income respondents also tended to report less favorable views toward police fairness than did their older, married, and higher-income counterparts.

Table 3.1 Favorable Attitudes Toward the Police by Demographic Factors (in percentages)

	Crime Protection	Crime Solving	Crime Prevention	Promptness	Friendliness	Fairness	Use of Force
Race							
White	77	79*	68*	86*	90*	87*	60*
Hispanic	83	74	73	83	85	83	42
Black	60	61	56	75	74	67	33
Other[a]	71	71	72	90	83	78	52
Gender							
Male	74	75	65	86	87	84	55
Female	77	78	69	83	89	85	55
Age							
18-29	69	67	59*	74*	76*	72*	54*
30-39	76	80	70	87	90	85	54
40-49	78	77	67	87	92	90	52
50-59	76	79	59	84	87	88	61
60-69	80	81	77	91	93	86	62
70 or older	83	81	74	94	96	96	59
Education							
Less than high school	74	76	71*	82	85	76	65
High school graduate	77	77	69	85	84	81	56
Some college	73	74	61	80	88	83	54
College graduate	76	79	68	90	94	92	52
Marital status							
Married	75*	77*	68*	87*	92*	88*	58
Widowed	90	89	81	89	94	91	57
Divorced/ separated	84	81	66	90	87	85	55
Never married	69	70	60	75	76	71	47

Use of Force

Research has shown that "the strongest single predictor of attitudes toward use of force by the police was race" (Williams, Thomas, & Singh, 1983, p. 42). African Americans are much more likely to hold negative perceptions toward police use of force than are whites (Flanagan & Vaughn, 1995). A 1992 Time/CNN national poll showed that two thirds of African Americans believed the police "are allowed to use too much

Table 3.1 Continued

	Crime Protection	Crime Solving	Crime Prevention	Promptness	Friendliness	Fairness	Use of Force
Household income							
Less than $15,000	77	79	65*	80	85	77*	50*
$15,000 to $30,000	74	70	67	81	83	78	56
$30,001 to $60,000	77	78	71	88	93	91	57
More than $60,000	74	80	59	87	90	86	50
Community type							
Rural	66	71	61	80	86	85	63*
Small town	78	76	72	84	90	84	67
Small city	79	79	70	85	87	81	47
Suburb	79	82	68	92	90	90	55
Urban	71	73	59	78	87	79	44
Political ideology							
Liberal	73	70	63	78	86	82	50*
Middle of the road	76	78	68	86	89	85	55
Conservative	77	79	68	85	89	87	59

a. Category contains fewer than 50 cases.
*Differences between groups are significant at $p \leq .01$ level.

force," whereas 39% of whites thought so. Results in Table 3.1 are consistent with prior research: 67% of African Americans thought police use of excessive force was a problem, whereas the majority of whites (60%) thought it was not a problem.

Table 3.1 also shows that public perceptions of police use of force varied with age, income, community type, and political ideology. Older, middle-income, rural, and conservative respondents tended to have more favorable perceptions about police use of force than did younger, urban, and liberal ones. This result is similar to research reported by Williams and colleagues (1983), who found older persons are more likely to approve of police use of force when compared to younger citizens.

In sum, the descriptive results showed that attitudes toward the police primarily varied by racial and marital background. Age was a significant factor in citizen attitudes toward the police. The curvilinear relationship between age and attitudes toward the police was not observed in these results. An examination of percentage differences between various age groups indicated that favorable attitudes toward the police did not decline in older respondents. Moreover, males and females did not differ significantly in their views about the police, although females tended to have more favorable attitudes toward the police. In addition, the following patterns were observed: Highly educated respondents tended to possess favorable attitudes compared to less educated respondents; suburban residents tended to hold favorable attitudes compared to urban residents; high-income respondents tended to express more positive attitudes than low-income citizens, and conservatives more than liberals held favorable attitudes toward the police.

Effects of Police Contacts on Attitudes Toward the Police

As discussed earlier, prior studies showed that citizen satisfaction with contact with the police explained more variation in attitudes toward the police than did other factors, including race, age, and marital status. It is therefore important to investigate whether significant variations of attitudes among racial and age groups still exist after controlling for satisfaction with contact with the police. To investigate the specific effect of police contacts on attitudes toward the police, analyses were conducted for those 547 respondents who had contacts with the police during the past 2 years.

Because the effect of one variable on attitudes toward the police may be mediated by many other variables, multivariate regression analyses were employed to control for influences of other factors. Ten individual variables were included in these analyses: male, African American, Hispanic, married, and urban are dichotomous variables coded as 0 and 1; education, income, conservatism, and satisfaction with police contact are categorical variables as defined by the survey; and age is a continuous variable, ranging from 18 to 89.

Findings for the Police Contact Cases

As expected, the *level of satisfaction with police contact* had a highly significant and consistent effect on the survey measures of attitudes toward the police. Table 3.2 shows that all the coefficients were positive, suggesting that the greater the respondents' satisfaction with the police contact, the more positive their attitudes toward the police. This result supports previous research (Scaglion & Condon, 1980; Zevitz & Rettammel, 1990) that reported a strong relationship between satisfaction with police contact and attitudes toward the police. More important, the analysis in Table 3.2 showed that the effects of race, age, and marital status were no longer significant (except in the fairness and use-of-force equations) after the citizen satisfaction factor was held constant. This suggests that African Americans and young citizens who experienced positive police contacts were as likely as non-African Americans and older respondents to report the police to be friendly, prompt, and effective at crime control.

However, the comparatively favorable views toward police promptness, friendliness, and crime control did not occur with the perceptions of police fairness and use of force. When experience with the police was considered, African Americans still believed that they were treated unfairly and that the police used too much force. These results confirm previous studies that found a strong subcultural belief about differential police treatment within minority groups (Hahn, 1971; Thomas & Hyman, 1977; Waddington & Braddock, 1991) and about police use of excessive force in African American communities (Brooks, 1993; Jacob, 1971; Lasley, 1994).

In addition to the above significant findings, Table 3.2 shows that Hispanics and urban residents hold less favorable views toward police use of force. Moreover, being conservative was significantly related to attitudes toward police fairness. The positive coefficient of conservatism suggests that conservatives are more likely than liberals to say that the police treat people equally. This finding supports Zamble and Annesley (1987), who reported that conservatism was a strong predictor of favorable attitudes toward the police.

Discussion and Conclusion

Confirming previous research, this chapter found that a majority of respondents held favorable views toward police friendliness, fairness, and promptness. More than half of the respondents possessed confidence in the ability of the police to control crime. Although citizens' support and confidence for the police were high, attitudes toward the police were mediated by a variety of individual characteristics. The analysis showed that young persons and African Americans, compared to older respondents and non-African Americans, were less likely to hold favorable attitudes toward the police. African Americans,

Table 3.2 Effects of Citizen Satisfaction With Police Contacts on Attitudes Toward the Police (regression coefficients)

Variable	Crime Protection	Crime Solving	Crime Prevention	Promptness	Friendliness	Fairness	Use of Force
Satisfaction with police contact	.345*	.282*	.273*	.400*	.394*	.386*	.214*
Black	−.150	−.228	−.184	.175	−.164	−.475*	−.595*
Hispanic	.043	−.253	−.040	−.155	−.400	−.192	−.439*
Male	.074	.043	.116	.140	.147	.033	.026
Age	.001	.001	−.001	.005	.003	.005	−.002
Education	−.009	−.006	−.003	.081	.099	.092	−.050
Urban	−.006	−.026	−.139	−.296	−.173	−.066	−.291*
Conservatism	−.001	.035	−.114	.033	.112	.186*	.105
Married	−.150	−.010	−.041	−.102	−.050	−.059	−.056
Income	−.032	.013	−.056	−.023	−.053	.015	.016
Constant	1.851	1.857	2.067	1.595	1.787	1.198	2.610
Adjusted R^2	.255	.200	.157	.262	.289	.309	.169

*Effect is significant at $p \leq .01$ level.

Hispanics, and urban residents are also specifically concerned about the excessive use of force by the police. These findings suggest that future research should focus on the types of community programs that improve positive attitudes toward the police among the young, those who live in urban areas, and minorities, particularly African Americans and Hispanics. Investigators should examine strategies proposed by Smith (1994), who detailed ways for police administrators to include these disaffected individuals in the police policy-making apparatus.

Experiencing a positive contact with the police was the strongest determinant of positive attitudes toward the police. The results suggest that contact with the police, more than race, explains variations in attitudes toward police friendliness, fairness, and confidence in the ability of the police to control crime (Jacob, 1971). As to attitudes about police fairness and use of force, African Americans continued to report lower favorable ratings on these items than did whites even after they had experienced positive contacts with the police. Both Hispanics and residents in urban areas also reported less favorable attitudes toward police use of force when considering police contacts.

Looking ahead, future community programs need to place a premium on increasing positive police-citizen contact and interaction. Recent research in community policing has shown that increased opportunity for citizens and officers to interact can enhance positive attitudes toward the police (Peak, Bradshaw, & Glensor, 1992; Trojanowicz & Banas, 1985). Programs aimed at youngsters also appear to increase positive interaction with the police. Blotner and Lilly (1986) found that programs such as DARE (Drug Awareness Resistance Education) and SPECDA (School Program to Educate and Control Drug Abuse) expose police officers to school-aged children as counselors and positive role models, which increases positive attitudes toward the police.[4]

In addition to the above programs, law enforcement professionals should also develop strategies to cultivate a positive atmosphere during the police-citizen encounter. Yarmey (1991) reported that crime victims have less support for the police if they experience an unsatisfactory contact with the police. Cox and White (1988) reported that it is not the negative contact with the police as much as the citizens' "perceptions and evaluations of the interaction" that affect attitudes toward the police (p. 120). To the extent that it is possible, police officers should attempt to foster a conciliatory atmosphere so citizens classify the police experience positively. To facilitate this process, law enforcement agencies should consider training programs and community outreach strategies to cultivate positive perceptions during police-citizen encounters.

Notes

1. Much of the polling data cited herein derives from the CD-ROM *Polling the Nations* (1986-1993).

2. Also see Sullivan et al. (1987), in which Cuban Americans in Miami possessed attitudes toward the police more similar to whites than Mexican Americans and other American Hispanics.

3. Because age is directly related to marital status, it is likely that age may mediate the effect of marital status on attitudes toward the police.

4. Some research did not support the positive relationship between police contact and attitudes toward the police. Kelly (1975) reported that previous efforts at police community relations programs have not significantly increased positive attitudes toward the police. Likewise, Decker, Smith, and Uhlman (1979) revealed that racial attitudes remained unchanged after a police-community relations program. Moreover, Smith and Hawkins (1973) found that positive minority-police contacts did not dramatically improve minorities' positive attitudes toward the police, suggesting that there are strong forces at play with racial minorities that create very negative attitudes toward the police irrespective of positive police contacts.

Bringing the Offender to Heel

Views of the Criminal Courts

LAURA B. MYERS

Public Opinion and the Courts

As a social institution, the courts have received high marks on overall satisfaction from the public. However, there is dissatisfaction with parts of the system, such as with perceived penalty leniency (Flanagan, McGarrell, & Brown, 1985; Hengstler, 1993). Previous studies indicate that related social attitudes and demographics are important in explaining public perception of the courts (Fagan, 1981; Flanagan et al., 1985). Court contact, knowledge, experience, and satisfaction are all related to perception (Flanagan et al., 1985; Hengstler, 1993).

The results of such studies suggest that people may expect too much from the courts. When expectations are frustrated through court contact, the public tends to become dissatisfied. This dissatisfaction has increased over the years. Of those polled in 1973, 24% had great confidence in the legal system. In 1978, confidence had dropped to 18%, 14% in 1988, and finally 8% in 1993 (Hengstler, 1993).

The factors related to perceptions of the courts are divided into three categories for discussion, similar to the categories in a 1978 (Yankelovich, Skelly, and White) public opinion study on the same topic. The first two categories are social attitudes about the courts: perceptions about the equality and fairness of the courts and perceptions regarding how the courts operate to protect society. The third category is public perceptions concerning quality and performance of courts.

Equality and Fairness of the Courts

Political Considerations Influencing Court Decisions

Courts often claim to be objective arbiters of social conflict. Consequently, political pressure should not be able to influence decisions made by the courts. Although there is a high degree of insulation in the courts, they are not impervious to political pressure. Two major factors affect judicial decision makers: the nature of the crime problem and the extent of media coverage. The more violent the crime problem and the more media scrutiny there is, the less latitude the court has and the more objective judges have to be. However, courts usually operate at low visibility with little outside scrutiny. Herein lies the avenue for political influence on judicial matters (Nardulli, Eisenstein, & Flemming, 1988).

In a national survey of the public, judges, lawyers, and community leaders (Yankelovich, Skelly, & White, 1978), only 26% of respondents felt that the influence of political considerations was a serious problem. However, African Americans were more likely to see it as a serious problem (38%), compared with whites and Hispanics, 24% and 28%, respectively. Those with less than a $10,000 income (in 1978 dollars) also were more likely to see it as a serious problem.

Treatment of Rich and Poor

Equality and fairness also can be measured in terms of the treatment of the poor and minorities. Studies indicate that people who believe such groups are treated inequitably are more likely to hold unfavorable views regarding courts (Sarat, 1977; Yankelovich, Skelly, & White, 1978). People who perceive courts this way are more likely to be African American, poor, or from urban areas.

Treatment of Minorities

According to Hagan and Albonetti's (1982) national survey, not only is there a perception that the poor are treated inequitably but that minorities receive differential treatment in the criminal justice system. Public perceptions of differential treatment of minorities appear to be conditioned by race, social class, and location. African Americans, those of lower social classes, and those from urban areas are more likely to perceive courts as discriminatory (Hagan & Albonetti, 1982; Yankelovich, Skelly, & White, 1978).

Disregard of Defendants' Rights

The due process rights of criminal defendants play a major role in public perceptions of the courts. A 1993 poll revealed that the public perceived the lawyer's role to be one of protecting citizen rights and society (Hengstler, 1993). However, the protection of rights is hard to balance with protection of society. Because of the emphasis on defendants' rights, courts often find themselves concerned with legal guilt more than factual guilt, resulting in a slow justice system. The public, on the other hand, places unrealistic expectations on courts to expedite justice and do more to protect society. The 1978 Yankelovich, Skelly, and White study found little concern for defendants' rights, except among African Americans.

Caba (1995) suggests that the public's perception is that the courts undo the work of the police to get criminals off the street. However, one public opinion study found little support for this perception (Fagan, 1981), and a more recent study found that when the public supports the police and corrections, they are just as likely to support courts (Flanagan et al., 1985). The perception that courts undo the work of the police in the name of societal protection may no longer be true.

Protection of Society

Bail for Those Previously Convicted

Concern for the protection of society through crime control can be measured with perceptions regarding offender treatment and court operations. The 1978 Yankelovich, Skelly, and White public opinion study found 37% of respondents surveyed felt granting bail to those previously convicted was a serious problem. The 1989 Gallup poll revealed 68% of respondents would deny bail to those accused of violent crime.

Courts That Do Not Reduce Crime

The Yankelovich, Skelly, and White (1978) public opinion study found that 43% of respondents felt courts that do not help reduce crime was a serious problem. Those with 1978 incomes over $7,500 were more likely to think so than those who earned less. In regard to race, Hispanics were more likely to think this way than were whites and African Americans.

Those who described their political orientation as liberal were the most negative (48%).

Harshness of Courts

In general, the public perceives that the courts are not harsh enough in the sentencing of criminal defendants. When asked about the O. J. Simpson case prior to the verdict, the public believed the jury would more likely be lenient than harsh. Only 47% of Americans believed the case would be handled properly (Saad, 1994). Fifty-three percent of the public responded that the Simpson situation could have been avoided if the court had been more harsh in the 1989 domestic dispute case.

The 1982 NORC General Social Survey (Wood, 1990) found 86% of respondents felt courts were not harsh enough on criminals. This number was a substantial increase from the 48% found in 1965 (Brown, Flanagan, & McLeod, 1984). The 1989 Gallup report (Shriver, 1989) produced a similar percentage, with 83% believing courts were too lenient. There was significantly more concern that criminals were being treated more leniently (79%) than about the disregard of defendants' rights (16%) (Wood, 1990).

Plea Bargaining

Even though a large number of cases are plea bargained in the courts, the public does not approve. Fagan's (1981) study revealed a large majority were opposed to the practice, and the 1989 Gallup poll (Shriver, 1989) reported a similar number.

Disregard of Crime Victims' Interests

In the past 20 years, there has been a growing concern for victims' rights. As citizens have become more concerned with their "outsider" status in the court system, various reformers have called for a responsiveness to the needs of victims (Karmen, 1984). Although victim/witness assistance programs and victim compensation programs have sprung up all over the country and public support has grown, the desire to spend tax dollars and to exert government control over the process has declined (McDonald, 1976).

Quality and Performance

Speedy Trial

With the promise of speedy trials, courts are creating much frustration for the public, especially for those who must use the courts. In the Yankelovich, Skelly, and White (1978) study, those with extensive, actual knowledge of courts were more likely to perceive a 6-month time period from arrest to trial as a serious problem (43%), whereas those with average (38%) and limited (26%) actual knowledge were less likely to see it as a serious problem.

Expensive Lawyers and Expensive Courts

The expense of hiring lawyers appears to be a major concern for the public. The public wants lawyers to be more responsive to their needs, and that means, among other things, being reasonably priced. The public is tired of high legal fees. They are willing to pay if the services are worth it. They want bills they can understand and they want to receive them in a timely manner (Levine, 1992). The public also perceives that courts are often priced beyond the reach of the average person. The infrequent user of the court may feel the court is the arena of the judges, lawyers, and litigants who use the courts most frequently, and citizens are just outsiders trying to get in (Nejelski & Wheeler, 1979).

Analysis

General Dissatisfaction With Courts

Respondents in the National Opinion Survey on Crime and Justice— 1995 (NOSCJ) were asked about their perceptions of the courts on the issues reviewed above. Most of the questions asked respondents if they felt these situations in the courts were a *serious problem, somewhat of a problem, a minor problem,* or *not a problem at all.* All responses were reclassified to reflect dissatisfaction, satisfaction, or lack of knowledge on the issue. Those with a lack of knowledge (*don't know*) were excluded from further analysis.[1] Eighteen demographic variables were analyzed with each of the issues.[2]

Equality and Fairness of the Courts

Fifty-seven percent of respondents answered that political considerations influencing court decisions was a problem (see Table 4.1). The 1978 Yankelovich, Skelly, and White study indicated race and income would condition the result, but neither factor was significant. However, respondents ages 30 to 69 were more likely to see the influence of political considerations as a problem than were the very young or the very old. Divorced or never-married respondents and respondents who felt their neighborhood streets were less safe were more likely to see it as a problem.

A similar relationship was found regarding the problem of differential treatment for the poor (57%). As in past studies, minorities were more likely to perceive this as a problem than were whites. The poor and those from urban areas, however, were just as likely as the rich and those from rural areas to see it as a problem. Democrats and liberals also were more likely to find differential treatment of the poor a problem compared to their Republican and conservative counterparts. The very old and those who were married or widowed were less likely to perceive differential treatment as a problem. Those who felt their neighborhood streets were less safe were more likely to see it as a problem, as were those who received their news from television or other people.

Interestingly, only 42% of respondents believed differential treatment of minorities was a problem. The previous literature indicated race and location would condition this perception. In the NOSCJ, minorities were more likely to see differential treatment of minorities as a problem, but location was not relevant. Democrats, liberals, the unmarried, those age 60 and above, college graduates, those who did not own guns, and those with religious preferences other than Protestant or Catholic were more likely to see it as a problem.

There also was a general lack of concern for the disregard of defendants' rights, with only 34% of respondents perceiving this as a problem. However, African Americans were more likely to see it as a problem. In addition, those who felt their neighborhood crime rate had increased, those divorced and those not married, and those under age 70 were more likely to see it as a problem.

Protection of Society

Seventy-three percent of respondents were concerned about courts that grant bail for those previously convicted (see Table 4.2). Minorities,

Table 4.1 Americans' Views About Courts in Their Community on Equality and Fairness Issues (percentage responding it is a problem)

Question: "Do you think each of the following is a problem or not?"

	Political Considerations Influencing Court Decisions	Treatment of Rich and Poor	Treatment of Minorities	Disregard of Defendants' Rights
National	57	57	42	34
Age				
18-29	46*	65*	50*	44*
30-39	65	58	44	33
40-49	59	53	40	33
50-59	56	58	42	35
60-69	58	62	38	31
70 or older	47	42	28	11
Race/ethnicity				
White	57	52*	35*	29*
Hispanic	53	74	67	45
Black	57	79	72	56
Other	48	58[a]	50[a]	32[a]
Sex				
Male	55	57	43	32
Female	58	57	42	36
Education				
Less than high school	45	58	42*	38
High school graduate	52	58	37	31
Some college	61	54	41	36
College graduate	62	58	53	33
Marital status				
Married	59*	52*	37*	30*
Widowed	54	59	37	27
Divorced/separated	69	62	49	41
Never married	43	65	57	41
Religion				
Protestant	57	53	40*	32
Catholic	57	57	41	31
None	50	61	49	39
Other	61	70	60	50

college-educated respondents, those under the age of 70 (especially ages 40-49), respondents who were married or divorced, those from suburbs or urban areas, and those who live with others were more likely to see it as a problem.

Table 4.1 Continued

	Political Considerations Influencing Court Decisions	Treatment of Rich and Poor	Treatment of Minorities	Disregard of Defendants' Rights
Party affiliation				
Republican	59	47*	34*	28
Democrat	63	64	52	38
Independent/other	51	59	43	35
Political ideology				
Liberal	60	68*	54*	43
Middle of the road	56	59	42	32
Conservative	55	49	37	31
Gun ownership				
Yes	59	52	38*	32
No	55	60	47	35
Neighborhood crime				
Increased	58	63	45	45*
Stayed the same	57	55	42	30
Decreased	49	55	41	28
Safe streets				
Safer	37*	51*	37	27
Not as safe	62	68	50	42
Same	58	54	41	32
TV news				
Television	57	60*	44	35
Newspapers	53	49	38	29
Radio	61	35	27	29
Other	56	69	51	37

a. Category contains fewer than 50 cases.
*Differences between groups are significant at $p \leq .01$ level.

Sixty-seven percent of respondents were concerned about courts that do not help reduce crime. Prior studies indicated race and income would condition this perception. In the NOSCJ, Hispanics and those with incomes of $60,000 and above were more likely to perceive this issue as a problem. In addition, respondents under the age of 70 (especially ages 40-49), and those who were either divorced or married, were more likely to be concerned.

Table 4.2 Americans' Views About Courts in Their Community on Protection of Society Issues (percentage responding it is a problem)

Question: "Do you think each of the following is a problem or not?"

	Bail for Those Previously Convicted	Courts That Do Not Reduce Crime	Harshness of Courts	Harshness of Courts on Drunk Drivers	Plea Bargaining	Disregard of Crime Victims' Interests
National	73	67	61	66	67	51
Age						
18-29	62*	62*	60	66	56*	44
30-39	77	69	68	65	67	52
40-49	83	75	60	64	72	54
50-59	79	62	56	68	72	54
60-69	72	81	61	60	72	62
70 or older	57	42	42	73	68	39
Race/ethnicity						
White	72*	66*	62	66	68	50
Hispanic	81	78	65	70	70	54
Black	78	67	55	66	59	60
Other[a]	51	46	49	42	63	56
Sex						
Male	70	66	60	58*	62*	49
Female	76	67	62	63	72	54
Education						
Less than high school	55*	65	62	65	64*	47
High school graduate	68	60	57	67	71	46
Some college	78	73	65	63	71	52
College graduate	81	70	61	66	60	58
Income						
Less than $15,000	67	59*	60	65	66*	53
$15,000 to $30,000	71	68	59	73	78	55
$30,001 to $60,000	75	63	63	61	63	48
More than $60,000	77	79	63	66	62	55

Sixty-one percent of respondents thought that courts did not sentence offenders appropriately. Ninety-four percent of this group felt criminals were not treated harshly enough. This finding, and the small concern for defendants' rights, supports prior studies that found the public to be more concerned with leniency than with a disregard for defendants' rights. Those respondents who felt their neighborhood streets were not safe and those who lived with others also were more likely to perceive courts as too lenient. When asked about the courts' handling of drunk

Table 4.2 Continued

	Bail for Those Previously Convicted	Courts That Do Not Reduce Crime	Harshness of Courts	Harshness of Courts on Drunk Drivers	Plea Bargaining	Disregard of Crime Victims' Interests
Marital status						
Married	77*	69*	63	67	69*	49
Widowed	65	58	51	67	73	64
Divorced/						
separated	74	74	61	64	67	58
Never married	65	59	55	63	59	51
Gun ownership						
Yes	74	69	65	62*	67	52
No	73	65	57	69	67	51
Community type						
Rural	71*	65	71	66	79	52*
Small town	63	61	55	67	66	38
Small city	74	70	62	62	63	51
Suburb	80	69	63	65	66	56
Urban	77	70	54	69	62	61
Safe streets						
Safer	67	55	53*	62	69	47
Not as safe	72	67	70	68	67	57
Same	74	68	60	65	66	50
Live alone						
Yes	62*	62	49*	62	66	48
No	74	67	62	66	67	51

a. Category contains fewer than 50 cases.
*Differences between groups are significant at $p \leq .01$ level.

drivers, 66% of the respondents were concerned, with 93% feeling drunk drivers were not treated harshly enough. Female respondents were more likely to be concerned than males, as were respondents who did not own guns.

As predicted by the literature, the respondents (67%) overwhelmingly opposed plea bargaining. Only 25% of the respondents thought it was a good idea, and 8% neither favored nor opposed it. Females, those age 30 and above, those with a high school diploma or some college (college graduates were least likely), those with incomes of $15,000 to $30,000, and those who were married, divorced, or widowed were most likely to oppose plea bargaining.

Only 51% of NOSCJ respondents viewed the courts' disregard for victims' interests as a serious concern. Those living in small towns were the least likely to see it as a problem, and those living in the suburbs were more likely to see it as a problem.

Quality and Performance

Given the significant amount of literature devoted to the quality and performance of the courts, it is not surprising the public would express much dissatisfaction with the courts and their personnel. Sixty-five percent of respondents were dissatisfied with courts that permit 6 months to pass between arrest and trial (see Table 4.3). The more educated the respondent, the more likely they were to be dissatisfied.

Respondents were especially dissatisfied with the cost of hiring a lawyer. Consistent with prior studies, 84% felt the cost of hiring a lawyer was a problem. The only factor that conditioned this perception was number of television hours watched per week, with those who watched 20 to 30 hours per week most likely to be dissatisfied. Those who watched over 30 hours per week were the least likely to be dissatisfied. Related to this finding, respondents also felt courts were too expensive for the people who use them (75%). Only Democrats were more likely than others to believe courts are too expensive for those who use them.

Satisfaction Scales

The dependent variables analyzed above were merged into an overall Court Satisfaction Scale (reliability test alpha = .77) and into three separate satisfaction scales representing perceptions of equality and fairness (reliability test alpha = .73), protection of society (reliability test alpha = .56), and quality and performance of the courts (reliability test alpha = .64). Low scores on each scale represented dissatisfaction and high scores represented satisfaction.

The demographic variables analyzed in the bivariate analysis of each dependent measure were used in the analysis of each scale. Table 4.4 yields the results of the regression analyses for each scale. The multiple R for the overall court satisfaction scale was .40 (R^2 = .16) and was statistically significant ($F = 7.96$, $p < .01$). Satisfaction with the police, living in a small town or a small city, being a Republican, and having less than a college education were all significantly associated with court satisfaction. Hispanic respondents, those who watched 20 to 30 hours of television per week, those who felt neighborhood crime had increased, and those who were divorced were more likely to be dissatisfied.

Table 4.3 Americans' Views About Courts in Their Community on Quality and Performance Issues (percentage responding it is a problem)

Question: "Do you think each of the following is a problem or not?"

	Speedy Trial	Expensive Lawyers	Expensive Courts
National	65	84	75
Sex			
Male	61	83	72
Female	68	84	78
Education			
Less than high school	56*	83	69
High school graduate	60	78	75
Some college	67	89	79
College graduate	71	85	75
Party affiliation			
Republican	59	79	67*
Democrat	70	88	82
Independent/other	67	85	77
TV hours per week			
Less than 10	62	83*	75
10 to 20	65	84	76
21 to 30	77	94	78
More than 30	59	70	69

*Differences between groups are significant at $p \leq .01$ level.

The multiple R for the equality and fairness scale was .31 ($R^2 = .10$) and was statistically significant ($F = 14.28$, $p < .01$). Respondents who were satisfied with the police, were white, were married, and lived in small towns were more likely to feel that courts promote equality and fairness. Those who believed their streets were less safe were less likely to believe that courts were equitable and fair.

The multiple R for the protection of society scale was .33 ($R^2 = .11$) and was statistically significant ($F = 8.71$, $p < .01$). Being satisfied with the police, being 18 to 29 years old, and living in a small town were all associated with the perception that courts were doing a good job of protecting society. Feeling that neighborhood crime had increased, being Hispanic, owning guns for protection or both protection and sport, and being female were all associated with the perception that courts were not doing a good job protecting society.

Table 4.4 Results of Stepwise Multiple Regression on Court Perception Scales

Overall Court Satisfaction Scale (N = 497)[a]			Equality and Fairness Scale (N = 724)[a]			Protection of Society Scale (N = 634)[a]			Quality and Performance Scale (N = 665)[a]		
Variable	R^2	Beta*	Variable	R^2	Beta*	Variable	R^2	Beta*	Variable	R^2	Beta*
Police satisfaction	.029	.15	Police satisfaction	.037	.15	Police satisfaction	.026	.14	Police satisfaction	.017	.11
Hispanic	.059	-.17	White	.065	.14	Age 18-29	.044	.17	Small town	.031	.10
Small town	.078	.16	Married	.081	.12	Crime	.060	-.11	Republican	.043	.13
TV hours 20-30	.093	-.17	Unsafe streets	.091	-.10	Small town	.076	.12	Age 18-29	.054	.13
Crime	.106	-.13	Small town	.097	.08	Hispanic	.087	-.10	Hispanic	.067	-.12
Republican	.117	.13				Protect/sport gun	.093	-.10	TV hours 20-30	.077	-.10
High school grad	.129	.12				Female	.100	-.09	Unsafe streets	.085	-.10
Small city	.139	.10				Protect gun	.110	-.08	High school grad	.093	.09
TV hours 10-20	.147	-.10									
Not high school grad	.154	.10									
Divorced	.162	-.07									
Constant (16.18)			Constant (5.59)			Constant (7.70)			Constant (3.27)		

a. Listwise deletion of missing cases.

*$p \leq .05$.

The multiple R for the quality and performance scale was .30 (R^2 = .09) and was statistically significant ($F = 7.74$, $p < .01$). Satisfaction with the police, living in a small town, being a Republican, being 19 to 29 years old, and having a high school diploma were all associated with the perception of good quality and performance by the courts. Being Hispanic, watching 20 to 30 hours of television, and feeling their streets were not safe were all associated with the perception that courts were not performing adequately.

Discussion

The Public's Views About Courts and Justice

The bivariate analysis revealed much dissatisfaction with the courts, and the overall satisfaction scale analysis revealed the nature of that dissatisfaction. Although African Americans were more concerned with specific issues, Hispanic respondents were more dissatisfied overall. Those who felt that neighborhood crime had increased were dissatisfied with only one specific issue, the disregard of defendants' rights, but overall they were more dissatisfied with the courts than those who thought that crime had decreased or stayed the same. Perhaps indicative of their direct experience with the courts, those respondents who were divorced were more likely to be unhappy with the courts.

Court satisfaction was directly related to satisfaction with the police, adding more evidence to the idea that the public does not believe the courts undo the work of the police. It also supports the assumption that satisfaction with other social institutions is indicative of court satisfaction.

Of the equality and fairness issues, the public perceived the influence of political considerations and the differential treatment of the poor to be more of a problem than differential treatment of minorities or the disregard of defendants' rights. In contrast, African Americans perceived the latter two as more of a problem than did respondents of other races.

Those respondents who were satisfied with the equality and fairness of the courts also were satisfied with the police and unlikely to suffer the potential inequities of the courts. Being white, married, and living in a small town are not the usual characteristics of those who feel mistreated by the courts. Such people are more likely to be minorities, single, and living in urban areas, which are also characteristics related to living in an area thought to be unsafe. People who felt that their streets were less safe were more likely to be dissatisfied.

The public was more concerned about protection of society issues than equality and fairness issues. A large proportion were dissatisfied with granting bail to those previously convicted, courts that do not help decrease crime, courts that do not sentence appropriately, and courts that permit plea bargaining. There was less concern about protection of crime victims' interests than about these generalized leniency concerns.

Satisfaction with the courts' ability to protect society was again related to police satisfaction. Young people and those living in small towns were less likely to be critical of the courts' ability to protect them. Older people and those who live in high-crime areas are perhaps likely to expect more from the courts.

Dissatisfaction resulted again from security concerns, with those who felt that neighborhood crime had increased and those who owned guns for protection concerned that courts were not protecting them. Women were critical of the courts' handling of drunk drivers and the courts' use of plea bargaining specifically, and more likely than men to believe that the courts were not protecting society sufficiently. Hispanic respondents were dissatisfied overall and also dissatisfied with the courts' ability to protect them.

The public also expressed concern about the quality and performance of the courts. They felt courts spent too much time between arrest and trial and lawyers and courts were too expensive. Satisfaction with quality and performance of the courts was related to many of the same factors associated with satisfaction with the courts' ability to protect society. Once again, Hispanic respondents and those who were concerned about their safety were more likely to be dissatisfied with court quality and performance.

Policy Implications and Future Research

Analysis of specific court issues and the major categories of issues reveals much about the nature of court perceptions. A primary issue for court policymakers is race. Hispanic respondents were more likely to be dissatisfied overall, with the courts' ability to protect society, and with the quality and performance of the courts. African Americans were more likely to be dissatisfied on specific issues of equality and fairness.

Fear of crime was the other major relevant factor associated with dissatisfaction. Public perceptions that neighborhood crime had increased, that their streets were less safe, and that there was a need to own guns for protection were associated with overall court dissatisfaction, and with the three areas of dissatisfaction.

Court satisfaction was associated with police satisfaction. Other factors indicated that those people who live in relatively safe and stable environments (living in a small town, being married, being white) were less likely to be unhappy with the courts, perhaps because they have less need for the courts' assistance. Those with less education and perhaps not enlightened to the plight of others were less likely to be dissatisfied.

It is clear that court satisfaction is continuing to decline. The results of this analysis indicate that race and fear of crime are major correlates of this dissatisfaction. Court reformers should respond quickly to this knowledge. Many courts have already initiated public education campaigns to attract those who feel alienated from courts. With the knowledge that certain segments of the population feel courts are not responsive to their needs, reformers can better tailor their campaigns to be more successful.

Why Hispanics stand out so much in their dissatisfaction with the courts and why those who feel unsafe are more likely to be unhappy with the courts is not so clear. Although this research should give policymakers the information they need to respond to these specific populations of people, further research should address why these people feel the way they do. Perhaps information on the actual knowledge and experience of the public with the courts would further clarify the relationships found in this study.

Notes

1. These data were excluded because the reasons for their lack of knowledge were uninterpretable given the data collected. The data ranged from a low of 3% *don't know* to a high of 20% *don't know* across the 13 issues.

2. The demographic variables included age, race, sex, education, income, marital status, religion, party affiliation, political ideology, gun ownership, reason for owning gun, community type, neighborhood crime, safe streets, live alone, TV hours watched per week, how respondent received news, and whether respondent was a TV crime show viewer.

Just and Painful

Attitudes Toward Sentencing Criminals

JURG GERBER

SIMONE ENGELHARDT-GREER

Four reasons exist why a society punishes offenders: (a) to discourage the same individuals from offending again in the future, or others from engaging in the same crimes (deterrence); (b) to prevent offenders physically from engaging in more crimes by locking them up (incapacitation); (c) to train, educate, and counsel offenders to help them become law-abiding citizens (rehabilitation); and (d) to inflict deserved punishment on people who harm society (retribution). In this chapter, we analyze data from the National Opinion Survey on Crime and Justice—1995 (NOSCJ) that focus on Americans' attitudes toward sentencing criminals.

Past Research on Attitudes Toward Sentencing Criminals

Evaluating public attitudes concerning the sentencing of criminals is difficult because our measures of public attitudes are often crude and we can only tap into relatively superficial domains. Research indicates, for instance, that public knowledge of crime and justice is quite limited, but this lack of factual information does not prevent people from having very strong attitudes (Roberts, 1992). The public has only the vaguest notions of crime-related statistics and vastly overestimates victimization rates for violent (Knowles, 1984) and property (Doob & Roberts, 1982) crimes. Furthermore, not only is there little factual information regarding crime and justice, often what the public "knows" is factually incorrect. Multiple reasons account for this. The media play a role in that they have a bias toward sensational crimes and therefore devote much attention to rare crimes such as murder (Liska & Baccaglini, 1990). Likewise, when asked about their response to a particular type of sentence for a particular offense, the public does not usually think of "typical" offenders, but rather of particularly hardened and vicious criminals, the type of offender most likely presented in the media.

The surveys themselves can be problematic. Roberts (1992) points out that questions are often relatively simple and do not reveal the complexity of crime and perceptions of fairness of punishments. Similarly, the amount of information presented to respondents affects their responses. Most surveys present little information, and most respondents indicate that they have relatively punitive attitudes. However, the more information concerning the offender, the victim, and sentencing options that is presented, the lower the degree of punitiveness (Doble & Klein, 1989). Finally, there is the possibility that questions that are designed to measure attitudes concerning criminal justice "are merely expressions of more general underlying attitudinal orientations" (Durham, 1993, p. 8).

Adults as Offenders

Until recently, the conventional wisdom among politicians, criminal justice professionals, educators, and pollsters was that the public was exceptionally punitive. Rehabilitation was believed to be unpopular, and the public was thought to support punishment for the sake of deterrence, but especially for incapacitation and retribution: "Lock 'em up because they deserve it (retribution), so they can't commit crimes for a while (incapacitation), and hopefully they will serve as a model for others who are thinking about committing crime (deterrence), but forget about reforming them (rehabilitation)." However, recent research indicates that the public, although undoubtedly punitive in some ways, is not uniformly so; rehabilitation still finds its support in public opinion surveys.

At first glance, the public seems to believe that the courts impose sentences that are too lenient (Stinchcombe et al., 1980) and that there is too much focus on rehabilitation, and not enough on "punishment." Politicians have subsequently jumped "on the punitive bandwagon" (Cullen, Clark, & Wozniak, 1985, p. 23) and passed laws mandating more punitive sentences, believing that is what the public wanted. McCorkle (1993) pointed out that this involved a misreading of public attitudes:

> Social science research has revealed, however, that public attitudes are anything but simple; indeed, they are "diverse, multidimensional and complex" (Flanagan and Caulfield 1984:41). To be sure, the public clearly holds a strong punishment orientation. At the same time, however, Americans appear to recognize the limits of a purely punitive response to the crime problem. Beyond punishment, studies show most believe some understanding, energy and resources should be devoted toward addressing the genesis of offending behavior (Cullen, Cullen, and Wozniak 1988; Duffee and Ritti 1977; Gottfredson and Taylor 1985; Riley and Rose 1980; Skovron et al. 1988; Warr and Stafford 1984). (p. 240)

More specifically, recent research indicates that respondents are not opposed to but rather support "programs that would enhance an inmate's chances, upon release from prison, for gainful economic employment" and generally support "educational and vocational training" (Cullen, Skovron, Scott, & Burton, 1990, p. 14). Similarly, McCorkle (1993) found considerable support, at least among some respondents, for rehabilitation programs for certain offenders. At the aggregate level, most respondents saw retribution and incapacitation as the primary reasons for sanctioning offenders. However, drug dealers were not seen as potential beneficiaries of treatment programs, but burglars and robbers were. With respect to categories of respondents, young, poor, and nonwhites were most likely to support some rehabilitation programs, a finding explained, according to McCorkle (1993), by the fact they were the individuals "most likely to find themselves in prison" (p. 250).

The relationship between sentencing attitudes and demographic characteristics is not clear: "Past research on the demographic and attitudinal correlates of punishment orientations has produced largely weak and inconsistent findings" (McCorkle, 1993, p. 243). Nevertheless, some tentative findings have been reported. Conservatives have been found to be somewhat more punitive than liberals, but people who have been victimized by crime were no more punitive than nonvictims

(Taylor, Scheppele, & Stinchcombe, 1979). Similarly, females were less punitive than males and African Americans were no more punitive than whites (Stinchcombe et al., 1980). According to research by Langworthy and Whitehead (1986), "Older people who favor government spending on social programs tend to be less punitive. People who are afraid about being crime victims and males tend to be more punitive" (p. 582). Finally, there is a "well-documented negative relationship between education and punitiveness" (McCorkle, 1993, p. 243).

Juveniles as Offenders

Young offenders in America have long been seen as different from adult offenders. The latter have often been seen as "hardened" criminals, whereas the public has long been more optimistic about the prospects for treatment for juveniles:

> Young people involved in crime were assumed to be less responsible for their actions, less inclined to benefit from punishment, and more hopeful targets of a therapeutic approach than their adult counterparts. A basic optimism concerning youth, the malleability of the adolescent, and the possibilities of successfully rehabilitating and changing youthful natures was the foundation on which the original juvenile court was built. (Cullen, Golden, & Cullen, 1983, p. 2)

Although Americans are somewhat ambivalent about rehabilitation for adult offenders, political rhetoric to the contrary notwithstanding, support for rehabilitation for juvenile offenders is still fairly high, and respondents consistently express a belief that juveniles should not be treated the same as adult offenders. In a 1982 survey by the Opinion Research Corporation (cited in Schwartz, Guo, & Kerbs, 1993), 73% of respondents supported the idea that the primary goal of the juvenile justice system should be rehabilitation (treatment). Similarly, in a Michigan sample, 66% of respondents believed that juveniles should be treated differently from adults (Schwartz, Abbey, & Barton, 1990).

There were some important differences in attitudes by demographic characteristics of respondents. Although many Americans wanted to see juveniles who engaged in serious crimes be treated as adults, the support for such treatment was not uniform. Schwartz and his associates (1993) reported that males were more punitive than females, whites more punitive than African Americans, parents less punitive than non-parents, but "African-American parents [were] more supportive of

punitive juvenile justice policies than other racial/ethnic groups with
and without children" (p. 5). Similarly, in a survey of criminal justice
professionals and the general public, Cullen and his associates (1983)
found that the public supported the idea of "child saving" (i.e., rehabilitation of youthful offenders), but that it was supported more by
criminal justice professionals (e.g., judges and correctional administrators) than by the general public.

In sum, the public has continued to support the idea of rehabilitation,
although perhaps less than it once did. What Cullen and his associates
called the "tenacity of rehabilitation as a correctional ideology" best
sums up public attitudes:

> Despite politicians' and criminologists' continual attempts over the past
> 15 years to undermine its legitimacy, the public believes that rehabilitation
> should be a goal of corrections. The data suggest that citizens do not feel
> that time in prison should be wasted; prisons should not be warehouses
> or places that inflict pain without clear purpose. Instead, most citizens take
> a more pragmatic stance: Inmates should be given the education, training,
> employment experiences, and, perhaps, counseling that will enable them
> to become productive citizens. Our respondents were not overly optimis-
> tic that treatment programs could help violent offenders, but they indi-
> cated that such interventions could be effective with nonviolent and many
> adult offenders. Juveniles were seen to be especially good candidates for
> rehabilitation. (Cullen et al., 1990, pp. 15-16)

Findings

The NOSCJ included five questions to test public attitudes toward
sentencing criminals. Respondents were asked whether deterrence,
incapacitation, rehabilitation, or retribution should be the most important purpose for sentencing adults (Question A1) and juveniles (Question A2). Next, they were asked if they thought legislatures should make
prison sentences mandatory for convictions for certain offenses or if
judges should have discretion in deciding who goes to prison (Question
A3). Respondents were then asked if the United States should spend
money on social and economic problems or on the criminal justice
system in an attempt to lower the crime rate (Question A4). Finally, we
asked them if the government should make a greater effort to rehabilitate or "punish and put away criminals who commit violent crimes"
(Question A5).

Consistent with past research, NOSCJ respondents were ambivalent in their attitudes toward sentencing criminals. They were punitive with respect to some issues, but made considerable exceptions in their beliefs that criminals should be punished harshly. More specifically, a majority of respondents, 53%, believed that the main purpose in sentencing adults should be retribution. However, Americans were much less likely to feel that simple punishment was the most appropriate purpose for sentencing juveniles. For juveniles, 50% chose the answer "to train, educate and counsel offenders" (rehabilitation) as the primary purpose of criminal sanctions. Our respondents thus were more likely to believe that juveniles are more malleable than adults. They also supported the idea of rehabilitation for juveniles, at least as long as the question did not include this term (cf. Innes, 1993).

This interpretation is verified by the two questions that focus on where the government should spend money to lower the crime rate and how the government should deal with violent criminals. Fifty-four percent of respondents indicated that money should be spent on social and economic problems, and only 31% chose the police, prisons, and judges, but 59% indicated that violent criminals should be punished, and only 31% supported the idea of rehabilitating them. Finally, when asked about the idea of making imprisonment mandatory for convictions "for some types of crimes," 55% of the respondents thought this was a good idea.

Demographic Differences

The NOSCJ included questions on respondents' age, race/ethnicity, gender, education, household income, marital status, religion, party identification, political ideology, gun ownership, reason for gun ownership, living alone, TV crime show viewing, TV hours per week, community type, region, perceptions of neighborhood crime, and perceptions of neighborhood gang problem. In general, we found support in the NOSCJ data for many findings of previous research. The demographic categories that had in the past been supportive of a punitive approach to sentencing tended to do so in the NOSCJ, but rehabilitation was supported by traditionally liberal respondents.

Five independent variables proved to be predictors of attitudes toward the sentencing of adults (see Table 5.1). Younger and well-educated respondents tended to be less punitive. The widowed, Republicans, and conservatives were more punitive than their demographic counterparts. With respect to sentencing juveniles, two independent variables were significant in regard to sentencing attitudes (see Table 5.1). The less educated respondents were, the more likely they were to support a punitive philosophy, and nonowners of guns were more likely to support rehabilitation. All differences were statistically significant at the .01 level of significance.

On the question of legislatively mandated prison sentences versus letting judges decide who serves time, differences on four demographic variables were statistically significant (see Table 5.2). Older respondents (but not those over the age of 70) were disproportionately in favor of mandated sentences. In terms of education, high school and college graduates supported mandated sentences, but not people with less than a high school education, or respondents with postgraduate college work. Similarly, people who have never been married, and Democrats, were more likely to support letting judges decide who serves time.

The findings on governmental spending to lower the crime rate were also consistent with past research. Respondents with postgraduate education supported spending money on social and economic programs and the same held true for liberals (see Table 5.3). Males and gun owners were more likely to support spending money on the criminal justice system.

Finally, clear demographic differences emerged in respondents' attitudes about whether greater effort should be made in rehabilitating or punishing violent criminals (see Table 5.4). At the aggregate level, 59% of respondents felt that punishing violent criminals is the most appropriate response, but this answer category was chosen disproportionately by whites, conservatives, and gun owners.

Consistent with the literature, we hypothesized that certain social characteristics of respondents might influence their attitudes toward sentencing criminals. For instance, we expected that TV-viewing habits would affect respondents' views: The more people watch TV, the more likely they would support punitive responses to criminal behavior. We expected this to be especially true for people who are regular viewers of "reality-based" crime shows on TV. Similarly, we expected respondents who live in poor neighborhoods, and are thus more likely to be confronted with street crime, to be more punitive than others. Also, individuals who fear being victimized might have attitudes toward sentencing criminals that are different from people who do not worry about being victimized. A series of questions were included in the questionnaire that let us test our expectations.

In general, we found relatively little support for the above hypotheses: The social characteristics of respondents were not good predictors

Table 5.1 Attitudes Toward Sentencing Adult and Juvenile Offenders (in percentages)

Question: "Which of these four purposes do you think should be the most important in sentencing . . . ?"

	Adults				Juveniles			
	Deterrence	Incapacitation	Rehabilitation	Retribution	Deterrence	Incapacitation	Rehabilitation	Retribution
National	13	13	21	53	15	4	50	31
Age								
18-29	11	9	29	51*	17	6	51	26
30-39	14	12	18	56	17	2	48	33
40-49	16	19	21	44	15	5	55	26
50-59	10	13	13	65	13	2	49	36
60-69	13	15	20	53	12	3	49	36
70 or older	6	11	21	63	10	9	42	39
Education								
Less than high school	5	6	23	66*	10	5	42*	42*
High school graduate	11	10	20	59	14	4	45	36
Some college	17	16	19	49	17	4	51	28
College graduate	9	19	33	39	11	5	68	17
Marital status								
Married	14	14	18	54*	15	4	49	33
Widowed	5	15	17	64	4	4	57	35
Divorced/separated	18	10	20	52	15	4	55	26
Never married	10	11	31	48	17	6	49	28
Party identification								
Republican	17	17	14	52*	17	4	48	32
Democrat	9	11	25	56	13	3	53	32
Independent/other	13	13	23	51	14	6	50	31
Political ideology								
Liberal	14	9	29	48*	16	3	49	32
Middle of the road	11	15	22	53	13	5	52	30
Conservative	15	13	15	56	18	3	48	31
Gun owner								
Yes	17	11	16	56	18	3	45	34*
No	10	14	25	51	12	5	54	29

*...ences between groups are significant at $p \leq .01$ level.

Table 5.2 Attitudes Toward Mandatory Sentences (in percentages)

Question: "Do you think mandatory sentences are a good idea or should judges be able to decide?"

	Good Idea	Judges Decide	Both	Neither
National	55	38	6	1
Age				
18-29	49*	45	6	0
30-39	54	36	9	0
40-49	61	37	2	0
50-59	51	38	4	6
60-69	63	29	6	2
70 or older	53	33	9	4
Education				
Less than high school	43*	48	5	5
High school graduate	55	37	7	2
Some college	58	35	6	1
College graduate	50	44	6	0
Marital status				
Married	58*	34	6	1
Widowed	50	35	11	3
Divorced/separated	54	40	4	2
Never married	46	47	5	1
Neighborhood crime				
Increased	51*	37	7	4
Stayed the same	56	37	6	1
Decreased	46	47	4	3
Protection by courts				
Dissatisfied	65*	29	5	1
Neutral	54	39	7	0
Satisfied	45	49	6	0

*Differences between groups are significant at $p \leq .01$ level.

of their attitudes toward sentencing criminals. The source of news about crime proved to affect none of the attitudes, and neither did the number of hours respondents watched TV. However, frequent viewers of TV crime shows were more punitive concerning the sentencing of juveniles and adults, although this correlation did not meet our stringent test of significance ($p \leq .01$).

The degree of neighborhood decay (Questions N1-N10) respondents witnessed also proved to be a weak predictor of sentencing attitudes. Those who believed that crime rates in their neighborhood decreased

Table 5.3 Attitudes Toward Spending Money in an Attempt to Lower the Crime Rate (in percentages)

Question: "Should money be spent on social and economic problems or on police, prisons, and judges?"

	Social Problems	Criminal Justice System	Both	Neither
National	54	31	13	2
Gender				
Male	55*	31	11	3
Female	53	30	15	2
Education				
Less than high school	51*	33	10	6
High school graduate	53	32	13	2
Some college	53	34	12	1
College graduate	68	13	17	2
Political ideology				
Liberal	66*	22	9	3
Middle of the road	57	29	13	1
Conservative	43	39	14	4
Gun owner				
Yes	51*	36	11	2
No	57	26	15	3

*Differences between groups are significant at $p \leq .01$ level.

during the past year wanted to let judges decide sentences instead of having legislatively mandated sentences for some types of crimes. Those who saw graffiti as a problem supported rehabilitation for juveniles. Finally, we constructed a scale of neighborhood decay and performed chi-square analyses between that scale and the five measures of sentencing attitudes. None of the differences proved to be statistically significant at the .01 level.

The extent to which respondents worry about being victimized (Questions W1-W7) only influenced attitudes about sentencing in one instance. People who worried about their homes being burglarized while they are away were more likely to support money being spent on the criminal justice system than those who did not. We also constructed a scale of worry about crime and tested its predictive power of sentencing attitudes, but similar to the neighborhood decay index, it failed to provide any significant differentiation in sentencing attitudes.

Table 5.4 Attitudes Toward Treatment of Violent Criminals (in percentages)

Question: "Where does the government need to make a greater effort these days: rehabilitate criminals who commit violent crimes or punish and put away criminals who commit violent crimes?"

	Rehabilitate	Punish	Both	Neither
National	27	59	13	1
Race/ethnicity				
White	23*	64	12	1
Hispanic	38	50	11	0
Black	46	39	15	0
Other[a]	25	48	25	3
Political ideology				
Liberal	41*	48	9	2
Middle of the road	27	59	13	1
Conservative	19	66	14	1
Gun owner				
Yes	21*	67	10	1
No	31	54	14	1
Protection by courts				
Dissatisfied	21*	66	12	1
Neutral	30	63	7	1
Satisfied	35	53	12	0

a. Category contains fewer than 50 cases.

*Differences between groups are significant at $p \leq .01$ level.

Finally, we used a scale developed by Myers (see Chapter 4 in this volume) on public perceptions of the courts' ability to protect the public against crime as an independent variable of attitudes toward sentencing. We found that it was a predictor in two instances (see Tables 5.2 and 5.4): The more dissatisfied respondents were with the courts' ability to protect society, the more likely it was they thought mandatory sentences were a good idea and that the government should focus on punishing rather than rehabilitating violent criminals.

Discussion

Our review of the literature on public attitudes toward sentencing criminals showed that there is more support for rehabilitation and less for retribution than political rhetoric and media coverage would indicate. The findings of this study support this conclusion. Notwithstanding evidence of some punitiveness, NOSCJ respondents supported rehabilitative efforts, especially for juvenile offenders. Twenty-one percent chose rehabilitation as the most important factor in sentencing adults, but 50% chose this answer for juveniles. Also, 55% indicated that more money should be spent on social and economic problems in an attempt to lower the crime rate, and only 31% wanted more money spent on "police, prisons and judges." NOSCJ respondents were much more punitive with respect to violent criminals, however: 59% wanted the government to place a greater emphasis on punishing these offenders, and only 27% wanted more emphasis on their rehabilitation.

These findings of combining punitiveness with some concern for treating inmates can be explained by an argument first advocated by Innes (1993). Innes argued that the public is concerned about safety first and thus supports the punitive treatment of criminals. But once offenders have been incarcerated and are no longer a threat to society, the public is willing to support treatment for prisoners. The current study supports such a conclusion. Our respondents wanted violent criminals punished, but they were quite willing to support the idea that most important in the sentencing of juveniles should be "to train, educate and counsel offenders."

Similar to McCorkle's (1993) finding, our research indicated that demographic characteristics of respondents were not good predictors of attitudes. We found few demographic correlates of sentencing attitudes that proved to be statistically significant. This finding indicates a remarkable robustness of public opinion regarding the sentencing of criminals. Whereas most political issues generate significant disagreement among various demographic categories, this topic does not. Members of the public were predominantly in favor of punishing criminals and treating prisoners.

The few demographic differences we found were all consistent with findings reported in the existing literature. Furthermore, we observed some correlations between demographic characteristics and sentencing attitudes that barely failed to meet the level of significance that we required ($p \leq .01$) but were also all consistent with our expectations. For instance, whites were less in support of rehabilitation for adult offenders than were other racial/ethnic groups, liberals were more in favor of letting judges decide who goes to prison than were conservatives, Republicans wanted money spent on the criminal justice system rather than on social and economic problems, and females were more likely to support rehabilitating violent criminals than were males.

The two demographic characteristics that were most consistently related to sentencing attitudes were educational achievement and gun ownership. These two independent variables were related to all five attitudinal measures we included, although not always at the .01 level of significance (but the correlations were in all instances significant at the .05 level). In general, the better educated respondents were, the less punitive their attitudes. Conversely, gun owners were more punitive than nonowners. All other demographic characteristics proved to be weak predictors of sentencing attitudes. Gender and race were significant in only one instance each.

Various social characteristics that we hypothesized might be related to sentencing attitudes proved to be weak predictors too. For instance, we expected that TV-viewing habits would be correlated with sentencing attitudes, but this proved not to be the case. Number of hours respondents watched television was not predictive of sentencing attitudes at all. To our surprise, frequent viewers of reality-based crime shows were not significantly more punitive than nonviewers of such shows either, although the correlations were in the expected direction and missed the .01 level of significance only barely in two instances.

Using our measures of fear of crime and neighborhood decay, sentencing attitudes cannot be predicted to any great extent either. Contrary to the findings of Langworthy and Whitehead (1986), respondents who were afraid of being victimized by crime were not more punitive than people who did not worry about being victimized. Similarly, the extent of decay that respondents witnessed in their own neighborhoods predicted sentencing attitudes only weakly.

Conclusion

This study reinforces the findings of recent efforts to understand public attitudes toward sentencing criminals. Our data show that the public continues to support some rehabilitative efforts. Prisons should not be just warehouses; offenders, juveniles in particular, should receive some form of treatment and money should be devoted to the social and economic problems that in the public's mind cause crime. Politicians, and the nation, would be served well if decision makers take the public's desire into consideration when setting policy.

6

Reform or Punish

Americans' Views of the Correctional System

TIMOTHY J. FLANAGAN

More than a decade ago, a colleague and I reviewed research and commentary concerning public opinion and prison policy (Flanagan & Caulfield, 1984). We observed that Americans' opinions about correctional policy and practices were much less fully developed than views about law enforcement or other components of the criminal justice system. We concluded that the cardinal function that the public assigns to the correctional system is the same as that expected of the larger criminal justice system: social defense or societal protection (p. 41). There was wide variation in support for specific programs and policies in corrections, but this variation was consistent with the perceived linkage between the program (e.g., good time, education programs, early release) and public protection. In 1996 as in 1984 and earlier, public support for correctional policies and proposals will be shaped by the prism of this linkage to public safety.

From the 1950s to the early 1970s, American penology was characterized by widespread optimism, indeed confidence, that intervention in the lives of convicted offenders was possible and could be effective in "changing" criminals into law-abiding citizens. Providing counseling, training, education, and treatment programs for offenders was a good investment, because such programs held promise of reducing the fiscal and social costs of recidivism.

A long series of research studies began to question the effectiveness of these programs, reaching an apex in 1975 with the publication of Lipton, Martinson, and Wilks's *The Effectiveness of Correctional Treatment*. The much-repeated conclusion of the "Martinson Report," as it came to be known, was that "with few and isolated exceptions, the rehabilitative efforts that have been reported so far have had no appreciable effect on recidivism" (Martinson, 1974, p. 25). The 735-page volume was reduced to the slogan "nothing works," a catchphrase that haunts correctional policy more than 20 years later.

Following a decade of relentless questioning, we were not surprised to find that by the mid-1980s many Americans had lost faith in the rehabilitative efficacy of correctional programs. By 1982, for example, 86% of Americans in an ABC News poll disagreed with the statement: "If a person spends time in jail, chances are good he won't commit more crimes after he gets out of jail." A corollary impact was unwillingness to trust discretionary decision making by corrections officials. For example, in the same 1982 poll 60% of Americans opposed the following statement: "Prison authorities should be allowed to free prisoners when they feel the prisoner will not return to a life of crime" (see Flanagan & Caulfield, 1984). Finally, loss of faith in the capacity of the corrections system to change offenders led to a shift in public opinion about the need for prisons and the purposes of incarceration. If criminals could not be changed, long determinate sentences would be justified on incapacitative grounds. The solution to crime might be found by investing in *more prisons* rather than investing *more in prisons*. In 1996 and beyond, America will struggle with the consequences of a crime control strategy founded on the cornerstone of imprisonment.

In this chapter, I review Americans' beliefs and opinions about prisons and correctional policies and practices. Special attention is focused on changes in public opinion since 1985. During the past decade, the correctional apparatus has grown to unprecedented levels. At year-end 1994, "more than 5.1 million Americans—or almost 2.7 percent of the adult population—were under some form of correctional supervision" during the year (U.S. Department of Justice, 1995). These included 2,962,000 adults on probation, 690,000 adults on parole, 484,000 in jails, and more than 1,053,000 in state and federal prisons. Both the absolute number and the rate of persons on probation and parole and in prisons and jails reached historic levels in 1994.

In addition to increases in the scale of correctional populations, corrections has become more complicated as new forms of supervision and new programs have developed. For example, probation agencies once had straightforward responsibilities of conducting presentence reports for courts and supervising offenders. Today, multiservice community corrections agencies operate drug treatment facilities, "intermediate confinement facilities" for probation violators, boot camps, and supervise offenders via electronic monitoring devices. They manage victim restitution programs, community service projects, drug testing clinics, and myriad other activities. Because of overcrowding in state prisons, local jails now hold thousands of convicted state felons who are "backed up" in local jail systems. In short, as correctional populations have soared since 1980, the dividing lines have blurred between local and state governmental functions, and between the community and institutional sectors of corrections.

There are many reasons underlying the tremendous increase since 1980 in the use of prisons and other forms of correctional supervision in America. Demographic changes in the population, increased drug use and drug law enforcement, structural economic shifts, improved efficiency of criminal justice agencies, and statutory revisions have each contributed to greater reliance on incarceration as a response to crime. In addition, Alfred Blumstein (1995) argued that "the loss of confidence in rehabilitation has contributed significantly to the growth in prison populations" (p. 396).

Clearly, the media, political leaders, and justice system officials have played an important role in shaping the policy debate. The view that dominates policy debates and neighborhood discussions about crime and punishment in 1996 is that more, longer, and tougher correctional sanctions are needed to deter offenders from drug use and crime. In Posner's (1995) view, "with even stiffer penalties, and greater resources devoted to police and prosecutors, we could undoubtedly make a minor dent in the existing crime rate" (p. 4).

In the current political and social environment, capital punishment plays a *symbolic role* in American thinking about crime control, but a minor role in practice because we so infrequently employ the death penalty. Prisons occupy the *central role* as the most visible, imposing, and expensive correctional program. Community corrections programs play a vast *supporting role*, encompassing millions of clients in programs that are less visible to, and less understood by, taxpayers.

In the sections that follow, I examine the results of the National Opinion Survey on Crime and Justice—1995 (NOSCJ) and other surveys to assess the current state of American thinking about faith in rehabilitation, prison programs, and other aspects of the "reform or punish" debate.

Confidence and Support for Correctional Rehabilitation

As Jurg Gerber and Simone Engelhardt-Greer reported in Chapter 5, Americans support multiple goals for sentencing and correctional policy. A majority of respondents in the NOSCJ felt that the government needed to focus *spending* on socioeconomic problems to reduce crime, but a slight majority thought that punishment should be the primary goal in *sentencing* adults. (This paradoxical situation is consistent with Leslie Wilkins's, 1984, observation that we must distinguish what we do about crime from what we do with criminals.) There is no logical inconsistency in supporting greater government efforts to ameliorate the so-called root causes of crime while calling for punitive sentences for those convicted of crime. Despite the primacy of the punitive sentencing goal, however, nearly one fifth of U.S. adults favored rehabilitation as the principal goal of sentencing, and one fourth favored deterrence and incapacitation as the most important goals.

Table 6.1 provides a measure of Americans' judgments of the prospects for rehabilitating offenders. The question asked, "Thinking of criminals who commit violent crimes, do you think most, some, only a few, or none of them can be rehabilitated given early intervention with the right program?" Nationwide, three fifths of America adults responded that *most* or *some* offenders could be rehabilitated under these conditions, and less than one tenth thought that *none* could be changed. The distribution of responses was similar to that of a Los Angeles Times poll conducted in 1994. In the Los Angeles Times poll, 64% of American adults responded that *most* or *some* violent criminals could be rehabilitated, and only 6% thought that *none* could be changed (Maguire & Pastore, 1994).

These views about the potential for rehabilitation of violent criminals were consistent across most demographic subgroups of the population. However, a few demographic differences were notable. Age was related to views about the possibility of rehabilitative change: Younger respondents were more inclined to believe that most or some offenders could be rehabilitated than were older persons. For example, 67% of 18- to 29-year-olds said that most or some violent criminals could be changed; in contrast, 54% of persons aged 60 to 69 expressed such faith in rehabilitation. Perspectives on rehabilitation were also modestly associated with place of residence (urban dwellers expressed greater support for rehabilitation) and political ideology (self-described conservatives were more likely to say only a few or none could be changed). There were no significant differences across subgroups in terms of race/ethnicity, gender, education, income, religion, political party affiliation, or level of worry about crime.

The dual themes of punishment and reform that characterize the popular view of correctional policy have persisted for years. For example, in 1982 Gallup asked Americans whether anything could be done to reduce recidivism among released prisoners. Nearly 70% believed that reducing recidivism was possible, and these respondents were evenly divided between "stiffer sentences" and "stronger rehabilitation" as the means to achieve this goal. Similarly, equal proportions of Americans favored "less leniency in prison" and "providing [prisoners] jobs when released" (McGarrell & Flanagan, 1985).

The Purpose of Prisons

Opinion pollsters periodically question the public concerning the primary goal of American prisons. This line of questioning provides a perspective on trends in public expectations concerning corrections. (Unfortunately, these data also illustrate the fact that minor variations in question wording and response categories in surveys complicate the interpretation of these trends.)

The Harris organization posed the question: "Now what do you think *should* be the main emphasis in most prisons—*punishing* the individual convicted of a crime, trying to *rehabilitate* the individual so that he might return to society as a productive citizen, or *protecting society* from future crimes he might commit?" In five surveys between 1968 and 1982, the proportion of Americans selecting rehabilitation as the main emphasis of prisons declined 40%; the proportion selecting punishment rose 171%, and the proportion selecting protection of society rose 166% (Flanagan & Caulfield, 1984). The Roper Organization asked the question differently: "Which one of the statements . . . comes closest to your point of view on prisons? . . . to *punish criminals and keep them away* from the rest of society, or . . . *to keep criminals separate from the rest of society until they can be rehabilitated and returned to society?*" The first option combines punishment and incapacitation goals (in that order), and the second combines incapacitation, rehabilitation, and reintegration goals.

Table 6.1 Americans' Views on How Many Violent Criminals Can Be Rehabilitated (in percentages)

Question: "Thinking of criminals who commit violent crimes, do you think most, some, only a few, or none of them can be rehabilitated, given early intervention with the right program?"

	Most	*Some*	*Only a Few*	*None*
National	15	46	30	9
Age*				
18-29	21	46	26	8
30-39	13	50	27	9
40-49	12	50	30	9
50-59	16	46	33	5
60-69	12	32	43	12
70 or older	13	43	29	15
Race/ethnicity				
White	13	45	31	10
Hispanic	17	46	31	7
Black	26	47	23	4
Other[a]	7	63	16	14
Sex				
Male	13	44	32	11
Female	17	48	27	8
Education				
Less than high school	17	42	31	9
High school graduate	13	44	30	12
Some college	18	48	28	7
College graduate	14	51	29	7
Income				
Less than $15,000	16	47	27	9
$15,000 to $30,000	13	45	32	10
$30,001 to $60,000	16	47	29	8
More than $60,000	12	53	27	8
Marital status				
Married	13	46	30	11
Widowed	16	44	28	11
Divorced/separated	17	41	32	9
Never married	19	51	24	6

Given this contrast, the percentage of the public who chose rehabilitation declined from 76% in 1971 to 53% in 1980. During the same period, support for punishment as the main goal of prisons rose from 15% to 32% (Pettinico, 1994).

In 1982, ABC News contrasted prisons as mostly a place to punish criminals or mostly a place to teach criminals how to be law-abiding,

Table 6.1 Continued

	Most	*Some*	*Only a Few*	*None*
Religion				
Protestant	15	47	28	10
Catholic	11	45	35	9
None	15	52	20	13
Other	24	43	28	5
Community type				
Rural	19	40	32	10
Small town	13	45	28	14
Small city	12	55	27	6
Suburb	11	52	28	10
Urban	24	35	34	6
Party affiliation				
Republican	12	48	32	8
Democrat	17	49	27	8
Independent/other	17	45	27	11
Political ideology				
Liberal	21	43	29	7
Middle of the road	14	51	26	9
Conservative	12	42	34	13
Gun ownership				
Yes	12	46	32	11
No	18	46	28	8
TV crime show viewer				
Yes	17	43	30	10
No	13	49	29	9
Police contact past 2 years				
Yes	14	46	29	10
No	16	46	30	8
Worry about crime				
Low	16	51	28	6
Medium	16	41	32	12
High	13	47	29	11

a. Category contains fewer than 50 cases.
*Differences between groups are significant at $p \leq .01$ level.

useful citizens. In this form, 75% of Americans chose the teaching response, and 16% chose the punishment response. The Gallup organization chose yet another variant of the question: "In dealing with those who are in prison, do you think it is more important to *punish them for their crimes* or more important to *get them started on the right road?*" In 1989, 38% of American adults chose the punishment alternative, and 48% chose the rehabilitation response. By the time the Los Angeles

Times poll asked, in 1993, "Where does the government need to make a greater effort these days: in trying to *rehabilitate* criminals who commit violent crimes or in trying to *punish and put away* criminals who commit violent crimes?" support for the punishment alternative rose to 61%, and support for the rehabilitation alternative dropped to 25% of respondents (Pettinico, 1994).

The most recent poll data on the purpose of prisons posed three alternatives: "to *keep criminals out of society, to punish criminals,* or to *rehabilitate criminals?*" In a national survey conducted by the Wirthlin Group in 1994, 61% of Americans chose the incapacitation response (to keep criminals out of society), 22% chose the punishment response, and 13% chose rehabilitation as the "main purpose of prisons" (Maguire & Pastore, 1995).

Tracing the trend in responses to these questions is complicated by the changing question wording, but two conclusions are warranted. First, public support for rehabilitation as the superordinate goal of prisons has declined precipitously during the past quarter century, although some of the decline may be attributable to public disaffection with the term *rehabilitation* itself. I will return to this point. Second, the apparent ascendance of punishment as Americans' choice for the chief goal of prisons may be a function of the fact that pollsters have not provided an alternative to the punishment response. The 1994 Wirthlin Group poll suggests that when provided with a option of choosing the social defense goal (incapacitation), Americans choose this objective over punishment by a wide margin.

Support for Prison Programs

In an important article published in 1993, Christopher Innes observed that Americans' attitudes about *criminals* are distinguishable from attitudes about *inmates.* That is, the apparent inconsistency in simultaneous public support for training and education programs within prisons and growing support for punishment as the primary goal of prisons may be explained by the fact that once held in secure confinement, the public is satisfied that the "social defense" function of prisons has been satisfied. Innes (1993) observed that

> there is no evidence in the available survey data that the general public shares the view that there is any necessary incompatibility among the

goals of justice in society, punishment of criminals, and teaching or training programs for inmates. (p. 232)

If providing education, training, and other treatment services to the incarcerated offers any hope of reducing recidivism, then Americans are supportive of providing such services to inmates. However, Innes notes that skepticism about the efficacy of such programs suggests that correctional administrators should use terms such as *teaching, training,* and other euphemisms rather than the term rehabilitation itself. Understanding this distinction in the public mind between criminals and inmates also provides insight into the limits of public support for correctional activities. Programs and services that are thought to make the prison walls more permeable, such as work release, early parole consideration, and others—which are perceived as compromising the social-protection function of prisons—will be resisted.

These observations are reflected in several surveys that indicate that the public supports efforts to train, counsel, and educate inmates, and in the responses to the NOSCJ. For example, Cullen, Skovron, Scott, and Burton (1990) found high levels of support among residents of two Ohio cities for "expanding the rehabilitation programs now being undertaken in the prisons" (p. 11). They found particularly strong support for education and vocational training programs. Similarly, Innes (1993) reported that Americans favor prison programs that "appear constructive and practical" (p. 230), especially programs that focus on upgrading educational and vocational skills. Similar findings have emerged from Canadian surveys (Adams, 1990).

Table 6.2 shows the responses to questions concerning correctional programs in the NOSCJ. For each, respondents were asked whether the proposal was a *good idea* or a *bad idea.* The highest levels of public support are for proposals to require "every inmate to have a skill or to learn a trade to fit them for a job before they are released from prison," and for requiring "every prisoner to be able to read and write before he or she is released from prison." For each of these items, there is overwhelming support that spans every subgroup of the American population. These efforts are strongly supported by liberals and conservatives and persons from all types of communities, regardless of other social and economic characteristics of respondents. Moreover, this high level of support is virtually identical to that found by the Gallup organization in 1982, using the same questions.

There is also very strong support for the idea of keeping "prisoners busy constructing buildings, making products or performing services

Table 6.2 Americans' Views Toward Selected Correctional Proposals (percentage responding good idea)

Question: "Tell me whether you think each of the following proposals are good ideas or bad ideas."

	Learn Trade	Literacy	Construction	Pay Prisoners	Spouse Visits	Re-Parole
National	92	94	88	80	49	75
Age						
18-29	95	96	87	75	62	72
30-39	90	94	87	83	42	80
40-49	95	92	87	83	49	79
50-59	89	92	91	85	46	70
60-69	89	93	92	82	42	69
70 or older	95	95	89	76	45	74
Race/ethnicity						
White	92	92	89	80	46	79*
Hispanic	94	94	85	85	60	65
Black	92	95	86	78	62	52
Other[a]	85	97	83	85	55	76
Sex						
Male	92	92	87	80	49	74
Female	93	95	88	81	48	76
Education						
Less than high school	93	96	87	77	55	60*
High school graduate	89	94	85	80	49	72
Some college	94	95	88	85	44	80
College graduate	94	91	91	77	52	81
Income						
Less than $15,000	90	95	85	81	53	66
$15,000 to $30,000	93	92	90	82	49	74
$30,001 to $60,000	94	94	90	80	48	81
More than $60,000	92	93	88	85	49	78
Marital status						
Married	91	93	90	80	44	78
Widowed	92	95	89	77	44	70
Divorced/separated	93	95	80	86	50	71
Never married	96	95	87	79	62	72

that the state would have to hire other people to do." Once again, support for inmate work programs cuts across all demographic subgroups of Americans. The only significant difference among subgroups is that 92% of Republicans favor inmate work programs, whereas 88% of Democrats and 86% of Independents and others favor this proposal.

Table 6.2 Continued

	Learn Trade	Literacy	Construction	Pay Prisoners	Spouse Visits	Re-Parole
Religion						
Protestant	92	94	89	80	49	76
Catholic	93	92	88	83	46	78
None	89	91	84	81	56	66
Other	91	97	89	81	54	77
Community type						
Rural	90	95	93	76	42	80
Small town	90	91	88	82	52	74
Small city	92	91	85	83	46	71
Suburb	95	96	86	83	50	78
Urban	93	95	88	76	50	72
Party affiliation						
Republican	91	95	92*	80	48	81
Democrat	93	92	88	81	49	76
Independent/other	94	94	86	83	49	72
Political ideology						
Liberal	94	94	88	82	61	75
Middle of the road	94	94	88	83	48	78
Conservative	89	92	88	77	43	73
Gun ownership						
Yes	92	93	89	79	46	80
No	93	98	87	82	51	72
TV crime show viewer						
Yes	91	94	86	82	51	73
No	94	93	90	79	47	77
Police contact past 2 years						
Yes	92	94	87	80	49	76
No	92	93	89	81	48	75
Worry about crime						
Low	93	93	88	81	50	70
Medium	90	92	89	77	47	76
High	93	95	87	83	49	80

a. Category contains fewer than 50 cases.
*Differences between groups are significant at $p \le .01$ level.

From time to time, the issue of paying inmates for their labor becomes controversial. In most state prison systems, inmates receive wages of a few cents per hour; some states, such as Texas, pay inmates nothing at all. The arguments for paying prisoners at least minimum wage focus on providing financial incentive structures that are similar to "real world" systems, motivating inmates to higher productivity and better quality of work, exacting charges against the salary to pay for the cost of incarceration, and enabling inmates to assist families and to allow for savings that could be relied on during the postrelease transitional period (Flanagan, 1989). The NOSCJ data show strong public support for the statement: "Pay prisoners for their work, but require them to return two thirds of this amount to their victims or to the state for the cost of maintaining the prison." Nationally, between three quarters and four fifths of American adults thought that the proposal was a good idea. Again, the findings of the NOSCJ were virtually identical to Gallup's survey on this question 13 years ago.

The final two correctional policy proposals illustrate the limits of Americans' support for correctional programs that may be perceived as reducing public safety. Nationally, less than half of the respondents thought the following statement was a good idea: "In some nations and in some states in the United States, in order to keep families together, spouses are permitted to spend some weekends each year with their husband or wife in special guest houses within the prison grounds." The strongest level of support for conjugal visits was among younger respondents (aged 18-29) and among self-described liberals. Ironically, respondents' marital status was related to support for conjugal visits— the highest level of support was among persons who were never married, and the lowest level of support was among married persons. (This item may be an important measure of marital bliss in contemporary America.) Finally, there was strong support for the proposal: "Refuse parole to any prisoner who has been paroled before for a serious crime." Three quarters of American adults thought this was a good idea. Significant differences in level of support for the "no re-parole" policy were found in relation to race/ethnicity (whites were most supportive of no re-parole, blacks were least supportive) and in relation to respondents' education level (college-educated persons were more likely than others to support the no re-parole policy). These findings coincide with the view that Americans expect prisons to provide programs that can assist inmates in preparing themselves for release, but they also expect the prison walls to serve as a means to keep criminals away from the rest of society.

Alternatives to Prison and Solutions to Prison Crowding

Table 6.3 shows responses to the following question: "Would you favor or oppose each of the following measures that have been suggested as ways to reduce prison overcrowding?" These data demonstrate that Americans react very differently to the three primary methods of dealing with overcrowded conditions in prisons. These methods are (a) "front-end strategies," which are designed to divert some offenders from prison through expansion of community-based corrections programs, or to shorten sentences so that prison beds become available more quickly; (b) "back-end strategies," which seek to reduce crowding by speeding up the release process through time off for good behavior, or by granting greater authority to parole authorities to release prisoners early; and (c) "capacity expansion strategies," which call for building more prison capacity to meet increasing demand.

Skovron, Scott, and Cullen (1988) found in earlier research on this issue that the public tends to support proposals that are least likely to reduce prison populations (and crowding) and is least favorable toward those strategies that are most effective in controlling prison population growth. That pattern is reflected in the responses in Table 6.3.

Different front-end prison population strategies received very different responses in the NOSCJ. There was strong and consistent support for "developing local programs to keep more nonviolent and first-time offenders active and working in the community." Nationwide, 90% of American adults favored that measure as a way to reduce prison overcrowding. At the same time, the proposal of "shortening sentences" was universally rejected by the poll respondents. Only 8% favored this measure, but several notable differences between demographic subgroups existed. Males favored shortening sentences more than female respondents did (11% vs. 4%), and poorer people were more supportive of this measure than were wealthier respondents (16% among those who earned less than $15,000, vs. only 4% among those earning more than $60,000). Finally, self-described liberals (15%) were more favorable toward shortening sentences than were those who described themselves as "middle of the road" (6%) or "conservative" (5%).

Differences in support for the two back-end strategies were also found. Almost two thirds of respondents favored "allowing prisoners to earn early release through good behavior and participation in educational and work programs." Support for this mechanism to accelerate the date of first parole eligibility was significantly higher among young respondents (aged 18-29), among males (72% in favor vs. 57% approval among females), and Republicans. At the same time, however, Americans strongly disapproved "giving the parole board more authority to release offenders early." Nationwide, only 21% favored this measure, although support was significantly higher among males (27%) and

Table 6.3 Americans' Views Toward Selected Proposals to Reduce Prison Crowding (percentage responding that they favor)

Question: "Would you favor or oppose each of the following measures that have been suggested as ways to reduce prison overcrowding?"

	Shortening Sentences	Allowing Early Release for Good Behavior	Develop Local Programs	Give Parole Board More Authority	Increase Taxes to Build More Prisons
National	8	64	90	21	33
Age					
18-29	12	67*	93	27	30
30-39	5	61	90	19	31
40-49	6	62	88	21	33
50-59	7	74	93	20	32
60-69	9	63	88	16	40
70 or older	10	72	90	18	32
Race/ethnicity					
White	6	64	89	18*	35
Hispanic	6	61	94	23	25
Black	15	71	97	37	21
Other[a]	20	59	88	34	21
Sex					
Male	11*	72*	88	27*	35
Female	4	57	92	15	29
Education					
Less than high school	18	68	88	30	25
High school graduate	6	62	92	21	29
Some college	8	63	89	17	31
College graduate	6	67	91	21	38
Income					
Less than $15,000	16*	66	90	26	31
$15,000 to $30,000	8	58	92	15	26
$30,001 to $60,000	6	66	89	22	34
More than $60,000	4	70	92	23	40
Marital status					
Married	6	63	88	19	33
Widowed	6	66	91	18	31
Divorced/separated	10	62	94	18	31
Never married	12	69	93	28	29

among self-described political liberals (35%). These findings indicate that the public supports the provision of incentive mechanisms within prisons, but does not approve giving parole boards greater release authority. Parole boards were the lowest-rated component of the crimi-

Table 6.3 Continued

	Shortening Sentences	Allowing Early Release for Good Behavior	Develop Local Programs	Give Parole Board More Authority	Increase Taxes to Build More Prisons
Religion					
Protestant	6	65	92	19*	30
Catholic	7	58	87	20	33
None	14	71	94	39	40
Other	11	69	91	21	30
Community type					
Rural	4	58	88	19	29
Small town	10	65	91	22	26
Small city	5	67	89	20	33
Suburb	8	66	91	21	36
Urban	9	63	92	21	34
Party affiliation					
Republican	7	67*	91	21	35*
Democrat	8	64	90	19	28
Independent/other	7	63	90	21	32
Political ideology					
Liberal	15*	70	94	35*	30
Middle of the road	6	64	91	19	34
Conservative	5	61	88	15	31
Gun ownership					
Yes	6	63	89	20	34
No	9	65	91	21	30
TV crime show viewer					
Yes	10	64	90	22	33
No	6	65	91	20	32
Police contact past 2 years					
Yes	8	64	89	19	34
No	8	65	92	23	30
Worry about crime					
Low	8	64	89	22*	32
Medium	6	66	90	26	28
High	8	63	91	15	36

a. Category contains fewer than 50 cases.
*Differences between groups are significant at $p \leq .01$ level.

nal justice system in terms of public perceptions of "accomplishing their part of the criminal justice mission," according to a 1991 poll conducted for the National Victim Center (Maguire, Pastore, & Flanagan, 1993), so resistance to granting additional discretionary authority to paroling authorities is consistent with lack of confidence.

Finally, we asked respondents to evaluate the proposal "Increasing taxes to build more prisons" as a measure to reduce prison overcrowding. This is a double-barreled question, insofar as we cannot determine unambiguously whether the response refers to willingness to increase taxes or willingness to build more prisons, but it is consistent with the way previous researchers have phrased the question. For example, ABC News pollsters asked Americans in 1982 whether they "would approve or disapprove of building more prisons so that longer sentences could be given to criminals," and 69% of respondents indicated approval. Of those, 62% said they would still approve of building more prisons if it meant their taxes would increase. Taken together, then, about 43% of Americans in 1982 would approve increasing taxes to build more prisons so that longer sentences could be imposed (Flanagan & Caulfield, 1984). A Gallup poll in 1982 found that 57% of Americans said that their state needed more prisons, but 49% were willing to pay more taxes to build them. In 1984, 75% of those responding to a Research and Forecasts, Inc. poll endorsed "build more prisons" as a solution to prison overcrowding, with no reference to the need to increase taxes to pay for them (Jamieson & Flanagan, 1987). A 1994 poll by the Wirthlin Group reported that 73% of Americans "approved of building more prisons so that longer sentences could be given to criminals" and that 85% of those who approved of building more prisons would approve of raising taxes to pay for them (Maguire & Pastore, 1995).

Our question introduced the idea of increasing taxes directly into the prison construction debate. When asked that way, only 33% of Americans indicated support for increasing taxes to build more prisons as a way to reduce prison overcrowding, about half the level of support found in the Wirthlin Group poll. The only significant demographic difference on this issue was in relation to party affiliation, where Republicans (35%) were more likely to favor increasing taxes to build prisons than were Democrats (28%) or Independents and others (32%).

It would not be surprising if Americans in 1996 are confused about the need to increase taxes to build more prisons. The late 1980s and early 1990s witnessed a historic expansion of prison capacity in the United States, and voters in most states have already approved tax increases or bond issues to fund this construction. Expenditures for corrections activities have been the fastest-growing segment of state budgets since 1985, outstripping increases in Medicaid, education, and other government functions (Irwin & Austin, 1994). Moreover, research by John

Doble (1987b), using focus groups in conjunction with surveys, suggests that although Americans are aware of crowded conditions in the nation's prisons, they do not understand how crowding affects the ability to deliver correctional services. Under these circumstances, the modest level of support in the current data for increasing taxes to build prisons as a means to reduce crowding may be interpreted as (a) a measure of exasperation with the seemingly unending increases in the cost of corrections, (b) a measure of doubt about whether prisons are actually overcrowded, (c) doubt about whether crowding itself is a real problem for the administration of prisons, or (d) some combination of these views. Regardless, it would seem that political leaders and correctional administrators may find greater resistance among citizens to continuing the spiral of prison expansion and its associated costs.

Conclusion

Americans hold the criminal justice system, and the corrections component of the system, to very high standards of performance. First and foremost, the correctional system is expected to protect the public from convicted criminals. This means that the correctional system is expected to be able to identify the appropriate level of supervision and custody for each offender that is consistent with public safety and deliver that surveillance and control. Surveillance is not the only function expected of the corrections system, however. The public also expects that efforts will be made within prisons and other correctional settings to provide services for offenders that may increase the odds that they will become law-abiding citizens. These include educational, training, and counseling efforts directed to reducing the deficits that are associated with involvement in crime.

In recent months, political leaders across the nation have seized the notion that prison conditions need to be much more harsh than at present. From the "No-Frills Prison Act of 1995" passed by Congress to calls for a return to striped uniforms, chain gangs, and breaking rocks, some political leaders argue that in addition to increasing the rate and length of incarceration during the past decade, we need to increase the punitiveness of imprisonment as well. These approaches are promoted on retributive as well as deterrent grounds. It is argued that Spartan, tough prisons will more effectively communicate society's revulsion of criminals and will serve as an effective deterrent to recidivism. Terminology such as *country club prisons* and *coddling criminals* peppers these calls for a return to the "good old days" when convicts were handled in a no-nonsense, stern manner (DiIulio, 1995). These positions appeal to a public that is frightened about crime and exasperated with the seeming inability of the criminal justice system to deal with the threat, but there is no evidence that a return to 19th-century prison philosophies and conditions will reduce recidivism.

It is difficult to determine who is leading and who is following in this recent effort to transform American correctional philosophy. That is, are political leaders and some correctional administrators *reacting* to changing public attitudes about the purpose and functions of prisons, or are they *leading* the public to a new position that equates tougher prisons with improved public safety? As always, "politicians who call for harsher punishments for criminal acts claim a mandate from the people" (Doble, 1987b, p. 4). However, there is evidence from previous research that political leaders often misjudge the mind of the public on criminal justice matters. And their misinterpretation is commonly in one direction—that of perceiving the public as more punitive and less accepting of community alternatives to prisons than is actually the case. Under these conditions, misinterpretation of the public mood becomes a needless obstacle to intelligent criminal justice reform (Gottfredson & Taylor, 1984; Riley & Rose, 1980). Moreover, some researchers find that the "vast majority" of Americans "believed that while prison life should be hard, it should also be humane and offer offenders a chance to rehabilitate themselves" (Doble, 1987b, p. 28). This view is not borne of Pollyannaish idealism. Rather, "respondents supported rehabilitation because they understood that most offenders eventually get out of prison. A Chicago woman explained, 'I've got to think: "He's coming back out." Don't send him out the way he went in' " (Doble, 1987b, p. 27).

Americans' Attitudes About the Ultimate Weapon
Capital Punishment

DENNIS R. LONGMIRE

Overview

Probably the most exhaustive review of death penalty attitudes among U.S. citizens was conducted by Bohm (1991). This review involved an analysis of death penalty attitudes as measured by a series of Gallup polls conducted between 1936 and 1986. In this analysis Bohm showed that in general, large proportions of the American public have always expressed support for the death penalty. During the 50-year period included in his study, Bohm reported that on average, 59% of the respondents in Gallup surveys supported the death penalty. Only 33%, on average, opposed it, and the remaining 9% were neutral. Levels of support for the death penalty among the general public ranged from a high of 75% in 1985 to a low of 42% in 1966.

Bohm (1991) also reported that trends in levels of support and opposition toward the death penalty varied depending on sociodemographic characteristics of respondents to the surveys. Differential patterns of support and opposition to the death penalty over time were associated with the respondents' race/ethnicity, income, gender, politics, and residential location. Bohm (1991) concludes that "whites, wealthier people, males, Republicans, and Westerners have tended to support the death penalty more than blacks, poorer people, females, Democrats, and Southerners" (p. 135). Over the 50-year period of time reviewed, there was little variation in death penalty attitudes among those from different age groups, education levels, occupations, religions, and city sizes.

Death Penalty Attitudes and Race/Ethnicity

Young (1991) reported that "one of the most persistent findings of public opinion polls is that blacks are more likely than whites to oppose capital punishment" (p. 67). He went on to demonstrate that racial differences in capital punishment attitudes might be explained by the different ways racial groups view issues of crime causation and questions of justice. According to his findings, whites are more likely than African Americans to subscribe to the "responsibility attribution" hypothesis of crime causation, whereas African Americans are more likely to draw on issues of trust in the police and perceptions of inequity. Support for the death penalty logically derives from the attribution hypothesis; opposition derives from the concerns about issues of procedural and distributive justice.

In an earlier study, Combs and Comer (1982) reviewed changes in levels of support for the death penalty among whites and African Americans over the 8-year period from 1972 to 1980. In each of these years, opposition to the death penalty was strongest among African Americans, and support for the death penalty was strongest among whites. During the latter part of the 1970s, support for the death penalty increased among both racial/ethnic groups. However, at no time did the level of support for the death penalty among African Americans reach beyond the 45% mark.

In one of the most recent studies of this kind, Barkan and Cohn (1994) examined the relationship between death penalty attitudes among whites and measures of racial prejudice. They reported that high levels of support for the death penalty among whites are associated with their antipathy toward African Americans and with practices of racial stereotyping. They further demonstrated that political conservatism, which is stronger among whites than other racial groups, is strongly associated with death penalty attitudes.

Death Penalty Attitudes and Religious Belief Systems

As with race/ethnicity, the relationship between death penalty attitudes and religious ideologies has been the subject of interesting research. In fact, Young's (1992) work examined the effect of both race and religious orientation on death penalty attitudes. Although limited in scope to data collected in a single year (1988), Young found that religious fundamentalism, evangelism, and devotionalism were significantly associated with death penalty attitudes. Furthermore, the nature and strength of these associations varied by race/ethnicity. Earlier research demonstrated that survey respondents who support the death penalty belonged to more conservative or dogmatic religious denominations (Curtis, 1991; Harvey, 1986; Moran & Comfort, 1986).

There is a small but interesting body of research examining the relationship between death penalty attitudes and religiously held attitudes about the sanctity of life in instances of both abortion and euthanasia (Finlay, 1985; Grandberg & Grandberg, 1981; Sawyer, 1982). The results of these studies are inconclusive at this time.

Death Penalty Attitudes and Sociopolitical Ideologies

The relationship between death penalty attitudes and sociopolitical ideologies is best represented by the work of Tyler and Weber (1982). In their effort to identify the root of people's strong levels of support for capital punishment, they examined whether death penalty attitudes are the function of reasoned responses to crime-related concerns or, instead, represent symbolic statements of an overall sociopolitical-ideological position. They found that those with conservative ideologies and high levels of both authoritarianism and dogmatism are more likely to support the death penalty, regardless of their attitudes about and/or experiences with other crime-related issues. Vidmar and Ellsworth (1974) reported similar findings, and Danigelis and Cutler (1991) demonstrated that trends toward both political conservativism and increased levels of support for the death penalty are not limited to older cohorts of survey respondents but, instead, span all age groups.

As has already been noted, Barkan and Cohn (1994) concluded that death penalty attitudes among whites are strongly associated with political conservatism as well as with an antipathy toward blacks. Curtis (1991) found that Republicans support the death penalty significantly more strongly than do either Democrats or independents and goes on to show that people with little faith in their fellow citizens are more likely to favor rather than oppose the death penalty.

Criminal Justice-Related Experiences and Attitudes

Whether death penalty attitudes are affected by criminal justice-related experiences remains unclear. Some studies support a thesis that attitudes toward the death penalty are affected by "environmental" factors. Rankin (1979), for example, found that death penalty attitudes were positively correlated with murder rates and fear of crime.

Handberg and Unkovic's (1985) research supported the "environmental effect" thesis. Seltzer and McCormick (1987) and Tyler and Weber (1982), however, concluded that the relationship between fear of crime and attitudes toward the death penalty was weak. Ellsworth and Ross (1983) concluded that attitudes toward the death penalty are more indicative of a person's general political and social ideology than a response to crime-related concerns or experiences.

Question Wording and Death Penalty Research

There has been some research showing that question wording influences responses to death penalty questions (Ellsworth & Ross, 1983; Harris, 1986; Williams, Longmire, & Gulick, 1988). There are slight, but significant, variations in the levels of opposition and support for the death penalty when questions are designed to be more salient to the respondent, when they posit mandatory as opposed to discretionary application of the sanction, or when they offer alternative sanctions for the respondents to consider. For example, support for capital punishment drops significantly when respondents are asked whether they would support the death penalty if a life sentence without the option of parole were available (Ellsworth & Gross, 1994). Such findings lead to the conclusion that support for the death penalty discerned through the use of single-item questions may overstate the actual levels of public support.

Smith (1978) studied the polling processes used by different survey research organizations to ascertain whether methodological variations in the interview protocol affects responses to a variety of different questions, including questions about the death penalty. By examining surveys conducted by three different research firms (Gallup-American Institute of Public Opinion, Michigan's Survey Research Center, and Roper), each of whom asked identical questions on 38 occasions during the 1970s, Smith was able to show that question order and position, sampling procedures, interview training, or field supervision do not influence measured levels of support or opposition to the death penalty.

The general consensus of those who have studied the methodological issues associated with death penalty attitudinal research supports two conclusions. First, when comparing levels of support or opposition to the death penalty over time or across different groups, care should be taken to rely on studies that used identically worded questions. Second, death penalty attitudes are complex and should not be measured through the use of a single question. Efforts should be made to include follow-up questions to determine how solidly respondents conform to their original position when faced with different circumstances.

National Opinion Survey on Crime and Justice—1995

The National Opinion Survey on Crime and Justice—1995 (NOSCJ) included nine questions concerning the death penalty. Respondents were first asked, "Do you favor or oppose the death penalty for persons convicted of murder?" Note that this is the same wording used in the majority of Gallup studies included in Bohm's 1991 study. Three groups of respondents emerged from answers to this question: those who favor capital punishment (supporters), those who oppose capital punishment (opposers), and those who are uncertain about their position on capital punishment for murderers (neutrals).

After assessing their initial position on the death penalty, respondents were told that there was additional "information that might influence some people's attitudes about the death penalty" and that we wanted to learn whether such information would cause them to change their positions. They were then given additional information designed to determine the constancy of their death penalty attitudes in light of eight different issues. The substance of these issues is described later. It is important to note here, however, that in an effort to distribute measurement error caused by fatigue and/or question order, the eight items were asked in random order throughout the interview process.

The design employed in this section of the NOSCJ most closely represents an expanded version of those studies focusing on efforts to understand the general public's attitudes about the death penalty. It updates the knowledge provided by Bohm (1991) about the level of support and opposition to the death penalty among U.S. citizens. However, the present study also attempts to better understand the consistency of people's attitudes about the death penalty by asking follow-up questions aimed at measuring the constancy of people's original positions. Ellsworth and Ross (1983) took a similar approach in their work.

Historical Trends in Death Penalty Support

Bohm's (1991) study is the most thorough assessment of the American public's position on the death penalty over a long historical period. Using Gallup poll data collected between 1936 and 1986, he showed that there has been considerable variation in support and opposition to the death penalty over this 50-year period. His data are included in Figure 7.1 along with the findings from three additional Gallup polls conducted since his study (Gallup, 1988, 1991, 1994a). The general findings of the NOSCJ (date of survey: June 26, 1995) are also reported for comparative purposes. Opposition to the death penalty reached its highest point in 1966 when 47% of the respondents stated that they were opposed to the death penalty for the crime of murder. Support for the death penalty reached its highest point in 1987 when 79% of Gallup respondents indicated support for its use. Since then, support for the death penalty, as measured by Gallup, has remained consistently high, and levels of uncertainty have declined.

The NOSCJ data show a decline in death penalty support (71%) in 1995 when compared with the most recent trends in the Gallup data. It is interesting to note that the drop in support did not coincide with an increase in levels of opposition to the death penalty. Instead, there has been an increase in people's uncertainty about the sanction. During the three Gallup studies conducted since Bohm's work, an average of 4.7% of the respondents were uncertain about their support for the death penalty. In the NOSCJ, this figure increased to 10%.

Figure 7.1 shows that in 1966 the proportion of respondents opposing the death penalty (47%) exceeded the proportion of respondents supporting it (42%). Since then, there has been a generally increasing trend in levels of support and a corresponding decrease in levels of opposition among survey respondents.

Bohm (1991) found significant variation in death penalty attitudes across different demographic groups. The NOSCJ confirmed this finding, showing statistically significant differences in death penalty attitudes along six different sociopolitical demographic dimensions. Figures reported in Table 7.1 show that males (74%) were significantly more likely than females (67%) to support the death penalty, and females (14%) were significantly more likely to be undecided on the issue. Similarly, African American respondents (40%) were significantly less likely to support the death penalty than were members of any other racial/ethnic groups. White respondents (77%) represented the group most likely to support the death penalty and least likely to oppose it.

The NOSCJ data show that respondents with higher levels of education (30%) were significantly more likely to oppose the death penalty than were those in other educational groups. There is, however, a curvilinear relationship among death penalty supporters along educational lines such that those with the lowest and highest levels of education were the least likely to favor its use (67% and 62%, respectively). Respondents with the lowest levels of education were not more likely

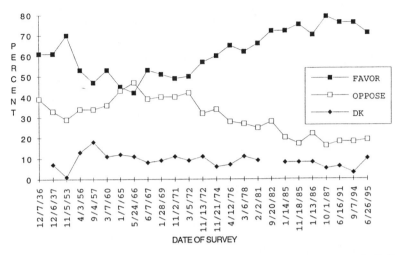

Figure 7.1. Americans' Attitudes About the Death Penalty, 1936-1995: Gallup Poll Data and NOSCJ Data

NOTE: Gallup poll data: survey dates 12/7/36-9/7/94; NOSCJ data: 6/26/95. DK = don't know.

to oppose the death penalty but, instead, tended to state that they were undecided about the issue (19%).

Community type relates to death penalty attitudes in that the strongest support came from those who resided in rural areas (82%), and the strongest opposition came from those residing in urban areas (25%). Urban residents also reported the lowest levels of support for the death penalty (58%) and the highest levels of uncertainty (17%) about its use.

Table 7.1 shows significant differences in death penalty attitudes among respondents with different political ideologies and among those who align themselves with different political parties. Liberals were significantly less likely to support the death penalty (61%) than were conservatives (76%). Similarly, the largest group of death penalty opposers were liberal (26%). Liberals were also significantly more likely to be undecided about the death penalty (13%) than were "middle of the roaders" (9%) or conservatives (11%). As has been established in previous studies, Republicans were significantly more likely to support the death penalty (76%) than Democrats (66%). It is interesting to note that in the NOSCJ study, independents were more like Democrats than Republicans. Although the largest group of death penalty opposers aligned themselves with the Democratic Party (26%), almost as many independents or "others" (20%) took a similar position.

Table 7.1 Attitudes Toward the Death Penalty (in percentages)

Question: "Do you favor or oppose the death penalty for persons convicted of murder?"

	Favor	*Oppose*	*Don't Know*
National	71	19	10
Age			
18-29	68	20	12
30-39	76	18	6
40-49	69	21	10
50-59	71	15	13
60-69	72	20	8
70 or older	65	15	20
Race/ethnicity*			
White	77	13	10
Hispanic	52	33	15
Black	40	48	12
Other[a]	67	29	5
Gender*			
Male	74	18	8
Female	67	19	14
Education*			
Less than high school	67	14	19
High school graduate	74	15	11
Some college	77	15	8
College graduate	62	30	8
Household income			
Less than $15,000	63	25	12
$15,000-$30,000	72	20	8
$30,001-$60,000	72	17	11
More than $60,000	77	19	4
Religion			
Protestant	74	17	9
Catholic	68	20	13
Other	59	22	6
None	72	28	13
Party identification*			
Republican	78	12	10
Democrat	66	26	8
Independent/other	68	20	12
Political ideology*			
Liberal	61	26	13
Middle of the road	71	20	9
Conservative	76	14	11
Community type*			
Rural	82	11	7
Small town	74	16	10
Small city	65	23	13
Suburb	73	19	8
Urban	58	25	17

a. Category contains fewer than 50 cases.
*Differences between groups are significant at $p \leq .001$ level.

There were no statistically significant differences in NOSCJ death penalty attitudes across any of the other demographic or sociopolitical lines. For the NOSCJ sample, attitudes about the death penalty did not vary significantly by income group as they did during the periods studied by Bohm (1991). Also, there were no significant differences in death penalty attitudes by age or religion.

Constancy of Death Penalty Attitudes

As was noted earlier, death penalty attitudes are much too complex to ascertain via a single-item question. Knowing what proportion of the population says that they "support" or "oppose" the death penalty tells us little about when, if, or how they really believe the ultimate sanction should be administered. Former U.S. Supreme Court Justice Thurgood Marshall argued that general public support for the death penalty reflects ignorance about its administration. In his concurrence with the *Furman v. Georgia* (1972) decision, Marshall claimed that although they may register support for the death penalty in general, an enlightened public would surely disapprove of it if they were informed that innocent people may be subjected to its application or that it is used in a discriminatory manner against people from particular groups such as racial minorities or the economically underprivileged. Marshall also claimed that even the most ardent supporter of the death penalty would abandon such support if they learned that it costs more than a term of life imprisonment without the possibility of parole. In essence, Marshall claimed that people are not firm in their support for the death penalty and that once enlightened about the realities that surround its administration, they would abandon their original positions and become abolitionists.

Both Bohm and Aveni (1985) and Ellsworth and Ross (1983) put Marshall's claims to an empirical test. Both tests confirmed Marshall's thesis that people are generally ignorant about the death penalty's administration, but they are not logical or consistent in their positions. Bohm's (1991) summary of this body of research concluded that "death penalty opinions are not the product of rational deliberation, but, instead, are the result of irrationality, emotion, ritualism, and conformity to reference group pressures" (p. 137). Death penalty attitudes are more or less "constant" depending on the circumstances surrounding its advocacy.

The NOSCJ included a series of questions designed to assess the level of attitudinal constancy of death penalty attitudes. After being asked whether they supported the death penalty for the crime of murder, respondents were queried about whether certain information about the death penalty would cause them to alter their original position by becoming "more likely to support" or "more likely to oppose" it. Respondents could also specify that the "new information" would not cause them to alter their original positions at all. Table 7.2 shows the categories of "new information" included in this study and what proportion of the sample selected each of the options. Table 7.2 also shows how respondents with different original positions (opposers, supporters, or neutrals) varied in their reactions to the new information.

Original Opposers

Respondents who originally identified themselves as death penalty opposers were the most likely to claim that new information would alter their original positions in some way. Only between 20% and 32% of the opposers specified that new information would not matter to them. Among those who originally supported the death penalty, between 30% and 53% claimed that the new information would not matter.

If they altered their original positions, opposers were more likely to become stronger in their opposition to the death penalty on learning the new information. Knowledge that innocent people might be executed caused the strongest affirmation of opposition, with 77% reporting that such knowledge would make them more likely to oppose the death penalty. Learning that the murderer is "severely retarded" (74%) or that poor people are more likely to receive the death penalty (72%) also affirmed positions in opposition to the death penalty. The information least likely to effect a change in attitudes among opposers was the deterrence issue and knowledge that the murderer is under the age of 18 (32% of opposers claimed that such information would not matter to them).

It is also interesting to note that between 3% and 13% of the opposers claimed that the new information would cause them to be more likely to *support* the death penalty. This group may represent those who believe that execution is too lenient and that a life sentence is actually a more sever sanction than is death.

Table 7.2 Effect of Information on Attitudes About the Death Penalty (in percentages)

If Respondent Learned That	Respondent Would Be		
	More Likely to Oppose the Death Penalty	More Likely to Favor the Death Penalty	Contingency Would Not Matter
Death penalty is not a deterrent			
Original opposers	62	5	32
Original supporters	23	25	53
Original neutrals	45	13	42
Minorities more likely to receive death penalty			
Original opposers	65	5	30
Original supporters	35	16	49
Original neutrals	55	6	39
Poor more likely to receive death penalty			
Original opposers	72	4	24
Original supporters	38	13	49
Original neutrals	55	7	38
Innocent people receive death penalty			
Original opposers	77	3	20
Original supporters	45	14	40
Original neutrals	66	5	29
Life sentence without parole as option			
Original opposers	64	11	25
Original supporters	2	33	45
Original neutrals	35	17	49
Life sentence cheaper than death penalty			
Original opposers	60	13	27
Original supporters	28	28	44
Original neutrals	49	13	38
Murderer is under 18 years old			
Original opposers	66	4	32
Original supporters	25	26	49
Original neutrals	47	6	47
Murderer is severely retarded			
Original opposers	74	3	24
Original supporters	61	9	30
Original neutrals	74	3	24

Original Supporters

Death penalty supporters were somewhat fixed in their opinions, with 53% unaffected by learning the death penalty was not a deterrent to murder. Almost half of supporters remained fixed in their support even if they learned the death penalty was likely to be administered more frequently to minorities and poor people. Similarly, 49% of supporters claimed the availability of a life sentence without the possibility of parole or knowledge that the murderer is under the age of 18 would not matter to them. Forty percent of supporters would not change their support even in the face of knowledge that innocent people might be executed. One third claimed they were likely to become more adamant in their support after learning that a life sentence without parole was available, and 28% became more adamant in support on learning that a life sentence is cheaper than the death penalty.

Original Neutrals

Some of the most interesting patterns of change demonstrated in Table 7.2 occurred among those who originally claimed to be neutral about the death penalty. Between 35% and 74% of neutrals claimed that the new information would cause them to become more likely to oppose the death penalty, and between 3% and 17% claimed that they would become more likely to support this sanction on learning the new information. Neutrals were also less likely than supporters to claim that the new information would not matter to them. The issues of most salience to neutrals included knowledge that the murderer is severely retarded and that innocent people might be subjected to the death penalty. Neutrals were least effected by knowledge that the death penalty is not a deterrent to murder, that a life sentence without parole is available as an option, or that a life sentence is cheaper than the death penalty.

Attitudinal Inconstants

A composite picture of all of the new information suggests that only 27% of the total sample were firm in their attitudes about the death penalty. The remaining 73% were inconstant in their attitudes about the death penalty (Figure 7.2).

The attitudinal inconstants group includes those whose original position was affected by at least one of the eight new facts. Death penalty supporters represent the largest group of inconstants. Fifty-nine percent

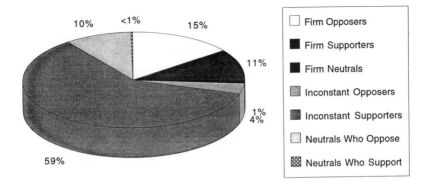

Figure 7.2. Attitudinal Constancy About the Death Penalty

of the total sample were inconstant supporters of the death penalty in that they were supportive of the death penalty but were likely to become "more opposed" after learning at least one of the new elements of information. This group represents 82% of all inconstants and 85% of all original supporters.

Only 4% of the inconstants were initially death penalty opposers who became more supportive of the death penalty after learning one or more of the new facts. This group represents 19% of all original opposers. Inconstant neutrals (10% of the total sample) include two different groups of respondents. Neutrals who oppose are those respondents who were initially neutral about the death penalty but later were "more likely to oppose" it after learning at least one new item (10% of the total sample, 92% of all neutrals). Neutrals who support (less than 1% of the total sample; less than 1% of all inconstants) include those few respondents who were initially "neutral" about the death penalty and became "more likely to support" it after learning one or more of the new items.

Attitudinally Firm

Twenty-seven percent of the respondents were firm in their positions about the death penalty. The largest group of firm respondents were firm opposers who represented 15% of the total sample and 57% of all firm respondents. This group includes those respondents who initially opposed the death penalty and either became more opposed to the death penalty as a result of at least one of the new items or stated that the items would not matter. Firm supporters (11% of the total sample,

40% of firm respondents) are those who were initially in favor of the death penalty and either claimed that the new information would not matter to them or that they would become more supportive of the death penalty after learning one or more of the new items. Firm neutrals (1% of the total sample, 3% of firm respondents) are those who initially claimed to be neutral about the death penalty and remained unaffected by any of the new information.

Summary and Conclusions

Since the late 1970s, Americans have become increasingly more supportive of the death penalty. The NOSCJ data show general support for such a trend with one major variation. According to the most recent data, Americans are becoming more uncertain about the death penalty. When asked whether they support the death penalty in the case of murder, 10% of the respondents were neutral on this issue. This represents a significant change in the previous trends showing increased levels of support for the death penalty and decreased levels of both opposition and uncertainty about the use of the ultimate sanction. Of course, no single study can prove the existence of a definitive shift in this trend. The existence of such a shift in attitudes needs additional confirmation.

This analysis also confirms previous patterns of association between demographic and sociopolitical variables and death penalty attitudes. Gender, race or ethnicity, education level, political ideology, political party affiliation, and type of community are associated with death penalty attitudes. Those most likely to support the death penalty are white males with less than a college degree but at least a high school degree. Supporters identify themselves as political conservatives who identify with the Republican Party and reside outside of urban areas. Death penalty opponents are more likely to be female, African American, politically liberal, either Democrats or independents, and residents of urban areas. Opponents of the death penalty are also more likely to have either very little formal education or to have graduated from college.

Death penalty attitudes are complex and need to be studied through more complex designs than those used in most of the simple, single-question public opinion polls. Positions on the death penalty are likely to change depending on the level of knowledge about its administration. There is a small group of people who remain firm in their death penalty positions, but 73% of the people are inconstant in attitudes toward this sanction. Learning that a murderer is severely retarded causes the highest levels of inconstancy, followed by knowledge that innocent people may be executed and knowledge that the death penalty may be administered in a discriminatory manner against the poor. People's attitudes about the death penalty are not greatly effected by knowledge about its deterrent effect or its cost effectiveness.

Public policymakers should note the generally high levels of inconstancy about the death penalty in America. It is a mistake to assume that the high levels of support for the death penalty reported in the typical, single-item public opinion survey are truly indicative of the "public mind" on this issue. People are not simply "in favor of" or "in opposition to" the death penalty. Instead, attitudes about this sanction vary with information about biases associated with its administration.

Those who advocate the abolition of the death penalty will have the greatest effect on supporters by emphasizing the potential that innocent people might be inadvertently subjected to this sanction and that some of those people given the death penalty are severely retarded. Cost-effectiveness arguments, deterrence, and the availability of a life sentence without the option of parole are not likely to have significant effects on death penalty attitudes of those who support its use. Abolitionists should also develop efforts to educate more fully the public about the potential biases in the administration of the death penalty. Those who are initially neutral about the death penalty are much more likely to become opposed when given information about its administration.

Those who advocate the death penalty must recognize the complexity of the public's mind on this issue and resist temptations to broaden its availability. People tend to be quick to stand in support of this sanction, but they are just as quick to back off their support when given specific information about its administration. Retentionists ought to be concerned about perceptions that innocent people might be executed and that the death penalty is administered unfairly against the economically underprivileged and minority group members.

The present study does not confirm the speculations made by former U.S. Supreme Court Justice Thurgood Marshall. He firmly believed that an "enlightened public" would stand in opposition to the death penalty. It is apparent from this research that "enlightenment" is not sufficient cause for all death penalty supporters to change their minds. This is clearly the case for 40% of death penalty supporters who continue to support the use of the ultimate sanction even if they learn that innocent people might be executed. Perhaps, as has been suggested by others, attitudes about the death penalty are symbolic of a more general conservative political ideology that is resistant to any information that might undermine its basic tenets. Further research into the sociopolitical dimensions of death penalty support is needed before this question can be finally put to rest.

8

Guns and Gun Control

KENNETH ADAMS

Guns are such an integral part of our society that proposals to limit access to firearms provoke contentious reactions. Gun control is controversial, in part, because guns have multiple purposes. They can be used for hunting, sport, protecting life and property, and committing crimes. This versatility complicates efforts at reducing firearms-related deaths and injuries, because action in one arena carries liabilities in another. For example, laws that attempt to curb the illegal use of guns by criminals, such as the Brady Bill, run afoul of the interests of hunters. The challenge, then, for criminal justice policymakers is to develop strategies that minimize the harm caused by illegal use of firearms while not unduly restricting legitimate use by law-abiding citizens.

Another reason that gun control efforts are controversial is that some types of violence, such as that in defense of life and property, are condoned, and even encouraged, by society. If guns are to be used for self-defense, they need to be readily accessible, which implies minimal restrictions on ownership. The possibility that law-abiding citizens dispossessed of guns may helplessly suffer injury or death at the hands of criminals strikes some observers as morally offensive (Snyder, 1993).

109

Finally, many uses of guns are congruent with notions of self-reliance that prevail in our culture. Hence, restrictions on firearms can strike at the core of our American identity.

This chapter examines issues of gun ownership and gun control as reflected in the National Opinion Survey on Crime and Justice—1995 (NOSCJ). First, the prevalence of gun ownership and the reasons for ownership are discussed. Second, opinions on gun control measures, the use of guns for self-defense, and liability for the misuse of guns are investigated. Third, opinions of persons who have actively promoted their views on gun issues are examined. Fourth, opinions of gun owners are investigated. Finally, the relation of fear of crime and confidence in police to gun-related opinions is considered.

Gun Ownership

The NOSCJ found that almost half (44%) of U.S. households own a gun. This finding is consistent with other surveys (Cook & Moore, 1995; Kleck, 1991). Gallup poll data indicate that the prevalence of gun ownership has been steady from 1959 to 1993, averaging around 47%.

In Table 8.1, we find that gun ownership is the norm in rural areas, with ownership more than twice as prevalent than in urban areas. Ownership levels were highest in the west-north Central and Mountain regions and lowest in the mid-Atlantic region. In addition, whites, males, married persons, high-income persons, and Republicans were more likely to own guns. Conversely, gun ownership was less prevalent among Democrats, Hispanics, blacks, and persons who live alone. These patterns are consistent with prior research (Kleck, 1991).

Gun owners were asked whether they owned a gun for "sport, protection against crime, both sport and protection, or neither." Sport was the most commonly given reason. As shown in Table 8.1, 45% of gun owners cited sport as the primary purpose of ownership. When this figure is combined with the proportion who cited both sport and protection, 72% of owners mentioned sport as a reason for ownership. Sport was more often the primary reason for ownership in the mid-Atlantic, west-north Central and Mountain regions, among upper-middle-income households, and among respondents who have never been married.

Although a minority of households (20%) indicated that protection against crime was the primary purpose for owning a gun, nearly half (47%) cited protection as a reason for ownership. Multiplying the own-

Table 8.1 Prevalence of Household Gun Ownership and Reasons for Ownership (in percentages)

	Household Gun Ownership		Reason for Ownership			
	No	Yes	Sport	Protection	Both	Neither
National	56	44	45	20	27	8
Race/ethnicity*						
White	52	49	49	17	27	8
Hispanic	72	27	27[a]	37[a]	33[a]	3[a]
Black	69	31	20[a]	46[a]	27[a]	8[a]
Other	71	29	40[a]	12[a]	48[a]	0[a]
Gender*						
Male	47	53	42	17	34	7
Female	64	36	45	24	17	15
Household income*						
Less than $15,000	76	24	41	24	25	10
$15,000 to $30,000	64	36	34	15	46	5
$30,001 to $60,000	47	53	55	20	17	7
More than $60,000	43	57	39	21	29	11
Marital status*						
Married	47	53	45	19	28	8
Widowed	72	28	30	35	6	29
Divorced/separated	70	30	33	20	38	9
Never married	69	31	55	19	22	4
Party identification						
Republican	48*	52*	41	19	33	7
Democrat	58*	42*	47	23	23	7
Other	58*	42*	49	16	24	11
Live alone*						
Yes	70	30	36	27	18	20
No	55	45	43	19	29	9
Community type*						
Rural	32	68	49	17	29	5
Small town	47	53	47	15	27	12
Small city	67	33	38	25	22	16
Suburb	62	38	42	19	33	5
Urban	69	31	31	29	23	17
Region*						
New England	60	40	54	11	31	3
Mid-Atlantic	75	25	59	10	18	12
East-north Central	64	36	43	24	23	10
West-north Central	41	59	61	9	21	10
South Atlantic	54	46	35	29	27	9
East-south Central	45	55	32	44	21	3
West-south Central	44	56	43	15	36	6
Mountain	40	60	61	4	26	10
Pacific	58	42	38	23	33	6

a. Category contains fewer than 50 cases.
*Differences between groups are significant at $p \leq .01$ level.

ership prevalence figures with those on reasons for ownership, we find that about one fifth of U.S. households were armed in defense of criminals. Nonwhites more often cited protection against crime as the primary purpose of ownership, as did residents of urban areas. Also, protection was more frequently a reason for ownership among households in the lower-middle-income bracket.

Again, these findings are consistent with prior research. A 1977 survey in Illinois found that 72% of owners have a gun primarily for hunting and recreation, whereas 29% have a gun primarily for protection (Bordua, 1984). A national survey conducted in 1975 found that 55% of owners cited self-protection as one of the reasons they own a gun (Bordua, 1984).

Gun Control Measures

Americans were asked two questions about gun control. The first question, used by the Gallup poll, asks about firearms sales laws. The second asks about concealed weapons laws.

Roughly, 6 out of 10 Americans wanted stricter firearms sales laws, and 3 in 10 favored the status quo. Only 1 in 10 wanted less strict sales laws. As shown in Figure 8.1, these findings are comparable to previous polls. However, in comparison with other surveys in this decade, the NOSCJ data suggest a shift in preference away from stricter laws.

In Table 8.2, we find that females, urban residents, liberals, Democrats, Hispanics, and blacks favored stricter sales laws. Americans from rural areas were more likely to be satisfied with the current situation. Changing proportions in the "more strict" and "keep as they are" categories accounted for most of the variation related to demographic characteristics.

In 1987, Florida began to issue permits for concealed handguns, and 2% of the state's population now has a permit. Given that predictions of soaring homicide rates failed to materialize, other states are considering fewer restrictions on concealed weapons. Recently, Texas passed a permit law that reversed a prohibition on carrying concealed handguns. Although roughly half of Texas's population opposes the new law, a recent poll found that 12% of adults are "very likely" to apply for a handgun permit (Ratcliffe, 1995).

As shown in Table 8.2, 61% of Americans oppose more liberal concealed handgun laws, whereas one third support such changes. Fewer restrictions on concealed handguns were favored most by persons in

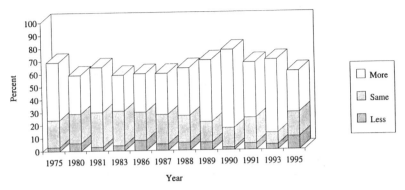

Figure 8.1. Americans' Views on Firearms Sales Laws, Gallup Poll, 1975-1993, and National Opinion Survey on Crime and Justice—1995
Question: "In general, do you feel that the laws covering the sale of firearms should be made more strict, less strict, or kept as they are now?"
NOTE: Prior to 1989, the Gallup poll asked about handgun, not firearms, sales.

rural areas and least by college graduates. Curiously, persons for whom radio is the primary source of information about crime strongly supported (42%) more liberal handgun laws. In contrast, females and Democrats were more likely to oppose freer access to concealed handguns.

Guns and Self-Defense

When our country was founded, private gun ownership was an important element in the nation's defense against foreign governments. Also, because the citizenry harbored an element of distrust toward the domestic government, private gun ownership was seen as a check on government abuse of power. Over time, the rationale for defensive gun ownership has shifted away from governments to criminals (Kennett & Anderson, 1975). Today, advocates for increasing the availability of firearms argue that widespread availability of firearms deters criminal activity. Rising violent crime rates, which highlight the inability of police to protect the citizenry, add credibility to the argument (Wright, 1984).

In Table 8.3, we see that a great majority (80%) of Americans did not agree that "an armed citizenry is the best defense against government

Table 8.2 Americans' Views on Gun Control Issues (in percentages)

	Question: "In general, do you feel that the laws covering the sale of firearms should be made . . .?"			Question: "It should be easier for law-abiding citizens to carry concealed weapons."				
	More Strict	Kept as They Are	Less Strict	Strongly Agree	Agree	Neither	Disagree	Strongly Disagree
National	61	29	10	7	26	6	51	10
Race/ethnicity								
White	57*	33*	9*	7	26	6	50	10
Hispanic	81*	12*	7*	4	25	5	57	9
Black	71*	15*	14*	9	22	3	54	12
Other[a]	87*	7*	6*	4	35	9	37	15
Gender*								
Male	51	35	14	10	29	5	47	8
Female	71	23	6	4	23	7	54	12
Education								
Less than high school	57	33	9	3*	34*	2*	58*	3*
High school graduate	61	29	10	6*	26*	6*	54*	8*
Some college	56	32	12	9*	31*	5*	47*	8*
College graduate	68	23	9	8*	17*	8*	51*	16*
Party identification*								
Republican	51	34	15	12	30	6	48	5
Democrat	73	22	5	5	25	6	50	15
Other	58	31	10	6	25	7	52	11
Political ideology								
Liberal	66*	23*	11*	5	29	2	53	11
Middle of the road	61*	32*	7*	6	24	6	51	14
Conservative	57*	28*	14*	11	27	8	50	4
Community type*								
Rural	45	43	11	10	33	5	45	6
Small town	56	33	11	4	29	7	55	5
Small city	66	25	9	6	23	6	51	13
Suburb	68	22	10	9	20	6	54	13
Urban	69	23	7	8	29	4	46	13
Primary source of news about crime								
Television	63	27	9	5*	26*	6*	52*	11*
Newspaper	61	31	8	7*	24*	7*	53*	11*
Radio	49	33	18	24*	18*	6*	43*	9*
Other	56	35	9	5*	37*	11*	47*	0*

a. Category contains fewer than 50 cases.
*Differences between groups are significant at $p \leq .01$ level.

abuse of power," with one quarter strongly disagreeing. Conversely, only 16% of Americans agreed, including 5% who strongly agreed. Females, Democrats, college graduates, and persons in the highest income category were more likely to strongly disagree. In contrast, conservatives, persons with low educational achievement, and persons who receive most of their information about crime from other than traditional sources (e.g., newspaper, TV, radio) were more likely to agree. This last finding suggests that a distrust of power extends to the mainstream media.

Also in Table 8.3, we find that 59% of Americans did not agree that "an armed citizenry is the best defense against criminals," whereas 34% agreed. Only a small proportion strongly agreed (9%) or strongly disagreed (14%). Conservatives, Republicans, persons with less than a high school education, and persons who think that the media pay too little attention to violent crime were more likely to agree. In contrast, females, liberals, and college graduates were more likely to disagree.

Liability

A solution to the gun control problem advanced by both sides of the debate is that of requiring liability, civil or criminal, for the misuse or illegal use of guns. Anti-gun control advocates tend to favor criminal liability, such as mandatory prison sentences for crimes committed with guns. They argue that this policy, which emphasizes personal responsibility, advances society's interests in reducing harm while preserving the legitimate interests of gun owners. A variation on this argument, inquired about in the NOSCJ, deals with parental liability for harm caused by a child's misuse of a gun. The issue speaks to the need to keep dangerous weapons out of the hands of those who are not competent to use weapons properly.

Gun control advocates, in contrast, have pushed for civil liability on the part of gun manufacturers, arguing that these companies should be held financially responsible for knowingly selling a dangerous product. The hope is that liability requirements will drain the financial resources of gun manufacturers, forcing them to go out of business or to impose severe restrictions on weapons sales. Although legal arguments for gun manufacturer liability have yet to prove successful, popular sentiment for this notion is explored in the NOSCJ.

As shown in Table 8.4, a majority (57%) of Americans agreed that "parents should be charged with a crime if their child injures themselves

Table 8.3 Americans' Views on the Defensive Use of Guns (in percentages)

	Question: "Armed citizens are the best defense against government abuse of power."					Question: "Armed citizens are the best defense against criminals."				
	Strongly Agree	Agree	Neither	Disagree	Strongly Disagree	Strongly Agree	Agree	Neither	Disagree	Strongly Disagree
National	5	11	5	55	25	9	25	7	45	14
Gender*										
Male	7	15	6	52	20	12	30	7	39	11
Female	3	8	3	57	29	6	21	6	51	17
Education										
Less than high school	5*	19*	5*	60*	11*	10	36	3	45	7
High school graduate	5*	9*	4*	58*	24*	8	27	7	45	12
Some college	5*	12*	5*	56*	22*	10	28	8	43	11
College graduate	4*	11*	4*	49*	32*	8	16	7	48	22
Income										
Less than $15,000	3*	9*	5*	66*	17*	8	33	4	45	9
$15,000-$30,000	5*	9*	5*	62*	19*	12	21	7	46	14
$30,001-$60,000	6*	12*	3*	50*	28*	8	25	8	43	14
More than $60,000	3*	13*	5*	47*	33*	7	26	5	45	17
Party identification*										
Republican	7	13	4	58	19	12	28	6	44	9
Democrat	3	11	2	50	34	7	23	4	44	22
Other	4	10	7	55	24	8	25	9	45	12

Political ideology*										
Liberal	3	14	3	53	28	9	21	4	45	22
Middle of the road	2	8	4	55	30	6	25	7	47	15
Conservative	10	14	6	55	15	14	28	7	43	8
Primary source of news about crime										
Television	4*	11*	4*	56*	25*	7	25	7	46	15
Newspaper	4*	14*	5*	49*	29*	8	24	7	44	17
Radio	4*	7*	15*	47*	27*	16	19	11	45	9
Other	10*	15*	0*	69*	5*	15	29	1	49	6
Media attention to violent crime										
Too much	4	13	5	53	26	6*	23*	9*	45*	16*
About right	3	10	3	58	26	9*	24*	6*	47*	14*
Too little	9	13	5	55	19	13*	33*	1*	43*	9*

*Differences between groups are significant at $p \leq .01$ level.

Table 8.4 Americans' Views on Parental and Manufacturer Liability for the Misuse of Guns (in percentages)

	Question: "Parents should be charged with a crime if their children injure themselves or others with a gun kept in their household."					Question: "Companies that manufacture guns with no hunting or sporting purpose should be held financially responsible when these guns injure or kill people."				
	Strongly Agree	Agree	Neither	Disagree	Strongly Disagree	Strongly Agree	Agree	Neither	Disagree	Strongly Disagree
National	12	45	10	29	4	14	32	5	40	9
Gender										
Male	11	45	9	31	4	14*	27*	5*	44*	11*
Female	13	45	11	26	5	14*	37*	5*	35*	8*
Education										
Less than high school	9	42	12	33	3	10*	25*	4*	58*	3*
High school graduate	10	44	9	31	6	12*	36*	6*	39*	7*
Some college	11	47	10	27	5	13*	31*	3*	37*	15*
College graduate	15	46	9	27	3	19*	32*	4*	35*	9*
Party identification										
Republican	14	45	7	30	4	9*	31*	6*	39*	15*
Democrat	9	46	13	28	4	17*	39*	3*	36*	5*
Other	11	45	10	28	5	16*	29*	4*	41*	9*
Political ideology										
Liberal	11	51	11	23	3	15*	35*	3*	39*	9*
Middle of the road	10	45	12	27	6	17*	35*	6*	36*	8*
Conservative	13	44	6	34	3	9	28*	9*	46*	13*

*Differences between groups are significant at $p \leq .01$ level.

or others with a gun kept in their household," with 12% strongly agreeing. A substantial minority (33%) did not support criminal liability for parents. The proportion neither agreeing nor disagreeing (10%) is larger than that for other questions, suggesting greater than average ambivalence on this issue. Finally, none of the demographic variables was related to opinions on parental liability. This finding suggests that views on the issue are formed through a socialization process that is either universal or was not measured.

No consensus emerged on the issue of whether "companies that manufacture guns with no hunting or sporting purpose should be held financially responsible when these guns injure or kill people." As shown in Table 8.4, Americans were almost equally split in terms of agreement (46%) and disagreement (49%). Democrats were more likely to favor manufacturer liability, and males, conservatives, and persons with low educational achievement were more likely to object. A lack of consensus may stem from differing views on the economic consequences of manufacturer liability or on the responsibilities of gun users.

Activism on Gun Issues

A major controversy in the gun control debate involves the role of activists, particularly well-funded lobbyist groups, in framing issues, shaping public opinion, and influencing legislation. We asked Americans if they had engaged in activities to express their views on gun issues within the past 5 years, and nearly one out of five (19%) indicated that they had made their views known. Activism on gun issues was highest in the Mountain regions (30%), a finding related to high levels of gun ownership. A previous national survey found that 8% of respondents had expressed their views on gun issues (Schuman & Presser, 1981a). Thus, the NOSCJ data suggest that activism has increased appreciably over the past decade and a half.

Table 8.5 compares opinions between Americans who were active in expressing their views and those who were not. Generally, those who promoted their views favored less gun control. They wanted fewer restrictions on firearms sales, and they also favored easier access to concealed handguns.

Persons in the active group were more inclined to view an armed citizenry as the best defense against criminals as well as government abuse of power. Forty-seven percent saw gun ownership as an effective means of dealing with the crime problem, and one quarter agreed that

Table 8.5 Opinions on Gun Issues by Whether Respondent Was Active in Expressing Views and by Gun Ownership

	Active in Expressing Views		Gun Owner				Nonowner
	No	Yes	Sport	Protection	Both	Total[a]	
Gun control (in percentages)							
Make firearms sales laws							
More strict*	64	46	49	46	27	43	74
Keep the same*	29	31	42	34	52	42	20
Less strict*	7	23	10	20	22	12	6
Make it easier to carry concealed handguns (percentage agree)*	32	41	34	53	73	48	22
Guns as "best defense" (percentage agree) Against government abuse*	14	25	13	22	36	22	12
Against criminals*	32	44	39	51	72	50	23
Liability for misuse (percentage agree)							
Parent-child	56	65	51	64	58	57	58
Manufacturer	47	43	45*	33*	24*	36*	53*
Active on gun issues (percentage yes)	NA	NA	21*	18*	37*	25*	12*

a. The group responding "neither sport nor protection" is not reported separately but is included in the total column. Chi-square tests of significance were run separately across categories of ownership and between owners and nonowners. In all cases, the results of the two tests were the same.
*Differences between groups are significant at $p \leq .01$ level.

civilian gun ownership is an important control on government abuse of power, a proportion almost twice that of the nonactive group. Persons in the active group also showed greater support for parental liability but were less likely to support manufacturer liability. These differences were not statistically significant.

In general, Americans who actively expressed their views on gun issues were in the minority, both numerically and in terms of the opinions they held. Compared to others, they wanted fewer restrictions on firearms and were more likely to view firearms as an important means of self-defense.

Gun Ownership and Views on Gun Issues

Gun owners presumably have different opinions on gun issues than nonowners. They have more at stake when it comes to gun control. They may also be more knowledgeable about current gun laws as well as about the effect of proposed changes in these laws. Some researchers have concluded that gun ownership is a critical determinant of opinions on gun issues, eclipsing most demographic and personal characteristics (Kleck, 1991).

In this section, differences in opinions between households that own guns and those that do not are examined. Gun ownership is subcategorized by reason for ownership.

Table 8.5 indicates that gun owners were much less likely to want stricter gun sales laws than nonowners (43% vs. 74%). The difference is most pronounced for households that own a gun for both sport and protection, with only 27% favoring stricter laws. A large proportion of gun owners (42%) favored keeping firearms sales laws as they are now. Support for less strict firearms sales laws was strongest among owners who cite protection from crime as a reason for ownership. These households were almost four times more likely to want fewer regulations on the sale of firearms compared to nonowners.

Households with guns were more than twice as likely to favor more liberal concealed weapons laws. "Protection" gun owners favored increased access to concealed weapons most, with roughly three out of four "sport and protection" owners supporting fewer restrictions on the carrying of concealed weapons.

Gun owners were more than twice as likely than nonowners to endorse citizen ownership of firearms as a defense against crime (50% vs. 23%). Americans who own guns for both sport and protection stood out in this regard, with 72% endorsing an armed citizenry. A similar pattern maintained for civilian gun ownership as a defense against government abuse. Gun owners were about twice as likely as nonowners (22% vs. 12%) to approve of an armed citizenry for this purpose, with "sport and protection" owners showing the greatest support (36%). However, a majority of Americans, owners and nonowners alike, did not agree that armed citizens are the best defense against government abuse.

The relation of gun ownership to opinions on parental liability was not statistically significant. However, the data suggest that Americans who owned guns solely for protection were most inclined, and those who owned guns solely for sport were least inclined, to hold parents criminally liable for the acts of their children. In contrast, gun owners were less likely than nonowners (36% vs. 53%) to hold manufacturers liable for the misuse of guns. Support for manufacturer liability was lowest among the "sport and protection" owners (24%).

Gun owners were more inclined to promote their opinions on gun issues than nonowners (25% vs. 12%). Again, "sport and protection" owners stood out, with 37% indicating that they had made their opinions known.

In sum, gun owners held opinions that differ substantially from those of nonowners. Some reasons for the differences in opinions are obvious. It is not surprising that persons who owned guns for protection against crime were inclined to think that an armed citizenry deters criminals and that firearms should be more widely available. They have acted on these beliefs. It is also interesting that the opinions of the "sport and protection" gun owners diverged most from those of nonowners as well as other gun owners. This group, which has multiple interests at stake, was most adverse to gun control and was most inclined to view guns as an important means of self-defense.

Fear of Crime, Confidence in Police, and Opinions on Gun Issues

Two theoretical perspectives have emerged to explain defensive gun ownership. The first links gun ownership to fear of crime and to victimization experiences (Lizotte & Bordua, 1980). The empirical evidence on this hypothesis has been mixed (Kleck, 1991). The second perspective, which has received broader empirical support, emphasizes notions of self-help and collective security (McDowell & Loftin, 1983; Smith & Uchida, 1988). Gun ownership is seen as a functional response to a lack of confidence in governmental agencies that are charged with ensuring the safety of the citizenry, most notably, the police. In this section, we examine these perspectives in relation to opinions on gun issues.

Several measures of fear of crime and confidence in police were included in the NOSCJ. Seven questions inquired about the frequency of worrying about being victimized by specific types of crimes. Among questions on confidence in the police, four addressed effectiveness at fighting crime, and three addressed police-community relations. In addition, the survey asked about perceptions of increasing or decreasing crime rates in the respondent's community.

Regarding firearms sales laws, five of seven measures of confidence in the police showed a significant relation. When confidence in the police to protect from crime, to solve crime, and to prevent crime was low, Americans were more likely to want less strict gun purchase laws (17%, 17%, and 14%, respectively). The fourth measure of police effectiveness, quickness in responding to calls, showed a similar, albeit nonsignificant, relation. Likewise, when perceptions of police fairness were low and when excessive force by police was seen as a problem, support for less strict gun purchase laws increased (19% and 16%, respectively). Perceptions of police friendliness showed the same pattern, although the relation was not significant.

Confidence in police ability to protect from crime was related to most opinions on gun issues. When confidence was low, Americans were more likely to favor relaxed access to concealed handguns (50%). They were also more likely to agree that an armed citizenry is the best defense against criminals (50%) as well as government abuse of power (30%).

Finally, Americans who lacked confidence in the ability of police to prevent crime were more inclined to favor easier access to carry concealed handguns. In addition, they were more likely to live in a gun-owning household and to cite protection from crime as a reason for gun ownership.

In contrast, only one of six measures of fear of victimization, that referring to mugging, showed a significant relation, with fear being inversely related to a preference for stricter gun purchase laws. Perceptions of a rising crime rate were unrelated to gun ownership and to opinions on gun issues.

The data indicate that perceptions of police effectiveness at fighting crime are related to gun ownership and opinions on gun issues. The findings support the self-help and collective security hypothesis. In contrast, fear of victimization and perceptions of rising crime rates were unrelated to gun ownership and to opinions on gun issues.

Summary

The results of the NOSCJ are consistent with other surveys in regard to the prevalence of gun ownership, the characteristics of gun owners, and opinions about gun control. About one fifth of U.S. households owned guns for protection against crime. In general, citizens preferred either more restrictions on firearms or maintaining the status quo.

Although only a small minority wanted less strict gun laws, the proportion appears to have increased over time.

The characteristics of respondents who wanted freer access to guns and who viewed guns as important for self-defense were similar. These characteristics also showed a coherent pattern with regard to lifestyle (e.g., region, community type), personal characteristics (e.g., race, gender), and political orientation (e.g., party affiliation, ideology). Also, Americans who actively expressed their views on gun issues and those who owned guns favored more liberal laws, indicating that the opinions of these groups diverged from those of the larger citizenry.

Americans tended to support the notion that an armed citizenry is the best defense against crime. In contrast, they generally rejected gun ownership as a means of protection against government abuse of power. Gun owners, particularly those who own guns for protection against crime, and activists were much more likely to view guns as important for protecting life and property from unlawful criminals or an abusive government. The fact that gun owners valued their guns in these essential respects helps to explain why they opposed gun control laws.

Regarding liability for the misuse of firearms, support was moderate for holding parents criminally responsible for the actions of their children, and no consensus emerged on holding manufacturers liable for injuries inflicted by guns. Gun owners and activists were more inclined to support parental liability and less inclined to support manufacturer liability.

Finally, confidence in police, rather than fear of crime, was an important correlate of attitudes toward gun issues. To the extent that police were seen as not carrying out their public safety mandate, gun ownership became more attractive and gun control laws less desirable. The collective security hypothesis, which predicts that individuals will assume responsibility for their safety when government is seen as failing at the task, is supported. Thus, successful implementation of gun regulations, which is frustrated by the perceived utility of personal gun ownership, can be promoted by increasing the public's confidence in the criminal justice system.

The Modern Plague
Controlling Substance Abuse

MYRNA CINTRÓN

W. WESLEY JOHNSON

The scientific evidence is strong regarding the negative health and societal effects associated with alcohol, illicit drug use, and cigarette smoking. This accumulation of scientific evidence, combined with government policies that target drug users and a general decline in the public's perception of their safety, has sustained public concern about illegal drug use during the 1980s and 1990s. Public concern over substance abuse has been reflected in the results of numerous opinion polls.

There is considerable public support for controlling substance abuse, but crime and drugs did not emerge as one of the "most important national problems" among opinion poll lists until the 1960s (Beckett, 1994; Erskine, 1974; Smith, 1980). The first government-sponsored national opinion survey of drug use among the general population emerged from the recommendations of the Commission on Marijuana and Drug Abuse (Shafer Commission) in 1973 (Bonnie, 1992; Musto, 1987). By the mid-1970s, an average of 10 problems had been itemized, under the crime category, by most polling agencies (Erskine, 1974). More recent surveys have focused more directly on the drug problem. For example, for the years 1978-1990, between 23% and 35% of the people surveyed responded in the affirmative to the question, "Do you sometimes drink more than you think you should?" (Gallup & Newport, 1990; Wood, 1990). In a survey of Americans' attitudes toward drug abuse, "nearly half (49%) of all Americans say they know a friend, relative, neighbor, or someone at work who became addicted to illegal drugs" (Center for Substance Abuse Research, 1995b).

It seems that the national focus on the drug abuse problem has been fostered by an interaction between the media and public opinion. Asher (1988) and Beckett (1994) suggested a "social constructionist-agenda setting hypothesis" whereby the power of public opinion is a function of the media and the political elite who control the issues brought to the public's attention. For example, the reported incidence of drug use declined during the 1980s, although public and political concern over the issue increased during this time period (Jensen, Gerber, & Bebcock, 1991; Johnston, O'Malley, & Bachman, 1993).

Asher (1988, p. 151) proposed that as the media and political leaders stop talking about drugs, the issue will recede from popular consciousness and citizens will be left with misguided feelings that somehow the problem was resolved. However, public opinion poll results, like the results presented here, are consistent in finding that in 1996 the public is still very much concerned about the drug problem.

Overview of Previous Opinion Polls

Marijuana Legalization Debate

Some political leaders, researchers, and analysts of the drug problem have argued that the war against illicit drugs is a lost cause and should be abandoned. It has been claimed that legalizing drugs, marijuana in particular, is a policy alternative worth trying. Although the marijuana legalization debate continues to capture the public's attention in public opinion polls, opposition to legalizing marijuana has increased since the late 1970s. It has been reported that slightly less than a third (28%-30%) of adult respondents oppose legalizing small amounts of marijuana for personal use, and the percentage of high school seniors favoring making marijuana use entirely legal peaked at about 34% in 1977 (ABC News/Washington Post, 1985; Gallup, 1985; National Opinion Research Center, 1986; Wood, 1990). By 1989, 38% of adults favored legalization, whereas only 17% of high school seniors favored marijuana legalization (Johnston et al., 1993). Results from the High School Senior Survey show that 19% responded that possessing a small amount of marijuana should be a minor violation like a parking ticket, but not a crime, and 50% felt it should be a crime (Johnston, O'Malley, & Bachman, 1991, 1992, 1993). The percentage of adult Americans who feel that possession of small amounts of marijuana should be treated as a criminal offense increased from 43% in 1980 to 74% in 1988. It is possible that the "war on drugs" rhetoric of the 1980s helped redefine public perceptions of the issue as a criminal offense.

Although the percentage of high school seniors favoring legalization of drug use has fallen, recent surveys show that many of the nation's youth are taking the attitude that drugs, especially marijuana and inhalants, are safe to try (Johnston et al., 1991, 1992, 1993; "Kids and Marijuana," 1994; National Institute on Drug Abuse, 1990). Marijuana use among high school seniors in 1993 rose for the first time in 14 years (Janofsky, 1994; "Kids and Marijuana," 1994). In 1991, 79% of 12th graders associated regular use of marijuana with "great risk"; in 1994 this figure dropped to 65% ("Drug Use Occupies," 1994; "Drug Use by Youth," 1995).

A majority of the seniors agreed that it should be legal to sell marijuana if it were legal to use it, but only to adults (Johnston et al., 1992, 1993). Adult respondents also favored stiffer penalties for the sale of marijuana than they did for the use or possession of marijuana. In the analysis of responses, researchers identified some trends that might reflect an increase in conservative attitudes about drugs in general, and marijuana in particular (Johnston et al., 1991, 1992, 1993). For example, fewer students support legalized sale, even if its use were to be made illegal (65% in 1979, 49% in 1992).

In sum, it seems that Americans continue to be interested in the debate over the legalization of marijuana. It is also true that public opinions and attitudes are not constant over time, especially when it comes to the use of marijuana. It is also interesting to note that although the official government attitude is one of user accountability and supply reduction, this policy is having little effect on public perceptions about the risks (and availability) of marijuana (Johnston et al., 1993).

Strategies to Reduce the Use of Illicit Drugs

Given the fact that the vast majority of the public rejects the legalization argument, what can be done to reduce illegal drugs in society? Public opinion surveys consistently indicate that the public believes that drug treatment programs will make a difference in reducing the demand for drugs, and especially so-called drug-related crimes. But only about 30% of the federal drug budget goes toward efforts that attempt to reduce the demand for drugs (treatment, prevention, and education). The rest goes to supply side efforts that emphasize control: more police, judges, prosecutors, and correctional facilities and boot camps. Responses to a telephone survey conducted by Peter D. Hart Research Associates found that the public feels that government-funded programs, either in or out of prison, make a major difference in reducing drug-related crimes (Center for Substance Abuse Research, 1995a). When respondents were given a choice of what to do with drug users, respondents preferred treatment over prison (Colasanto, 1990). The consensus of opinion appears to be that prison should be reserved for major drug dealers (drug kingpins).

Survey respondents have also been asked about the effectiveness of the approaches used in the war on drugs. Despite the "tough" current political rhetoric on drug-related issues (drug-screening tests, longer prison terms for convicted felons, and boot camps for first-time offenders), the public prefers a balanced approach between law enforcement, prevention, and treatment ("Drug Use Occupies," 1994; Treaster, 1994). The public prefers spending money on programs in their own communities rather than on border and international interdiction programs; court supervised treatment over prison terms; and prison time for drug dealers rather than for drug users ("Drug Use Occupies," 1994).

However, Americans believe that the institutions engaged in the supply reduction efforts are ill equipped, have limited resources, and lack the ability to be effective in the war against drugs. The public has confidence in federal drug agents than in local police officers. Survey respondents have some confidence in drug treatment centers, the educational system, and the police and have little or no confidence in the border patrol (Colasanto, 1990). These responses might reflect the public's perceptions of which agencies have the resources, ability, and preparedness to be effective (e.g., the Drug Enforcement Administration and the Border Patrol).

Although the public believes that federal drug agents are most effective, they still believe that education about the dangers of drugs is the best way to win the war against drugs (Colasanto, 1990). This belief is supported by a study by the RAND Corporation that quantified the relative merits of demand-side and supply-side strategies. It was found that for every $34 million allocated to treatment, the government would have to spend $246 million on domestic law enforcement, $366 million on drug interdiction, or $783 million on source-country control (Center for Substance Abuse Research, 1995a; Treaster, 1994).

In brief, it seems that the public is able to distinguish between the alternatives they feel can be applied to an individual drug user and the overall national drug control strategy. Strategies such as military intervention and law enforcement are being rejected over such policies as drug education and drug treatment programs.

Effectiveness of the War on Drugs

Are Americans optimistic about the effects of the war on drugs in their communities? In an ABC News/Washington Post (1985) poll, 36% of the respondents said that in their community, drugs were a bigger problem than alcohol, whereas 38% said alcohol abuse was more threatening than drug abuse, and only 15% said the two were equal. Research conducted for the Drug Strategies organization revealed that 52% of the respondents indicated that drug abuse is an *extremely serious* or a *quite serious* problem in their community (Center for Substance Abuse Research, 1995b).

In brief, survey respondents were not optimistic about the effects the recent war efforts had on drug use in their communities. Seven out of 10 Americans reported that the drug abuse problem is worse than it was 5 years ago. Respondents also felt that money spent on overseas and border interdiction efforts would be better spent on direct aid to American communities (Center for Substance Abuse Research, 1995a).

Survey Results

During the previous decade, heightened public concern and media attention concerning the use of drugs in American society produced a variety of public policy responses. Particular emphasis, during this time, was placed on the use of criminal justice resources. This section of the survey, in the aftermath of the 1980s war on drugs, provides empirical evidence of the public's opinion of contemporary drug control efforts. The survey questions in this section focused on the legalization of marijuana, the use of the military in controlling national borders, street-level police efforts, drug education programs, drug treatment programs, and the depiction of drug use in the media.

Table 9.1 summarizes survey results regarding the regulation of marijuana. National survey percentages indicate overwhelming sup-

Table 9.1 Attitudes Toward Marijuana Legalization (in percentages)

Question: "Changing topics, there has been a great deal of public debate whether marijuana use should be legal. Which one of the following would you favor?"

	Legalize	Prescription	Minor Violation	Crime
National	11	49	13	26
Age*				
18-29	14	43	15	28
30-39	11	44	15	28
40-49	9	47	16	27
50-59	15	54	9	21
60-69	38	61	9	21
70 or older	10	61	3	24
Race/ethnicity				
White	11	49	12	26
Hispanic	6	54	9	32
African American	11	38	22	26
Other[a]	0	59	14	19
Education				
Less than high school	12	47	15	25
High school graduate	10	50	11	29
Some college	9	46	16	26
College graduate	13	51	13	22
Household income*				
Less than $15,000	7	54	11	25
$15,000-$30,000	9	51	9	31
$30,001-$60,000	10	48	14	26
More than $60,000	15	46	19	17
Party identification				
Republican	8	47	12	32
Democrat	12	51	15	22
Independent/other	12	51	13	24
Political ideology*				
Liberal	14	50	17	17
Middle of the road	11	49	14	25
Conservative	7	49	11	33

a. Category contains fewer than 50 cases.
*Differences between groups are significant at $p \leq .01$ level.

port for public policies enabling the prescription of marijuana for medical purposes. These data also indicate that a larger percentage of the respondents favored making marijuana use a crime (26%) or a minor violation (13%) than those who favored its legalization (11%). Age, income, and political ideology were the only demographic variables significantly associated with marijuana policy. As with the national results, regardless of income level, medical prescription was the overwhelming policy choice, and marijuana legalization was the least-favored response. Respondents in the higher income groups were more in favor of marijuana legalization than those in the lower income groups. Similarly, respondents among the highest income group were less likely (17%) to favor marijuana being a crime than those among the lowest income groups (25%) and more favorable toward it being treated as a minor violation than any other income group. In terms of political ideology, conservatives were more likely than liberals to favor making marijuana a crime.

The questions that yielded the data in Table 9.2 asked which policy—military border control, police street-level efforts, drug education, or drug treatment—was most effective and which policy was least effective. The answers to these questions were recoded to provide comparison of supply-side antidrug efforts (military border control and police street-level efforts) and demand-side reduction efforts (drug education programs and drug treatment programs). The national data indicate that the respondents were almost evenly split over which policies were the most effective drug control policy: 48% supported supply-side strategies, and 47% supported demand-side efforts. Analysis of these data produced significant associations between respondents' attitudes and age, education, income, and political ideology. In summary, respondents who were less educated, in lower income groups, and conservative were most likely to support supply-side efforts over demand-side efforts.

When respondents were asked which policy was least effective, they were more likely to support demand-side policies and less likely to favor supply-side strategies (50% vs. 43%). Respondents who were younger, had more education, and conservative were more likely to support demand-side efforts and view supply-side efforts as less effective. The survey responses on these questions were cross-tabulated, revealing that those who chose drug treatment (demand side) as the most effective policy approach were more likely to indicate that military border control (supply side) was the least effective policy approach. This dichotomy between those who choose supply-side efforts and those who choose demand-side approaches was not as distinct when police street-level efforts (supply side) were similarly examined. Among those who chose police street-level efforts as the most effective

Table 9.2 Attitudes Toward Most and Least Effective Drug Control Approaches (in percentages)

Question: "Which of the following approaches to dealing with drug use in American society do you think would be most effective, least effective?"

	Most Effective Policy		Least Effective Policy	
	Supply Side	Demand Side	Supply Side	Demand Side
National	48	47	50	43
Age				
18-29	46	52	51	45
30-39	47	49	55	41
40-49	47	49	51	42
50-59	50	42	52	37
60-69	59	36	43	49
70 or older	52	36	43	36
Race/ethnicity				
White	50	46	50	43
Hispanic	50	48	44	46
African American	42	53	59	34
Other[a]	38	53	46	41
Education				
Less than high school	60*	38	42	49
High school graduate	57	41	47	46
Some college	45	48	52	42
College graduate	35	59	59	36
Household income				
Less than $15,000	57*	41	55*	36
$15,000-$30,000	57	41	42	52
$30,001-$60,000	46	50	55	40
More than $60,000	39	53	56	40
Party identification				
Republican	49	47	46*	48
Democrat	49	47	54	40
Independent/other	45	51	54	39
Political ideology				
Liberal	39*	59	61*	32
Middle of the road	49	47	50	44
Conservative	53	44	47	46

a. Category contains fewer than 50 cases.
*Differences between groups are significant at $p \leq .01$ level.

policy choice, approximately one third (31%) chose military border control as the least effective policy. This anomaly suggests that respondents may view police efforts as focusing not on dealers (supply side) but on users (demand side). Despite these discrepancies, there is some evidence to suggest that there is a difference between those who support supply-side efforts and those who support demand-side efforts.[1]

Table 9.3 summarizes respondents' attitudes toward the impact of the recent drug control efforts on drug use. The response (64%) indicates that the recent war on drugs had no effect on the perceived amount of drug use in the respondent's community. Significant associations were identified between age, political ideology, and judgments of the effectiveness of drug policy. More of the younger respondents (66%) than older respondents (57%) believed the war on drugs had no effect on drug use. Also, respondents aged 40 to 60 were more likely than the other older and younger age groups to indicate that the war on drugs had no effect on drug use. When political ideology was considered, liberals and those who identified themselves as middle of the road were more likely than conservatives to believe the war on drugs had no effect on drug use. These data suggest an overall negative view of the success of the war on drugs. There were respondents who answered *don't know* to the question of effects of recent drug control efforts, and there were some respondents who believed the war on drugs actually increased the amount of drug use in their community.

Table 9.4 shows attitudes toward the depiction of illicit drug use in the movies or television programs. The vast majority of respondents (60%) supported the prohibition of showing illicit drug use in the movies or television programs. Significant associations were identified for age, education, income, and political ideology. In summary, those who were older, less educated, reported less income, and conservative favored legislation that prohibited the depiction of illegal drug use in the media.

In summary, these individual-level data indicate that Americans do not favor marijuana legalization, but instead believe marijuana use/possession should remain a crime. Although there was some limited support for making marijuana use/possession similar to a parking violation—the user would be cited, but not arrested for a crime—there was substantial support among the respondents for making marijuana available for medicinal uses as a prescription drug. Although the national survey results demonstrate that Americans favored supply-side drug control strategies, there were significant differences within the

Table 9.3 Attitudes Toward the Effects of Most Recent War on Drugs on Illicit Drug Use (in percentages)

Question: "From what you can tell in your community, has the government's most recent war on drugs . . . ?"

	Reduced the Amount of Drug Use	Increased the Amount of Drug Use	Had No Effect on Drug Use	Don't Know
National	18	7	64	11
Age*				
18-29	17	9	66	7
30-39	18	8	65	8
40-49	21	3	67	9
50-59	20	13	57	10
60-69	11	8	59	23
70 or older	14	9	57	19
Race/ethnicity				
White	17	7	65	10
Hispanic	17	9	57	17
African American	24	7	64	5
Other[a]	8	7	61	24
Education				
Less than high school	21	9	52	19
High school graduate	18	5	69	8
Some college	19	10	62	10
College graduate	17	6	66	11
Household income				
Less than $15,000	23	5	58	14
$15,000-$30,000	18	8	63	11
$30,001-$60,000	15	7	69	8
More than $60,000	23	7	64	6
Party identification				
Republican	20	7	60	13
Democrat	17	6	68	10
Independent/other	17	9	67	8
Political ideology*				
Liberal	15	5	67	13
Middle of the road	16	9	66	9
Conservative	22	8	61	9

a. Category contains fewer than 50 cases.
*Differences between groups are significant at $p \le .01$ level.

Table 9.4 Attitudes Toward Laws That Would Prohibit Depiction of the Use of Illicit Drugs in the Media (in percentages)

Question: "Would you support legislation that prohibited the depiction of the use of marijuana or other illicit drugs in movies, on television, or in music videos?"

	Yes	No
National	60	37
Age*		
18-29	45	52
30-39	57	39
40-49	64	35
50-59	68	30
60-69	70	22
70 or older	76	19
Race/ethnicity		
White	62	35
Hispanic	48	48
African American	52	42
Other[a]	62	38
Education*		
Less than high school	70	27
High school graduate	60	35
Some college	64	35
College graduate	53	44
Household income*		
Less than $15,000	69	29
$15,000-$30,000	66	31
$30,001-$60,000	59	38
More than $60,000	51	49
Party identification		
Republican	63	35
Democrat	58	39
Independent/other	60	37
Political ideology*		
Liberal	50	47
Middle of the road	61	37
Conservative	64	33

a. Category contains fewer than 50 cases.
*Differences between groups are significant at $p \leq .01$ level.

various demographic categories. Survey responses also indicated a very strong interest in regulating illicit drug use on television and in films.

Conclusion

Taken as a whole, the opinions held by the respondents toward the drug issue were complex. Although survey respondents were against the legalization of use and sale of marijuana, there was strong support for public policies enabling the medical prescription of marijuana. The survey suggests that respondents favor medical treatment rather than punishment as the best alternative to reduce the use of illegal drugs. It should be noted that there was limited support for making marijuana use/possession similar to a parking violation, where the user would be cited, but not arrested, for a crime.

Survey results indicated that respondents were not optimistic about the success of the war on drugs and were not convinced that either demand reduction or supply reduction strategies were superior. The survey data revealed that respondents believe that the recent war on drugs had little effect on the amount of drug use in their community. It is also possible that the public is losing faith in supply-side strategies. The vast majority of respondents supported legislation prohibiting the depiction of marijuana and other illicit drugs in the movies and on television programs.

In general, it seems that Americans want to see a change in drug control strategies. The public has traditionally preferred a balanced approach to the problem, one that includes drug prevention, treatment, and law enforcement, with more funds spent on prevention and treatment and less on jails and overseas programs. Of the six basic demographic variables examined in this analysis, age, education, income, and political ideology exerted the most influence on responses and should be considered relevant in similar future analyses.

Note

1. Less than 2% of the respondents selected the same responses as both the least effective and most effective policy choice. One possible explanation for these responses may be that they simply misunderstood the question.

10 ■ The Growing Threat
Gangs and Juvenile Offenders

RUTH TRIPLETT

Public concern over serious juvenile crime such as gang activity and increasing questions about the mission of the juvenile justice system have sparked interest among researchers who, until recently, have given little attention to public opinion on these issues. In this chapter, the public opinion literature on juvenile crime and juvenile justice will be reviewed followed by a report on the findings from the National Opinion Survey on Crime and Justice—1995 (NOSCJ).

Public Opinion and Juvenile Justice

One way of discovering public opinion on the juvenile justice system is to ask what the court's purpose should be—rehabilitation and treatment or punishment. Studies that asked respondents about the purpose of the juvenile justice system have found that the majority of the public supports a rehabilitative mission. The Public Opinion Research Corporation (1982, as reported in Schwartz, Guo, & Kerbs, 1993) found that 73% of respondents believed that the juvenile court's primary purpose should be rehabilitation and treatment. Similar findings are reported by Steinhart (1988) in his poll of Californians and Schwartz (1992) in a nationwide survey. However, it is interesting to note that when asked specifically how society should deal with juveniles who commit crimes, Gallup (1994a) found only 31% of the respondents supported rehabilitation, whereas the majority, 52%, reported that society should deal with juveniles by giving them the same punishment as adults.

Cullen, Golden, and Cullen (1983) conducted a survey of the Illinois public, prison guards, legislators, judges, lawyers, correctional administrators, and prison inmates. When asked to report their level of agreement with the statement "The best way to stop juveniles from engaging in crime is to rehabilitate them, not punish them," 47% agreed. The majority, however, viewed punishment as more effective than rehabilitation, but 82% of those surveyed agreed that "it would be irresponsible for us to stop trying to rehabilitate juvenile delinquents and thus save them from a life of crime."

The public, then, is supportive of rehabilitation for juveniles but apparently sees no inconsistency in the use of punishment. Further evidence of support for both punishment and rehabilitation comes from public opinion surveys concerning how serious juvenile offenders should be treated. Schwartz (1992) found that 97% of respondents supported punishment for juveniles who commit serious property crimes or who sell large amounts of drugs; 99% felt the same for juveniles who commit serious violent crimes. However, punishment does not necessarily mean placement in secure facilities. Of the same respondents, only 45% favored secure placement for first-time violent offenders, with 70% favoring it for a second violent offense. Thus, even in the case of serious offenses where the public favors punishment, they support placement of these youthful offenders in facilities or programs usually considered to be aimed at rehabilitation and treatment. Schwartz (1992) also found that between 88% and 95% of those surveyed want juveniles who commit serious property crimes, serious violent crimes, or who sell large amounts of drugs rehabilitated, if possible. Similarly, only 22% of those surveyed by Steinhart (1988) agreed that "youths who commit serious crimes cannot be rehabilitated and should be locked up without any attempt at rehabilitation for as long as the law allows."

Another way of uncovering public opinion about the juvenile court and its mission is to query the public about juvenile waiver to adult court. Waiver lies at the heart of the juvenile court because trying a juvenile in adult court means we are effectively giving up on the ability of the court to help this particular youth.

Surveys have reported a great deal of support from respondents for waiving serious offenders. They also found that the more serious the offense, the greater the level of public support for waiver. For example, Schwartz, Abbey, and Barton (1990) reported that 76% of a sample of Michigan residents agreed that juveniles charged with serious violent crimes should be tried as adults. In a national survey, Schwartz (1992) found somewhat less agreement, 68%, although the majority were supportive of waiver.

The findings also suggest that although the majority of the public supports trying juveniles in adult court, they are not necessarily supportive of treating juveniles like adults in terms of sentence length and place of confinement. Steinhart (1988) and Schwartz (1992) found that less than half of those surveyed agreed that sentences for juveniles should be the same as those for adults for all crimes, or that juvenile offenders should be confined in the same institutions as adult prisoners. Gallup (1994a) found more support, with 50% of respondents agreeing that juveniles convicted of their first crime should be given the same punishment as adults convicted of their first crime, 40% responded with "less harshly," and 9% said "it depends." However, when asked "what should be used for first-time juvenile offenders committing a major crime, but not murder?" 66% chose boot camps, 19% job training, and only 12%, prison (McAneny, 1993).

Public opinion supports severe treatment of serious juvenile offenders, but there are many indicators that public faith in the juvenile justice system and rehabilitation is not gone. For example, Steinhart (1988) reported that 82% of respondents agreed that "we should focus less on long terms of confinement for juvenile offenders and more on programs and treatments that will help these youth become law-abiding citizens."

Ironically, the public does not view rehabilitation programs as successful in reducing youth crime. When asked how successful rehabilitation programs have been at controlling juvenile crime, only 1% said very successful, and 24% said moderately successful, leaving two thirds reporting these programs to be unsuccessful (Gallup, 1994a).

Although belief in rehabilitation for juveniles varies, it appears that the public supports rehabilitation more for juveniles than for adults. Cullen et al. (1983) found only 10% of those surveyed agreed that "the rehabilitation of juveniles just does not work" compared to 27% who agreed with the statement that "the rehabilitation of adult criminals just does not work." Similarly, Steinhart (1988) discovered that almost two thirds of respondents, 71%, agreed it is more important to emphasize rehabilitation for juveniles than it is for adults.

The continuing belief of the public in the potential of rehabilitation is demonstrated by questions on funding these programs. When Gallup (McAneny, 1993) followed questions about the successfulness of reha- bilitation programs with questions about monetary support ("Do you think that these programs have been given the necessary money and other support to be successful . . . ?"), only 39% answered yes, and 48% said no. Steinhart (1988) and Schwartz, Kerbs, Hogston, and Guillean (1992) found that although the public supports spending more on a variety of programs for crime reduction, there is more agreement about the need to spend more on rehabilitation programs.

If concerns about serious juvenile offenders are driving policy, then concerns about youth gangs could be critical in understanding public opinion on juvenile justice policy issues. Although youth gangs have long been at the center of attention among criminologists, only recently have questions about them been incorporated into public opinion re- search. A literature review finds only three studies involving public perceptions or opinions on youth gangs. Two of these use surveys only to uncover public perceptions of gang problems in the community (see Pryor & McGarrell, 1993; Takata & Zevitz, 1987, 1990). The third study examined public opinion on how to deal with youth gangs.

Public opinion on policy for dealing with youth gangs derives from a national survey conducted in 1993 by the Research Network (reported in Maguire, Pastore, & Flanagan, 1993). A national sample of adult Hispanics was queried about the seriousness of youth gangs in their communities. Thirty-nine percent responded that it was a *very serious* problem, 31% answered *somewhat serious*, 20% *not very serious*, and only 8% responded it was *not a problem at all*. When then asked their opinions on what should be done to discourage youth gangs among Hispanic youth, 19% of the respondents said, "There should be stiffer sentences"; 8% supported the improvement of security at schools; and 20% said, "Government should increase aid to youth centers." The largest per- cent, 44%, however, believed that having more employment opportu- nities for Hispanic youth would discourage youth gangs. Thus, even for youth gangs, the policies that received the most support were nonpunitive—employment and increased aid to youth centers.

As Krisberg and Austin (1993) note, public opinion polls show the average citizen holds conflicting views about both the goals of the juvenile justice system and effective policies for reducing serious juve- nile crime. The public sees no apparent contradiction in attempting to rehabilitate juveniles at the same time that they are being punished for the crimes they commit. Nor does the public see a contradiction in calling for punishment of serious juvenile offenders while preferring placement for offenders in community-based programs or those oriented toward rehabilitation. The research also suggests that the public is supportive of the use of rehabilitation programs and nonpunitive responses for members of youth gangs. The literature supports Cullen et al.'s (1983) conclusion that rehabilitation will remain a dominant correctional ideology for juvenile justice along with continued support for punitive measures in the disposition of juvenile cases.

The National Opinion Survey on Crime and Justice—1995

In this section, findings from the NOSCJ on two general issues related to juvenile justice policy are explored. The first is public support for the juvenile justice system as shown through opinions on waiver and rehabilitation. The second is public perceptions of gangs and policies for discouraging them.

Public Support for the Juvenile Justice System

The first series of questions in the NOSCJ on juveniles asked respondents to report their level of agreement with statements involving waiver of juveniles who have committed serious offenses (see Table 10.1). When asked to report their agreement with the statement "A juvenile charged with a serious property crime should be tried as an adult," a clear majority, 62%, agreed or strongly agreed. When the crime was selling illegal drugs, support for waiver was stronger; 69% strongly agreed or agreed. When asked their level of agreement with trying juveniles as adults when the crime was a serious violent offense, 87% strongly agreed or agreed. Thus, in agreement with past findings, the NOSCJ found strong support for waiver. The more serious the offense, the greater the level of support.

The relationship between respondent and neighborhood characteristics and the level of support for waiver was examined. Respondents' views of the purpose of sentencing in the juvenile court was the only variable consistently associated with level of agreement on issues of waiver. On whether serious property offenders should be tried in adult court, those who view the purpose of sentencing in the juvenile justice system to be punishment were more likely to agree than those who view

Table 10.1 Attitudes Toward Waiver of Juvenile Offenders (percentage responding strongly agree or agree)

Question: "Tell me for each of the following statements whether you strongly agree, agree, neither agree nor disagree, disagree, or strongly disagree:
(1) a juvenile charged with a serious property crime should be tried as an adult;
(2) a juvenile charged with selling illegal drugs should be tried as an adult;
(3) a juvenile charged with a serious violent crime should be tried as an adult."

	Serious Property Crime	Selling Illegal Drugs	Serious Violent Crime
National	62	69	87
Age			
18-29	61	68*	87
30-39	61	69	87
40-49	67	70	91
50-59	61	67	82
60-69	67	75	88
70 or older	74	76	86
Race/ethnicity			
White	64	71	88
Hispanic	67	67	86
Black	57	65	81
Other[a]	60	78	91
Gender			
Male	69	71	89
Female	58	70	86
Education			
Less than high school	73	67	85
High school graduate	67	73	88
Some college	61	71	86
College graduate	59	67	87
Income			
Less than $15,000	60	65	82
$15,000 to $30,000	66	73	86
$30,000 to $60,000	63	69	89
More than $60,000	64	73	88

the purpose to be rehabilitation. On whether juveniles accused of selling drugs should be tried as adults, there was a significant association with age and ideological alignment, as well as views of the purpose of sentencing. Respondents 60 years of age and older were significantly more likely to agree that juvenile drug sellers should be tried as adults. Those who saw the purpose of sentencing for juveniles as punishment were significantly more likely than those who have a rehabilitation orientation to support waiver for juveniles selling drugs. And those

Table 10.1 Continued

	Serious Property Crime	Selling Illegal Drugs	Serious Violent Crime
Party affiliation			
Republican	68	72	88
Democrat	58	65	87
Independent/other	64	71	87
Political ideology			
Liberal	59	61*	81
Middle of the road	63	71	90
Conservative	65	74	87
Purpose of sentencing juveniles			
Discourage	65*	70*	90*
Separate[a]	83	89	93
Rehabilitate	53	62	82
Punish	77	81	93
Neighborhood crime			
Increased	62	73	87
Stayed the same	63	68	86
Decreased	69	78	93
Neighborhood safety			
Safer	72	67	95
Not as safe	61	72	84
About the same	64	70	87
Neighborhood gang problem			
Serious problem	65	67	87
Somewhat/minor	65	73	90
Not a problem	61	68	85

a. Category contains fewer than 50 cases.
*Differences between groups are significant at $p \leq .01$ level.

who identified themselves as conservatives were also significantly more likely to agree than liberals. Finally, on whether violent juvenile offenders should be tried as adults, the purpose of sentencing was also significant.

The next two items asked respondents about the funding and successfulness of rehabilitation programs for juveniles. The first question was, "In most places, there are juvenile justice programs that emphasize protecting and rehabilitating juveniles rather than punishing them. Do you think these programs have been given the necessary money and other support to be successful?" (see Figure 10.1). Fifty-four percent of respondents said not enough money had been given to these programs for them to be successful. It is interesting to note that 22% of respondents reported they did not know whether these programs had been provided with enough resources.

The follow-up question asked, "Would you say these programs have been very successful, somewhat successful, not very successful, or not at all successful at controlling juvenile crime?" (see Figure 10.2). Approximately 2% felt the programs had been very successful, 28% said successful, 42% said not very, and 12% said not at all successful. Once again, a substantial proportion, approximately 16%, reported they did not know. Thus, of those who felt they had enough information to say, 54% said the programs were not very effective at controlling juvenile crime.

Policies for Discouraging Youth Gangs

The first question in the area of youth gangs asked, "How serious a problem are gangs in your community?" Thirteen percent of those surveyed said they were a serious problem, 44% said they were somewhat of or a minor problem, and 42% said gangs were not a problem in their community (see Table 10.2). Thus, a majority of the respondents viewed youth gangs as less than a serious problem in their community.

When respondent and neighborhood characteristics were examined, two respondent and two neighborhood characteristics were found to be significantly related to views of gangs as a community problem. Respondents aged 40 to 49 were significantly more likely to report youth gangs as a serious problem in their communities. Whites were significantly less likely to report gangs as a serious problem, and Hispanics consistently viewed them as more of a problem. Those who viewed their neighborhood crime rate as higher and those who viewed their neighborhood as not as safe as the previous year were significantly more likely to view youth gangs as a serious problem.

Finally, respondents were asked to respond to a series of suggested measures to discourage youth gangs—stiffer sentences, improving school security measures, increasing government aid to youth centers, having more employment opportunities, and holding parents legally responsible for their children's actions (see Table 10.3). A total of 81% either strongly agreed or agreed that stiffer sentences for juvenile offenders would discourage youth gangs. But support for increased punitiveness did not exclude support for other types of programs. When asked about the improvement of school security measures, 78% either

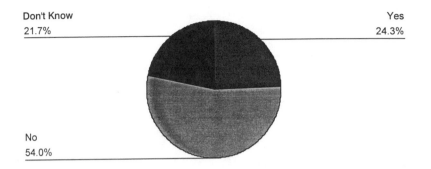

Figure 10.1. Percentage of Respondents Who Believe Rehabilitation Programs Have Enough Resources

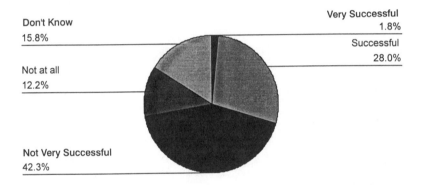

Figure 10.2. Percentage of Respondents Who Believe Rehabilitation Programs Have Been Successful

strongly agreed or agreed. Similarly, 77% strongly agreed or agreed that increased government aid to youth centers could discourage youth gangs. But the greatest level of support (87% strongly agreed or agreed) was for more employment opportunities. The proposal receiving the least agreement was holding parents legally responsible for their children's actions, although 59% still agreed with the idea.

We next examined the relationship between respondent and neighborhood characteristics, and level of support for each of the policy items. Education, party affiliation, ideological alignment, and views on

Table 10.2 Attitudes Toward the Problem of Youth Gangs (in percentages)

Question: "How serious a problem are gangs in your community?"

	Serious Problem	Somewhat or Minor Problem	Not a Problem
National	13	44	42
Age*			
18-29	10	44	46
30-39	10	55	35
40-49	20	39	41
50-59	13	43	44
60-69	12	44	44
70 or older	13	26	61
Race/ethnicity*			
White	11	45	44
Hispanic	21	51	28
Black	18	38	44
Other[a]	21	21	58
Gender			
Male	13	43	44
Female	12	46	42
Education			
Less than high school	12	36	52
High school graduate	11	43	46
Some college	16	46	38
College graduate	13	47	40
Income			
Less than $15,000	20	32	48
$15,000 to $30,000	14	48	38
$30,000 to $60,000	13	44	43
More than $60,000	8	49	43

the purpose of sentencing were associated with the suggested use of stiffer sentences. College graduates, Democrats, liberals, and those who view the purpose of juvenile sentencing to be rehabilitation or separation were significantly less likely to agree that stiffer sentences would be effective in reducing youth gangs. Only one characteristic was associated with the item asking if improving school security would discourage youth gangs—political alignment. Democrats were significantly more likely than Republicans or others to agree that this would be effective.

On whether increasing aid to youth centers would discourage youth gangs, there were significant differences by age, gender, education,

Table 10.2 Continued

	Serious Problem	Somewhat or Minor Problem	Not a Problem
Party affiliation			
Republican	12	51	37
Democrat	13	49	38
Independent/other	14	38	48
Political ideology			
Liberal	11	42	47
Middle of the road	12	50	38
Conservative	16	40	44
Purpose of sentencing juveniles			
Discourage	14	45	41
Separate[a]	20	30	50
Rehabilitate	12	48	40
Punish	10	44	46
Neighborhood crime*			
Increased	23	49	28
Stayed the same	9	44	47
Decreased	17	42	41
Neighborhood safety*			
Safer	13	40	47
Not as safe	24	46	30
About the same	10	45	45

a. Category contains fewer than 50 cases.
*Differences between groups are significant at $p \leq .01$ level.

party affiliation, ideological alignment, and sentencing purpose. Younger respondents (aged 18-29) were significantly more likely to agree than were older respondents, and females more than males. High school graduates, Democrats, liberals, and those who view the purpose of sentencing to be rehabilitation were also significantly more likely to agree with this policy of increasing funding for youth centers. When asked if increasing employment opportunities would discourage youth gangs, significant associations were found with ideological alignment and views on sentencing. Liberals were significantly more likely than conservatives to agree that this would be effective, as were those with a rehabilitation orientation. Finally, on the issue of whether holding parents legally responsible for their children's actions would be effec-

Table 10.3 Attitudes Toward Policies for Discouraging Youth Gangs (percentage responding strongly agree or agree)

Question: "People have suggested a variety of measures that could be used to discourage youth gangs. Please tell me whether you strongly agree, agree, neither agree nor disagree, disagree, or strongly disagree with each of the following":

	Stiffer Sentences	Improve School Security	Increase Aid to Youth Centers	Increase Employment Opportunities	Hold Parents Legally Responsible
National	81	78	77	87	59
Age					
18-29	81	81	88*	90	45
30-39	89	82	81	90	62
40-49	81	77	74	88	62
50-59	79	80	74	83	66
60-69	78	82	69	86	72
70 or older	77	83	77	83	70
Race/ethnicity					
White	84	81	76	86	62
Hispanic	88	89	93	100	64
Black	69	80	91	96	46
Other[a]	80	79	78	86	61
Gender					
Male	79	79	74*	87	62
Female	85	83	84	89	58
Education					
Less than high school	82*	91	81*	93	50*
High school graduate	86	85	85	91	55
Some college	85	77	75	87	62
College graduate	76	77	76	85	69
Income					
Less than $15,000	82	87	87	89	61
$15,000 to $30,000	83	83	80	92	61
$30,000 to $60,000	84	82	79	89	62
More than $60,000	81	73	73	86	62

tive in discouraging youth gangs, significant differences were found by age, education, and party affiliation. Younger respondents (aged 18-29) were more likely to disagree that parents should be held responsible than were older respondents. Those with higher education levels were more likely to agree. Republicans were significantly more likely than

Table 10.3 Continued

	Stiffer Sentences	Improve School Security	Increase Aid to Youth Centers	Increase Employment Opportunities	Hold Parents Legally Responsible
Party affiliation					
Republican	91*	79*	71*	84	68*
Democrat	77	88	88	94	59
Independent/other	80	76	77	85	56
Political ideology					
Liberal	72*	74	92*	95*	56
Middle of the road	84	82	84	89	60
Conservative	88	84	65	84	64
Purpose of sentencing juveniles					
Discourage	92*	84	76*	85*	64
Separate[a]	70	79	70	91	58
Rehabilitate	79	79	83	91	61
Punish	86	83	75	84	58
Neighborhood crime					
Increased	87	85	73	85	61
Stayed the same	81	81	80	88	61
Decreased	78	78	83	92	48
Neighborhood safety					
Safer	80	77	83	90	52
Not as safe	79	86	75	86	65
About the same	84	80	79	88	60
Neighborhood gang problem					
Serious problem	83	79	82	88	66
Somewhat/minor	85	81	80	87	61
Not a problem	80	82	77	89	59

a. Category contains fewer than 50 cases.
*Differences between groups are significant at $p \leq .01$ level.

Democrats to agree that increasing employment opportunities would effectively discourage youth gangs.

It is interesting to note the pattern of significant and nonsignificant associations. Democrats were significantly more likely to agree with improving school security measures and increasing aid to youth centers than were other parties. Republicans, on the other hand, were significantly more likely to agree with the use of stiffer sentences and holding parents legally responsible.

Most interesting perhaps is the relationship of respondents' perceptions of neighborhood crime rates, neighborhood safety, and the severity of the gang problem in their community to opinions of policies for discouraging youth gangs. None of these items was significantly associated with any of the policy items. Thus, respondents' views on policies for discouraging youth gangs were not associated with their perceptions of the crime problem in their neighborhood.

Discussion and Conclusion

The NOSCJ findings are consistent with those from past research in public opinion on issues of juvenile justice and gangs. They illustrate the public's desire for harsher treatment of serious juvenile offenders within the context of a rehabilitation framework.

The findings on waiver support the public's desire for harsher treatment of serious juvenile offenders. The majority of the respondents agree with waiver for serious juvenile offenders. The more serious the offense, the greater public support. These findings do not mean, however, that the public is not supportive of rehabilitation. Over half of those surveyed believe we have not given enough money to rehabilitation programs. Combined with the results from past surveys, this suggests the public is supportive of greater funding for programs aimed at rehabilitating juvenile offenders. At the same time, over half of those surveyed believe rehabilitation programs are not very successful at controlling juvenile crime.

The findings on policies for discouraging youth gangs also illustrate the desire for punishment and rehabilitation. Each of the five policy items suggested for discouraging youth gangs received support from the majority of respondents. The policy most agreed on was more employment opportunities for youth, followed by the use of stiffer sentences, improvement of school security, increased aid to youth centers, and holding parents legally responsible.

The NOSCJ findings suggest a number of interesting questions future researchers might pursue. One important issue is the need to discover specifically when the public wants punishment to be emphasized and when it wants rehabilitation. Also, it is obvious that researchers need to move beyond respondent's demographic or personal characteristics and even neighborhood characteristics to uncover what drives public opinion on the issues of juvenile crime and juvenile justice.

11

Public Opinion and Public Policy in Criminal Justice

TIMOTHY J. FLANAGAN

In this brief chapter, I examine the "so what?" question in relation to public opinion on crime and justice. Does the evidence indicate that surveys of the public on crime-and-justice-related issues "matter" in any meaningful way? Do political leaders and criminal justice administrators take heed of public opinion when designing justice policies, developing programs, or passing criminal laws? A related concern is whether these public officials are themselves capable of influencing public opinion on justice issues. Finally, I consider the role played by the media as a transmitter, an amplifier, and a filter between the people and their criminal justice leaders.

One of the most important historical figures in criminal justice had strong views on these questions. Sir Robert Peel, law enforcement pioneer and the architect of the London Metropolitan Police (whose officers are called bobbies in his honor), referred to "that great compound of folly, weakness, prejudice, wrong feeling, right feeling, obstinacy, and newspaper paragraphs which is called public opinion" (cited in Lippmann, 1922/1965, p. 127). Presumably, Peel thought that crime and justice matters were best left to the experts and that a uninformed and unenlightened citizenry was ill prepared to contribute to such policy discussions. The idea that common citizens are ignorant of the complex knowledge bases and administrative nuances needed to fashion justice policy has existed for centuries. The alternative view is best expressed by Thomas Jefferson (1955), who argued that

> I know of no sage depository of the ultimate powers of the society but the people themselves, and if we think them not enlightened enough to exert their control with wholesome discretion, the remedy is not to take it from them but to inform their discretion by education. (p. 97)

This tension between those who see a role for public opinion in debates about crime and justice and those who would "leave it to the experts" remains with us today. Leslie Wilkins (1984) observed that "public opinion has few friends, but many who would exploit its power" (p. 122). Perhaps no other topic in contemporary America better illustrates the potential, the use, and the misuse of public opinion in policy and program development than crime, delinquency, and criminal justice.

There are several reasons why crime and justice issues provide an exemplar for examining the role of public opinion. First, crime and justice issues are *relevant and salient* to Americans. Second, public safety and punishment of wrongdoers are at the core of the political and *ideological doctrines* that unite and divide Americans and their political parties. Third, there is substantial disagreement about methods to achieve them, but Americans know and can articulate the *results* that they want from crime policy and from the criminal justice system. Fourth, political leaders are *highly responsive* to public concerns about crime-related issues. Skogan (1995) commented that the nation's leaders are "obsessed with reaping the most political advantage from popular concerns about crime" (p. 9).

Who's Leading, Who's Following?

If survey data on Americans' attitudes about crime and justice are to contribute to the development of enlightened justice policy, political leaders must be sincerely interested in understanding the will of the people. We sometimes think that citizens only give voice to that will in the electoral process. Having won at the ballot box, some political leaders profess to understand the hopes, dreams, fears, and preferences of their constituents. Survey data are seen as a poor substitute for the "messages" that voters deliver through the ballot box. But Wilkins reminds us that "don't know" and "no opinion" responses in surveys are typically much *lower* than nonvoting rates in elections. Ironically, we worry about the statistical validity of survey results, but not the validity of election results!

This does not mean that political leaders should design and construct their positions on crime issues solely on the basis of poll data. As Michael Traugott (1992) observed, few would wish to live in a nation in which the government was "of the polls, by the polls, and for the polls" (p. 144). The proper and most effective uses of polls in this context are as a mechanism to examine preferences between alternative policy options, to understand the diversity of views on justice issues within the citizenry, and to understand the public's evaluation of justice system components.

In assessing the influence of public opinion, Converse (1987) said, "It goes without saying that the political impact of public opinion data would be quite muffled indeed if politicians themselves gave such data no credence" (p. S16). There is little doubt that public opinion surveys on crime and justice issues are influential among political leaders. It appears, however, that this influence is tempered by the fact that leaders' *understanding* of the public mood is limited and selective. Two problems are at work: Opinion researchers only sporadically assess public opinion on criminal justice issues (except for isolated questions), and political leaders consider the results in a highly selective manner. When used properly, careful examination of survey data should both clarify and fight "the tendency to oversimplify the public's attempt to reach judgment on public issues" (Dionne, 1992, p. 163). In contrast, it is said that politicians use public opinion surveys in the manner that a drunk uses a lamppost—for support rather than illumination. Uslaner and Weber (1979) coined the term *poorly informed elites* to describe the incomplete and inaccurate perceptions of their constituents that many public officials maintain. To be informed, careful development and analysis of poll data must go substantially beyond fielding one-sided survey questions or seizing idiosyncratic results that buttress preexisting positions.

There is substantial evidence that political leaders misperceive the public mind on crime and justice issues (Gottfredson & Taylor, 1984; Riley & Rose, 1980). Moreover, these misperceptions appear to be in one direction: that of assuming that citizens are more conservative and resistant to innovation in criminal justice than they actually are. These errors dampen imaginative thinking about crime control policy, cause premature rejection of promising policies and programs, and make certain policy options (e.g., decriminalization of some offenses) taboo subjects.

What of influence in the opposite direction? Are political and community leaders effective in influencing the public about crime and justice? Finckenauer (1978) argued that crime and criminal justice became a national political issue in the 1964 Goldwater presidential election campaign's focus on "law and order" issues. He contended that the crime issue had been monopolized by political conservatives and that this definition of the problem and its solution gave rise to the "more cops, more prisons, more punishment" approaches that have characterized recent decades.

The growth of electronic media outlets in the past two decades has increased the channels available to political leaders to define the problem, prescribe the solution, and rally support behind positions. The Willie Horton scare campaign that was the hallmark of the Bush-Dukakis election contest in 1988 demonstrated the capacity of political leaders to take an image and its accompanying impact directly to the people and to use fear of crime as a political weapon. And the congressional debate over the 1994 Crime Bill amply illustrated the capacity of politicians to reduce complex, nettlesome policy decisions to histrionic debates about midnight basketball leagues and shrill arguments about prevention versus punishment. In sum, it appears that on crime and justice issues, political leaders readily use the communication outlets available to them to advance positions and policies, but rarely and ineffectually use those resources to educate the public about the costs and effectiveness of policy options.

The Role of the Media

The recently completed O. J. Simpson trial provided a chilling lesson in the effect of media coverage on Americans' views of crime and criminal justice. In a phenomenon that combined soap opera, prime-time drama, and unprecedented media coverage and analysis, Americans were simultaneously assaulted with information from the trial and asked to evaluate all aspects of the proceedings. They were asked to offer opinions on guilt or innocence, the character and reliability of trial participants, the professionalism and effectiveness of justice system employees, and the consequences of the trial for criminal justice, jurisprudence, race relations, and presidential politics in America. The intensity of this "media phenomenon" was so outsized that one must be very careful in evaluating its effect.

One early finding that provides a warning to all concerned with criminal justice was that Americans who most assiduously watched the Simpson drama unfold reported declining respect and confidence for law enforcement, the courts, and other aspects of the justice process. As Laura Myers discussed in Chapter 4 of this volume, the defining characteristics of the Simpson trial process—excessive delay, excessive cost, and perceptions that the judicial process fails to deliver justice—were preexisting fixtures of public attitudes toward American courts. For many, the Simpson trial simply confirmed what they believed to be true about America's courts. Blaming lowered public assessments of the justice system on the uncommon media coverage of the trial is tantamount to blaming the sports pages for the decline in American interest in baseball.

Political scientist V. O. Key, Jr. (1961) observed that the effect of media is conditioned on the strength with which views are held. In the short run, he contended, effects of media coverage are greater on topics or issues for which citizens have undeveloped internalized norms or standards. Given that public opinion on many crime issues is deeply and firmly held (see Dennis Longmire, Chapter 7 in this volume), the short-term effect of media attention is likely to be lessened. The media's greatest effect may be in bringing an issue to the attention of the public and in helping to place the issue on the public agenda (Bennett, 1980, p. 305). In a similar vein, Surrette's (1992) studies of the effect of the media on crime and criminal justice issues led him to conclude that the media affect citizens' "factual perceptions of the world" rather than their evaluations of social conditions.

Surrette's (1992) observation that the media influence perceptions of crime and justice is important, because ample evidence indicates that the image of crime and justice presented in newspapers and television news, in prime-time television, and in movies is highly distorted. In newspaper coverage of crime, for example, research indicates that reporting focuses disproportionately on violent crime, especially homicide, and underrepresents less serious and property offenses (Antunes & Hurley, 1977). The same biases have been shown in local television news coverage of crime (Garofalo, 1981a; Graber, 1980). In television crime dramas, the storylines focus on "trackdown and capture," but subsequent justice processes such as arraignment, grand juries, pretrial hearings, jury selection, and others receive scant attention (Dominick,

1978). Movies present a similar image of Dirty Harry-style police pursuing (and always defeating) violent criminals.

If media present a distorted image of crime and criminal justice, they nevertheless focus attention on crime and justice issues. In some cases, concerted attention moves from "agenda setting" to "agenda building." A recent case illustrates the dramatic, if short-term, effect of heightened media attention to crime on public assessment of the problem. For many years, pollsters have asked samples to name the "nation's most important problem." Jeffrey Alderman (1994), director of polling for ABC News, reported that "until [Fall 1993], no ABC/Washington Post poll had ever shown more than 5% of the public naming crime as the most important problem (MIP) facing the country" (p. 26). Suddenly, in November 1994, crime jumped to the top of the list of the nation's ills, with 21% of Americans saying that crime was the top concern. By January 1995, the percentage had leaped to 31%, displacing traditional economic concerns. Alderman argued that a confluence of highly visible justice-related events (including a multiple homicide on a Long Island commuter train, the Reginald Denny beating in Los Angeles, and the attack on Olympic skater Nancy Kerrigan) and intensive media attention produced the poll results. The media responded, according to Alderman, with an impressive series of "special editions and broadcasts on the subject of violent crime." These included cover stories in the major weekly newsmagazines and special reports on network and local news programs. "Add to that mix the so-called 'reality-based' police programs on the 'news' no matter where you look" (Alderman, 1994, p. 26). The effect of this energetic and focused media attention is shown in Figure 11.1, which presents findings from Gallup polls from 1981 to 1994. Alderman (1994) concluded that the media can "make the public focus on a problem they are not feeling in their own lives only for as long as the media attention is maintained. As soon as the spotlight moves on, the problem moves down the public's MIP list" (p. 26).

In summary, the cumulative effect of media coverage and popular culture depiction of crime and the criminal justice system is an important intermediary between citizens and elected officials. Idiosyncratic events can touch off a media feeding frenzy (see Flanagan & Vaughn, 1995), which, in addition to raising fear, worry, and concern about crime, becomes a media story itself. The rising tide of media attention captures the attention of political leaders, which promotes even more coverage and which may further increase public concern. Action is demanded from political leaders and the criminal justice system, and the salience

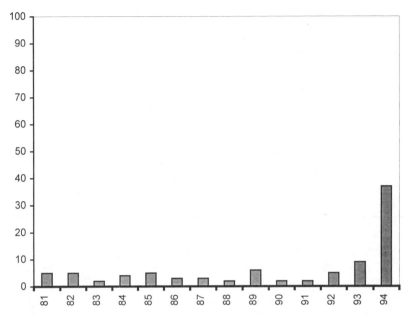

Figure 11.1. Rating of Crime as Nation's Most Important Problem, Gallup Polls, 1981-1994

of crime and justice issues is temporarily increased. Recurring cycles of this amplification process may lead to ill-considered, reactive, and dysfunctional legislation. If public opinion is to play a positive role in shaping crime policy, it must be less a reaction to specific events and more a regular assessment of the many dimensions of this critical quality-of-life issue.

Popular Justice

What changes or initiatives might be implemented in the American criminal justice system if public opinion were systematically incorporated? Preceding chapters have suggested several such developments, so the review here will be brief. In addition, Erickson, Wright, and McIver's (1993) research strongly suggests that state-level public policy on justice and other issues already corresponds closely to public opinion in the states. They concluded that "across an impressive range of policies, public opinion counts, and not just a little" (p. 95).

First, recent Gallup (1994b) polls in the United States indicate that the public supports hiring more police, broader application of the death penalty, repeat-offender legislation modeled after the "three strikes and you're out" laws, more stringent policies and procedures within the juvenile justice system, and bans on automatic weapon manufacture, sale, and possession. In this regard, the public clearly distinguishes between serious and nonserious crimes, repeat offenders versus others, and weapons designed for sport or protection versus weapons designed for street crime applications.

Second, at the same time that "get tough" proposals such as those just mentioned receive widespread support, the public also supports early intervention programs for high-risk youth, spending federal funds to provide positive social programs for poor youth, and provision of community-based correctional programs for nonviolent offenders.

Third, the public strongly supports efforts to reduce what is perceived to be excessive delay and leniency in processing cases in the court system. Efforts to reduce or eliminate pretrial release and plea bargaining for serious offenders and to restrain the sentencing discretion of judges would be strongly supported.

Fourth, studies in Canada (Himelfarb, 1990) and the United States indicate that citizens would demand "tougher" and more productive prisons, but would also support the provision of various "treatment" (education, training, counseling) programs within the correctional system. These views coincide with a general perception, in both countries, that the justice system is lax, lenient, inefficient in its use of resources, and ineffective in protecting citizens from victimization.

If these are the boundaries of the crime control debate in the public mind, criminal justice leaders, political decision makers and scholars should heed them, study them, and incorporate them into their educational and administrative responsibilities. These findings indicate that the American public appreciates that "doing something about criminals" is different than "doing something about crime." Although recognizing that it is a Herculean task, the public demands that its political leadership and its criminal justice system work hard on both fronts.

12 ■ The Art and Science of Survey Research

JAMES A. DYER

The objective of this chapter is to examine the current art and science of doing surveys in the contemporary environment and to consider the implications for making accurate inferences based on survey research. It is not intended as a survey of issues relating to the validity of survey data, but centers on topics that are relevant to the development of survey research at this time. This is particularly relevant in the context of a research volume reporting on what may be the first of a continuing series of surveys that looks at public views of issues relating to crime and criminal justice.

The title of this chapter, "The Art and Science of Survey Research," was suggested by the editors. The use of the word *art* is interesting in the context of discussing research techniques that are a central part of virtually all of social science.

The *science* of survey research is reasonably well known and involves things such as sampling to make inferences about populations and estimating the error with which such inferences can be made. It involves methods for constructing and evaluating questions that involve estimating the reliability and validity of questions. Although the basics of the science of survey research have been well established, the technology for carrying out the science and the environment in which surveys are conducted have changed significantly.

I once heard a well-known social scientist observe that he thought that people who wrote methods books must surely not have done research. Having coauthored a methods book and done a fair amount of research, I do know that the process of science often does not reflect the reconstructed logic of science that is usually imposed on the exposition of process after the fact and is set forth in methods books. At some points, the discrepancy between the formalized science and what is done as research involves an element of "art."

One of the dictionary definitions of art is "a sphere in which creative skill is used" (*New Lexicon Webster's Dictionary of the English Language*, 1989). Clearly, there is much room for the use of "creative skill" in survey research. Dealing with the problems of developing questions, designing samples, overcoming obstacles to doing field work, and accurately interpreting the aggregates of responses to questions involves creation.

The first section deals with the survey environment, and the next three deal with developing survey methodologies of computer-assisted interviewing, sampling, and questionnaire design. In the final section, the question of the utility of surveys given the environment and the available technologies is considered.

Survey Environment

The environment in which surveys are conducted has changed markedly and continues to do so. On the positive side, a long-term shift has been the increased penetration of telephones. In 1960, it was estimated that 78.5% of households had telephones, compared to 87% in 1970. The estimate is about 90% now. Of course, we still have to be concerned about the biases produced by the nontelephone households, but sampling using the telephone has been cost-effective and has proven to be reasonably accurate. It is likely that given usual household sample designs, a number of households would not fall into a sampling frame for in-person surveys either.

It should be noted that the bias due to nontelephone households, as well as other biases in representation, does not necessarily significantly alter conclusions from surveys. For example, suppose 75% of households with telephones answer yes to a question and 25% answer no. At the same time, the households without telephones would have responded 25% yes and 75% no. The conclusion based only on the telephone sample estimates 75% yes instead of the correct 70%. For the bias to influence the conclusion significantly, the variable has to be strongly related to the difference between the over- and undersampled respondents, and the size of the undersampled group has to be a large fraction of the population being studied.

A more serious concern than the lack of telephones is the increasing reluctance on the part of people to participate in interviews and the improved technologies for screening calls in telephone surveys. It is difficult to get accurate information on the decline in participation, but there is undeniable evidence that it has declined. In his presidential address to the American Association for Public Opinion Research on the problem of nonresponse, Norman Bradburn (1992) cited information that response rates had declined from the 80% range in the 1970s to around 60% today in national telephone samples. In a meta-analysis of in-person surveys, John Goyder (1987) found that response in the 1970s was lower than in any decade since 1940. In our own telephone surveys, much of it in Texas, we were always able to get the cooperation rate above 70% in the 1980s and early 1990s. Now, it is frequently between 60% and 70%.

The reluctance to participate may stem from a number of causes: a decrease in leisure time, increasing number of polls, and a decline in willingness to contribute to collective activities. A major reason may be the increase in telemarketing, which results in people being inundated with unsolicited calls.

The technologies for screening calls are developing as well. Many people routinely use the inexpensive answering machine to screen calls. National figures put the estimated number of answering machines in use at 43% in 1991, and a large-scale survey in California found that 31% of the households contacted were using an answering machine (Xu, Bates, & Schweitzer, 1993). In the survey reported here, 10% of the numbers were ones where answering machines responded in all attempts.

In general, however, answering machines have not proved to be an insurmountable barrier. The rate of completing surveys with respondents whose phones were answered once or more by machine is higher than that of phones with no answer. Furthermore, leaving messages introducing the organization and purpose of the survey appears to help cooperation rates (Oldendick & Link, 1994; Piazza, 1993).

Caller identification, where the person can see the telephone number of the caller before answering the phone, is becoming more widespread and will no doubt further increase the opportunity to reject a call. A potential threat in the future are proposed laws that limit unsolicited telephone calls. Although largely directed at telephone solicitation, the language in some of the proposals would eliminate most telephone interviews as well.

At the same time telephone surveys have become increasingly difficult, in-person interviewers within a household have become more problematic. Although far from typical experiences, in one project this year we had field workers present in an apartment building while a shooting was going on, and workers returning to their car to find a gang fight going on in the parking lot! In many areas, we have to anticipate the additional cost of having two interviewers working together.

There is considerable evidence that nonresponse produces serious biases in the final sample. Research has demonstrated the fact that noncontacting (not being able to reach a household to talk to) and noncooperation (refusing to talk once the household is contacted) are related to predictable demographic variables. But it also suggests that cutting across demographics are differences in attitude that affect participation, and these attitudes are likely correlated with other attitudes and behaviors being measured (Goyder, 1987).

One of the many issues raised in Wesley Skogan's (1990) critical review of the National Crime Survey is the severe underrepresentation of young blacks and the implications that this has for underestimating victimization. The underrepresentation is a function of sample problems, noncontact, and possible noncooperation. The common way of dealing with these undersampling problems is to weight the undersampled part of the sample. But the problem goes beyond what weighting will fix if the basis of the underrepresentation is not defined by a demographic characteristic that can be used as a weight. For example, weighting the sample so that the sample has the same ethic distribution as the population will not necessarily improve the representation of the sample of people who are attitudinally predisposed not to respond to surveys.

Changing Technology of Surveys

Computer-assisted telephone interviewing (CATI) and computer-assisted interviewing (CAI) have produced a major revolution in survey research (see Saris, 1991, for a general discussion of CAI). Both systems allow more accurate administration of a questionnaire and more accurate recording of the data. The computer program controls what the interviewer sees and reads. Questions skipped on the basis of a response to another question are always skipped accurately (assuming correct programming). Responses are checked to make sure that they are on the list of allowed responses to a question. Responses can thus be immediately checked for consistency with other responses and rejected if not consistent. Data do not have to be reentered by a data entry operator, which, even with complete double entry for verification, produces the potential for error.

Data collected using CAI are immediately accessible for analysis. This allows checking of the data early in the collection and also for quick access of completed data at the end of the survey. It also allows for monitoring of possible sample biases (e.g., ratio of males and females) while the survey is under way so that some corrective action can be taken.

But the real advantage of CAI is that we can now do things that were difficult or impossible to do with paper and pencil. For example, to randomize the effects of order in responses or questions, we often want to randomize the order in which a series of responses or questions are presented. On paper, this was often accomplished by reading the list starting at a random starting point, which is not true randomization.

CAI can easily randomize questions or groups of questions. In the current survey, the substantive questions were divided into three groups that consisted of about the same number of questions and constituted logically distinct groups of questions. The CATI was used to randomize the order of presentation to the respondents. The main reason for this was to reduce the effect of respondent fatigue so that no single subject matter would be affected disproportionately by growing restlessness or lack of attentiveness by the respondents.

CAI also has the ability to allow much more sophisticated decision rules than is practical using a paper-and-pencil questionnaire. For example, based on responses to several questions, the computer can determine whether a respondent would be classified as likely to have a drug or alcohol problem and then either skip or ask an additional sequence of questions based on that evaluation. Fairly sophisticated analysis, such as conjoint analysis, can be applied to the data, and the later questions asked the respondent can be based on the analysis of his or her earlier responses. CAI can also be used to force respondents to resolve discrepancies.

For example, we have used a series of questions to get the respondent to allocate water resources by indicating what percentages of a pie the respondent would assign to each of the uses noted. At each step, the respondent could be told how much he or she had already used and how much was remaining. The respondent was not allowed to allocate more than 100% of the pie, and the CAI made certain this did not happen. In addition, when using CAI in person, the computer can be used to provide graphic displays of information as part of the questioning.

As with almost all technologies, there are trade-offs. Undetected CAI programming errors can produce systematic errors in data collection that can be far more devastating than most unsystematic interviewer errors. Programming the CAI requires a trained person and can require many hours of work. Interviewers must be better trained because of the additional requirements of handling the computer, and at least minimal keyboard skills are required of interviewers. And although all good CAI systems have redundant data storage and other protections against losing information, an ill-timed power outage or machine failure can lose interviews.

Using CAI and portable laptop computers, we collected data on over 1,500 adult inmates and 1,000 youth inmates in the Texas Department of Corrections and 3,500 interviews with probationers and jail inmates. The survey was extremely long (in many cases it took over 2 hours to complete) and very complex. Data for the survey reported in this book were gathered in a survey facility using 36 stations of a centralized CATI system. It made considerable use of the ability of the CATI to randomize the order of responses and of the ability of the system to manage and monitor the sample. Furthermore, the supervisors constantly monitored the interviewers by not only listening to the telephone call but also watching a duplicate of the interviewer's screen. This provided for a more thorough monitoring of the interviewing process than would be possible with a paper-and-pencil questionnaire because the supervisor saw the question and the response entered by the interviewer while monitoring.

The important conclusion of this is that the development of practical CATI systems has not only reduced the errors in conducting surveys but also allowed development of measurement strategies that are impossible with paper-and-pencil interview protocols.

Sampling

Good sampling methodologies for surveys have generally been used for the past 50 years or so, but there have been some major improvements in the kinds of samples available that mean typical surveys can be based on better samples. Firms specializing in sampling, new databases, and a merging of those databases and technologies for prescreening not only make sampling more cost-effective but also make it possible to target effectively populations that could not have been done before, at least without unreasonable cost.

Companies that specialize in producing samples have invested a great deal of effort into producing databases and sampling methodologies that are beyond the resources of most survey research projects. The results of these efforts are available at relatively modest cost to any researcher. Thus, the quality of samples used in many surveys is likely to be superior to those in use just a few years ago.

Consider the sample in this project. The sampling frame was all telephone households in the United States. We used Survey Sampling, Inc. to produce the sample of telephone numbers used. Briefly, a data file of all listed numbers in the United States is used to identify "working blocks" of numbers (a contiguous group of 100 numbers that has listed numbers among them). It is assumed that all numbers in a working block may be working, even though not listed. Working blocks are sorted by the county they are in and sampled by using a fixed skip interval.

The resulting sample is stratified by county and drawn from among numbers that are near known working numbers. The sample is much more efficient to use than a pure random-digit process.

There are two added features to the sample. Based on a database of the likely ability to reach a household in the different regions of the United States, areas with low completion rates are sampled at a higher rate. Furthermore, numbers are screened against business listings to eliminate business numbers. Finally, Survey Sampling can prescreen numbers to eliminate a large number that are detected as being disconnected.

The ability to produce specialized samples is another improvement. Samples can be generated for specified small geographic areas defined by census tracts or zip code areas. If the researcher is willing to use listed numbers, the sample can be precisely limited to the area. Estimates of the overlap between telephone exchanges and the geographic area (based on listed numbers) can be used to construct a random-digit sample with a known "hit rate" in the designated area. Using census data, along with the mapping of numbers into tracts, allows oversampling of selected respondents by oversampling in tracts where a larger concentration of the respondents live. For example, in other surveys we have conducted, we have doubled the hit rate for finding African Americans by sampling numbers from areas where there is an estimated 30% African American population. Most deviations from a "pure" random sample involve trade-offs. This sampling technique oversamples blacks living in areas with higher concentrations of blacks. In several studies, we find little difference in attitudes and behaviors between samples drawn this way compared to a random sample of all households. The relatively high degree of racial segregation in housing undoubtedly contributes to the representativeness of the sample. Using this technique for less segregated populations, such as Hispanics, is more questionable, however.

Other samples can be targeted when using listed numbers and other databases. We have conducted a survey of Asian populations in Texas by using a sample created by matching listed names with dictionaries of names from several areas in Asia. In another survey, we have contacted households with adolescents, finding such households with a much higher hit rate than would have otherwise been possible.

Even the process of sampling households in person has been made more manageable by the availability of map-based databases. Files containing maps detailed down to individual blocks linked to detailed census-level data are published on CD-ROM. The entire state of Texas is contained on a part of a single disk. The process of drawing a multistage cluster sample and providing appropriate maps for field workers has been infinitely simplified by the availability of these databases.

Measurement

The problem of eliciting reliable, valid data from respondents is a central problem in survey research. There is the problem of people willing to be honest or responsive at all, particularly if a question is sensitive. Even more of a problem than lying are the subtle biases in response as those being surveyed formulate their responses to appear socially acceptable. The respondent may not be lying, but simply sees things differently in responding to a survey than in other contexts. Another problem is eliciting responses from people who really do not have the ability to respond. We may elicit "opinions" from people who really do not have opinions. These responses may be particularly subject to response biases of various kinds. Finally, there are a variety of communications problems that are involved. Do all respondents understand the question in the same way? Does the researcher interpret the response as the respondent intended it?

Casual readers of survey research are often led to conclude that the accuracy of surveys as indicated by the reported sampling error reflects all of the error involved in the survey process. In fact, of course, it only represents the error due to sampling and then assumes that the sampling is not tainted by biases due to noncompletion. It does not reflect any measurement error at all.

Errors due to measurement are probably far more serious than sampling errors, but there is little we can do to estimate such error, so we often choose to ignore it even while scrupulously reporting the error due to sampling. There are formalized procedures for item analysis and other forms of response analysis, but these analyses primarily involve the measurement of consistency across a series of interrelated items used in developing a scale.

A measure based on internal consistency is limited by the fact that it assumes that a respondent's general response is basically correct and only allows items not consistent with the general measure to be identified and eliminated. If the overall measure is not basically a valid measure, the item analysis is a useless effort. There are some developments in questionnaire and question construction growing from theories of cognitive psychology. The object is to use principles of cognitive psychology in the development of approaches to asking questions to obtain responses that are more likely to be valid (Tanur, 1991).

There are methods of determining the extent to which different measures of the same concept are actually classifying respondents in the same way. In addition, survey measures may occasionally be verified by nonsurvey methods, such as using hair samples to evaluate self-reported drug use or police records to look at survey reports of crime (Embree, 1993; Falk, Siegal, & Forney, 1992; Harrison, 1995; Miller & Groves, 1981).

However, the opportunity to measure behavior, or even the consequences of behavior, is often limited. Even when observation can be made, the measurement error involved in the observation may be more serious than that of the survey. The presence of the observer may influence behavior; the behavior that can be observed is a biased subset of all behaviors. Consider use of drug testing to confirm measured use. We know there is significant underreporting in a self-report. On the other hand, methods of providing better data are flawed also. Urine tests are terribly intrusive and cooperation is problematic. It also is reasonably accurate for only a few hours of use. Hair analysis is intrusive and unavailable for a significant segment of the population with very short hair. (Using body hair instead of head hair is suggested, but the intrusiveness and cooperation factors become major issues.)

Implications for Survey Research

Given all of the problems and possible sources of error in survey research, it might be easy to conclude that social science cannot rely on such data. The further observation that even the "harder" social science data are similarly flawed may simply lead to the conclusion that social science cannot be done at all. The more appropriate perspective is that although almost all measures are subject to significant error, even enormous error, carefully interpreted social science data can lead to important understanding. This is true of survey data no less than of harder social science data.

We know there is error, but appropriate analysis, often involving creative skill, is often the key. For example, we know that there is significant underreporting of drug and alcohol use. On the other hand, the dynamics of change over time indicated by these surveys have been confirmed by other indicators as well as other findings on the relationship between reported use and other behaviors. Some of the problems with lack of correspondence between findings from the National Crime Survey and the Uniform Crime Report and other methods of estimating crime and victimization are not simply indications of problems of measurement, but allow the exploration of factors influencing people's perception of crime and the willingness to report crimes. The discrepancies have to do with the fact that different things are being measured, and those different measures are valuable in their own right (for a sample of the discussion, see Blumstein, Cohen, & Rosenfeld, 1991; Koss, 1992; O'Brien, 1990; Scott, 1992).

It is also helpful to remember that for many appropriate and important conclusions, a great deal of error will not significantly influence the findings. This is not an apology for the inaccuracy of social science data, but it is important to realize that the policy consequences of

60% of people believing something may not be much different if 75% believe it.

We have some important new tools in survey research: refinements in questionnaire development and sample design and improvements in the ways in which the data can be collected. On the other hand, the environment for conducting surveys is becoming increasingly hostile. Undoubtedly, we will continue to be challenged in using our creative skill to produce useful surveys in the future.

13 ■

The National Opinion Survey on Crime and Justice—1995

Development and Methods

BARBARA SIMS

The National Opinion Survey on Crime and Justice—1995 is a national assessment of public attitudes toward crime and criminal justice. The survey was designed and commissioned by the Criminal Justice Center's Survey Research Program at Sam Houston State University during early 1995.

The purpose of this chapter is to discuss and outline (a) the development of the instrument used in the survey, (b) the sampling design, and (c) the sample weighting procedures. In addition, a description of the respondents will be included along with a discussion of various statistical methods used to prepare the data for analyses.

Instrument Design

The purpose of the survey was to query a nationally representative sample about attitudes toward a wide variety of crime and criminal justice issues. To assess how the public might have changed its thinking about crime and criminal justice, it was important to include questions that have been the mainstay of public opinion polls on crime over the past 30 years. Several sources were examined, including the annual *Sourcebook of Criminal Justice Statistics,* Gallup and Harris surveys, Los Angeles Times polls, the National Opinion Research Center's (NORC) General Social Survey, Research Network, and the U.S. Department of Health and Human Services.

In addition to the national polls, scholarly journals were examined for related questions on crime and criminal justice to allow for the testing of different perspectives on the correlates of crime or criminal justice and public opinion. For example, much of the literature discusses the relationship between neighborhood disorder and fear of crime (LaGrange, Ferraro, & Supancic, 1992), so eight questions designed to tap citizens' perception of *incivilities* in their neighborhoods were included. Several studies examined the level of congruence between the public's seemingly punitive attitudes toward offenders and support for prison expansion and solutions to prison overcrowding (Skovron, Scott, & Cullen, 1988). The five questions in Chapter 6, asking citizens if they favor or oppose various measures to relieve prison overcrowding, provide an opportunity to examine these questions with more recent data.

A review of the national polls and journals produced the following topical areas:

- ☐ The public's fear of crime
- ☐ Attitudes toward police and courts
- ☐ Citizens' perceptions about sentencing criminals, and the purpose of prisons
- ☐ Public attitudes toward the use of the death penalty
- ☐ The public's views on gun possession and gun control legislation
- ☐ Perceptions of what to do to curb drug supplies and use in American society
- ☐ Citizens' attitudes toward juvenile gangs and what should be done about them

Some of the questions were used verbatim from their original source (national poll or journal article). This allows for consistency in reporting results and for comparing changes in public attitudes over time. However, many questions drawn from previous studies were designed for a mail survey, so word or sentence structure changes were needed to transform the question into use for a telephone survey.

The expected length of time to complete the telephone interview was a major concern. Obviously, in a field as broad as criminal justice, many more issues and topics could have been included, and dozens of additional questions could have been added to the instrument. One of the disadvantages of the telephone survey, however, is its "limitations on the complexity and length of the interview" (Lavrakas, 1993, p. 6). Lavrakas (1993) suggests that the average length of the telephone interview should be no more than 20 to 30 minutes. The average length of time for the telephone interview in the present study was 26 minutes.

Because of the length of the telephone interview, the questions were divided into three separate modules. The modules were randomly sequenced in an effort to minimize potential bias due to respondent fatigue that would be expected in questions asked at the end of the interview session.

Drafts of the proposed questions for the survey were evaluated by the study team and reviewed by each contributor. Additional reviews by the study team produced a draft instrument.

While the questionnaire was in development, requests for proposals (RFP) for data collection services were sent to organizations across the United States capable of conducting a national telephone survey. These organizations were identified in the American Association of Public Opinion Research's *Bluebook* directory. The RFP specified that the selection of a contractor would be on the basis of (a) experience in national opinion research on social science issues, (b) the ability to adhere to project deadlines, (c) references from previous clients, (d) total cost for services provided, and (e) the quality and thoroughness of the proposal. A total of 21 responses to the RFP were received and reviewed by the study team. On the basis of the above criteria, the contract for the study was awarded to the Public Policy Research Institute (PPRI) of Texas A&M University.

The final questionnaire was evaluated by the staffs of the Sam Houston State University's Criminal Justice Center and Texas A&M's PPRI. After further revisions, the draft instrument was assessed again during interviewer training. Finally, the instrument was pretested in the field. Problem questions were identified as those questions that were not readily understood by a majority of the respondents, or that were ambiguous or required repeating the question to solicit a response. Those questions were either discarded or revised.

Anticipating a significant number of Hispanic households, PPRI drafted a Spanish version of the survey instrument. When the respondent was more conversant in Spanish than in English, the interviewer either turned the interview over to an individual who was able to converse in Spanish, or arranged for the respondent to be contacted at a later time to be administered the Spanish version of the questionnaire.

The final version of the questionnaire used in the National Opinion Survey on Crime and Justice—1995 is included as the appendix.

The Sample

The basic design of the sample was a random sample of all telephone numbers in the 50 states of the United States. The approach was to determine working telephone numbers (listed or not) and draw a sample from those numbers.

The sampling frame for the survey was provided by Survey Sampling, Inc. (SSI). Through the use of a massive database, specialized computer programs, and classical statistical techniques, SSI produces a sampling frame that consists of highly efficient and unbiased samples of telephone numbers drawn along recognized geographic boundaries. In this approach, the sampling frame is constructed to produce proportionate stratified random samples from working blocks of numbers. To equalize the probability of selection, samples were stratified to all U.S. counties in proportion to each county's share of telephone households in the survey area. In this way, the sample is distributed across all counties in proportion to their share of the total population of telephone homes.

Random-Digit Dialing

To randomly sample respondents within households, the "last birthday method" of sampling was employed. Modified to correct for the undersampling of males in telephone surveys, the interviewer asked to speak with the male over 18 years of age with the most recent birthday. Once the known ratio of males in the target population was reached, interviewers no longer asked to speak with a male. This procedure allowed for the correction of the undersampling of males and, at the same time, maintained random selection within the household.

According to the U.S. Bureau of the Census, approximately 92% of all U.S. households have a telephone. With the saturation of telephone lines in American households, it is possible for a telephone survey of the United States to reach any household with a telephone (Lavrakas, 1993). One of the disadvantages of the telephone survey, however, is the fact that 8% of households are not eligible to be sampled, and households without telephones differ substantially from those with telephones. According to Lavrakas (1993), not having a telephone is related to very low income, low education, rural residency, younger ages, and minority racial status.

The inability to reach all U.S. households in a telephone survey is clearly a disadvantage. Yet with the exception of the U.S. Census of Population and Housing, few surveys reach the entire population of the United States. To do so, it has long been recognized, would be cost and time prohibitive. As Dillman (1978) observed, the available lists for sampling frames for *mail* surveys are often incomplete and tend to misrepresent the general public.

The advantages of telephone surveys far outweigh these disadvantages. The most important advantage of telephone surveys is quality control over the entire data collection process (Lavrakas, 1993). The researcher is able to closely control respondent selection, for example, through conversing with individuals within households by telephone. Once the individual within the household has been selected, has agreed to conduct the interview, and the interviewing process begun, the interviewer can maintain control over the interview. Questions can be repeated at the request of the person being interviewed, and the interviewer can make every attempt to get a response from the individual. The use of the computer-assisted telephone interviewing (CATI) system allows for control over the gathering of the data. When monitored correctly, corrections can be made with regard to problems identified with the interviewing process. This high level of quality control ensures the gathering of data through which more accurate estimates can be provided (Lavrakas, 1993). (See Chapter 12 for an elaboration on telephone surveys and the CATI system.)

The Survey

Telephone interviews were conducted between June 2 and June 26, 1995, using the CATI system during the hours of 8:00 a.m. to 11:00 p.m. on Mondays through Fridays, 10:00 a.m. to 6:00 p.m. on Saturdays, and 1:00 p.m. to 11:00 p.m. on Sundays. The CATI system prevented any chance of a misdial or inadvertently contacting a respondent in an

Table 13.1 Disposition of the Sample

Total sample	6,000
Less:	
Disconnects/bad numbers	2,023
No answer/busy/answering machine	946
Call backs not completed	944
Deaf/language	103
Business/government	367
	1,617
Less:	
Refusals/terminates	612
Completed interviews	1,005
Cooperation rate	62.2%

incorrect time zone or region of the country. Every attempt was made to convert all refusals, which helped to raise the cooperation rate. The total number of completed interviews was 1,005, with a cooperation rate of 62%, calculated as 100 × completed surveys/(completed surveys + refusals/terminates). Table 13.1 shows the disposition of the sample.

A national distribution by region of U.S. households with telephones and the percentage of survey completions by region (unweighted sample) is displayed in Table 13.2. The Pacific states yielded the highest percentage of completed surveys (19%), followed by the south Atlantic states (17.3%), and the east-north Central states (14.3%). The lowest percentage of completed surveys came from states in the New England area (4.2%). The Pacific states, in addition to yielding the highest percentage of completed surveys, were responsible for a greater amount of variance between number of telephones in households (15.6%) and completed surveys (19%)—a difference of 3.4%.

Weights

Two weighting techniques were applied. The first weighting procedure is dictated by the sampling design, and it controlled for the unequal probability of selection in homes where there are a number of people in the household and in homes with more than one telephone number. This is necessary because the larger the number of people in the household, the *lower* the probability of any one of them being

Table 13.2 Regional Distribution and Sample Variance (in percentages)

	Regional Distribution of U.S. Households With Telephones	Distribution of Survey Completions by Region
New England	5	4
Mid-Atlantic	15	14
East-north Central	17	14
West-north Central	7	8
South Atlantic	18	17
East-south Central	6	5
West-south Central	10	12
Mountain	6	7
Pacific	16	19
United States	100	100

Table 13.3 Estimated Population Distribution by Gender and Ethnic Group (in percentages)

	Ethnic Group				
Gender	White	Hispanic	Black	Other	All
Male	38	4	5	1	48
Female	41	3	6	2	52
All	79	7	11	3	100

selected. The larger the number of telephone numbers within the household, the *higher* the probability of those households being reached.

After applying the weight dictated by the sampling design, the data were further weighted to adjust for discrepancies between the sample and population on ethnic group and gender differences. Using census data from 1990 (U.S. Bureau of the Census, 1990), PPRI estimated the number of aged-18-and-older adults by ethnic and gender groups and adjusted the sample distribution to those population distributions shown in Table 13.3.

A weight to adjust the sample distribution to those population distributions was computed by dividing the percentage found in the population by the percentage found in the sample (with the previous weight applied). This weight was then multiplied by the weight based on the sampling design to produce a combined weight. That weight was normalized so that the weighted sample was the same size as the original unweighted sample.

Description of Respondents

As shown in Table 13.4, the weighted data reveal that the majority of respondents came from the 30 to 39 age category (28%). Examining the unweighted data, the percentage of respondents from that age category drops to 23%, which aligns exactly with the reported percentage for that age group found in U.S. census figures.

By computing the mean age of the sample on the continuous data, it was possible to compare the mean age of the sample, 42, with that of the population, 33. The finding that the average person in the sample is older than the average person in the general public is not unexpected given the fact that individuals below the age of 18 were excluded from the sample.

The weighted data reported in Table 13.4 reveal that the majority of the respondents were white (80%), 10% were African American/Black, 7% Hispanic, and 3% said they belong to "other" ethnic groups. Forty-eight percent of the respondents were male and 52% were female. These figures compare closely with 1990 census data as depicted in Table 13.3.

Sixty-two percent of the respondents reported having either at least a high school education or some college, with 28% responding that they have a college degree or have completed some graduate work. Examining the distribution of education in the census data, it appears that the sample was somewhat more educated than the general population. Census figures reveal that 38% of the public reported having at least a high school or "some college" education, with 14% reporting they have a college degree.

Thirteen percent of survey respondents reported annual household incomes of less than $15,000. According to the census, 24% of U.S. households have incomes under $15,000. In the higher income brackets, however, the differences diminish somewhat. Sixty-six percent of the respondents to the survey reported annual household incomes of $15,000 to $60,000. Census figures reveal that approximately half (51%)

Table 13.4 Description of Respondents (in percentages)

	Unweighted Data	Weighted Data
Age		
18-29	20	22
30-39	23	28
40-49	21	23
50-59	12	9
60-69	12	10
70 and over	12	8
Race/ethnicity		
White	82	80
Hispanic	8	7
Black	8	10
Other	2	3
Gender		
Male	52	48
Female	48	52
Education		
Less than high school	10	10
High school graduate	32	33
Some college	27	29
College graduate	31	28
Household income		
Less than $15,000	15	13
$15,000 to $30,000	26	26
$30,001 to $60,000	37	40
More than $60,000	22	21

of the general population report annual household incomes in the $15,000 to $50,000 category, and 15% report incomes between $50,000 and $74,000.

Because the categories used in the study on the income variable differ from those used by the U.S. census, it was not possible to compare exactly the sample distribution with the population marginals for those characteristics. It was possible, however, to compute the mean household income for both the sample data and the U.S. census data. The mean household income for the sample was $32,781, and the mean household income from census data is $30,056.

The Data

In several of the preceding chapters, the responses in the "don't know" and "refused" categories were recoded as "missing." It is always possible that respondents may not have enough information about the question's subject to form an opinion, or some questions, such as ones regarding income, may be viewed by the respondent as too sensitive to answer (Schuman & Presser, 1981b). In small sample sizes, the refusal of respondents to respond to questions can pose major problems. In larger samples, however, treating "don't know" or "refused" responses as missing information is not likely to affect the outcome (Schuman & Presser, 1981b). These responses are also less of a problem in simple reporting of item marginals than they would be in multivariate analysis (see Jones, 1994, however, for a different perspective on treating "don't knows" as missing information).

Most data analysis treats weighted samples as if they were simple random samples. This is not likely to be misleading as long as the weighted sample is approximately the same size as the unweighted sample and the weights are close to one. There is a slight clustering effect on the present sample because households, rather than individuals, are sampled, but this clustering effect is minimal. In order not to be misleading in reporting results of tests of significance, however, tests of association/correlation were conducted on the unweighted data and a more conservative estimate of statistical significance ($p < .001$) was used. The analysis was repeated on the weighted data and the results reported accordingly.

Hello, this is _____calling from the Public Policy Research Institute at Texas A&M University. We are conducting a nationwide survey of people's opinions about crime and justice in America. May I speak with the man or lady of the household who is 18 years of age or older who had the most recent birthday?
(if under 18 then terminate)

M1 First of all, I would like to get your opinions about issues dealing with crime and justice in America. Concerning media coverage of crime, how much attention does the local media in your community give to violent crime? Would you say it is: too much, too little or about right?

    1   Too much
    2   About right
    3   Too little
    8   Don't know
    9   Refused

M2 Do you get most of your news about crime from television, newspapers, radio, co-workers or friends and neighbors?

    1   Television
    2   Newspapers
    3   Radio
    4   Co-workers
    5   Friends and neighbors
    6   Other, specify _____
    8   Don't know
    9   Refused

M3 Are you a regular viewer of television programs that deal with crime or criminal justice issues, such as COPS, Real Stories of the Highway Patrol, Justice Files or America's Most Wanted?

    1   Yes
    2   No
    8   Don't know
    9   Refused

M4 Approximately how many hours do you watch television per week?
(record exact response)

    _____
    888   Don't know
    999   Refused

Changing topics, I would like to ask you about various aspects of your neighborhood. For each of the following would you say it is a serious problem, somewhat of a problem, a minor problem or not a problem at all?

N1   Trash and litter lying around

    1   Serious problem
    2   Somewhat of a problem
    3   A minor problem
    4   Not a problem at all
    8   Don't know
    9   Refused

N2   Neighborhood dogs running loose

    1   Serious problem
    2   Somewhat of a problem
    3   A minor problem
    4   Not a problem at all
    8   Don't know
    9   Refused

N3   Graffiti on sidewalks and walls

    1   Serious problem
    2   Somewhat of a problem
    3   A minor problem
    4   Not a problem at all
    8   Don't know
    9   Refused

N4   Vacant houses and unkempt lots

    1   Serious problem
    2   Somewhat of a problem
    3   A minor problem
    4   Not a problem at all
    8   Don't know
    9   Refused

N5   Unsupervised youth

    1   Serious problem
    2   Somewhat of a problem
    3   A minor problem
    4   Not a problem at all
    8   Don't know
    9   Refused

N6   Too much noise

1   Serious problem
2   Somewhat of a problem
3   A minor problem
4   Not a problem at all
8   Don't know
9   Refused

N7   People drunk or high on drugs in public

1   Serious problem
2   Somewhat of a problem
3   A minor problem
4   Not a problem at all
8   Don't know
9   Refused

N8   Abandoned cars or car parts lying around

1   Serious problem
2   Somewhat of a problem
3   A minor problem
4   Not a problem at all
8   Don't know
9   Refused

N9   In the past year do you feel that the crime rate in your neighborhood has
      increased, decreased or stayed the same?

1   Increased
2   Stayed the same
3   Decreased
8   Don't know
9   Refused

N10   In the past year do you feel safer, not as safe or about the same on the streets in
      your neighborhood?

1   Safer
2   Not as safe
3   About the same
8   Don't know
9   Refused

Next, I want to ask you how much you worry about each of the following
situations. Do you worry very frequently, somewhat frequently, seldom or never
about:

W1   Yourself or someone in your family getting sexually assaulted

    1   Very frequently
    2   Somewhat frequently
    3   Seldom
    4   Never
    8   Don't know
    9   Refused

W2   Being attacked while driving your car

    1   Very frequently
    2   Somewhat frequently
    3   Seldom
    4   Never
    8   Don't know
    9   Refused

W3   Getting mugged

    1   Very frequently
    2   Somewhat frequently
    3   Seldom
    4   Never
    8   Don't know
    9   Refused

W4   Getting beaten up, knifed or shot

    1   Very frequently
    2   Somewhat frequently
    3   Seldom
    4   Never
    8   Don't know
    9   Refused

W5   Getting murdered

    1   Very frequently
    2   Somewhat frequently
    3   Seldom
    4   Never
    8   Don't know
    9   Refused

W6   Your home being burglarized while **someone** is at home

    1   Very frequently
    2   Somewhat frequently
    3   Seldom
    4   Never
    8   Don't know
    9   Refused

W7   Your home being burglarized while **no one** is at home

    1   Very frequently
    2   Somewhat frequently
    3   Seldom
    4   Never
    8   Don't know
    9   Refused

P1   Changing topics, I would like to ask you about the police in your community.
      How much confidence do you have in the ability of the police to **protect** you
      from crime? Would you say: a great deal, some, little or none at all?

    1   A great deal
    2   Some
    3   Little
    4   None at all
    8   Don't know
    9   Refused

P2   What about the ability of the police to **solve** crime?

    1   A great deal
    2   Some
    3   Little
    4   None at all
    8   Don't know
    9   Refused

P3   What about the ability of the police to **prevent** crime?

    1   A great deal
    2   Some
    3   Little
    4   None at all
    8   Don't know
    9   Refused

P4   Please rate the police in your community on the following aspects, such as responding quickly to calls for help. Would you rate the police very high, high, average, low or very low?

1   Very high
2   High
3   Average
4   Low
5   Very low
8   Don't know
9   Refused

P5   What about the **friendliness** of the police?

1   Very high
2   High
3   Average
4   Low
5   Very low
8   Don't know
9   Refused

P6   How would you rate the **fairness** of the police in dealing with people?

1   Very high
2   High
3   Average
4   Low
5   Very low
8   Don't know
9   Refused

P7   In some places in the nation there have been charges of excessive use of force by the police. In your community would you say this is a serious problem, somewhat of a problem, a minor problem or not a problem at all?

1   Serious problem
2   Somewhat of a problem
3   Minor problem
4   Not a problem at all
8   Don't know
9   Refused

P8   Have you had any contact with the police during the past two years?

1   Yes
2   No   (SKIP TO C1)
8   Don't know   (SKIP TO C1)
9   Refused   (SKIP TO C1)

P9   Would you say you were very satisfied, somewhat satisfied, neither satisfied nor dissatisfied, somewhat dissatisfied or very dissatisfied?

1   Very satisfied
2   Somewhat satisfied
3   Neither
4   Somewhat dissatisfied
5   Very dissatisfied
8   Don't know
9   Refused

Moving to another topic, I would like to ask your opinions of the courts in your community. Do you think each of the following items are a serious problem, somewhat of a problem, a minor problem or not a problem at all in your community?

C1   Court decisions that are influenced by political considerations

1   Serious problem
2   Somewhat of a problem
3   Minor problem
4   Not a problem at all
8   Don't know
9   Refused

C2   Courts that do not treat the poor as well as they treat the rich

1   Serious problem
2   Somewhat of a problem
3   Minor problem
4   Not a problem at all
8   Don't know
9   Refused

C3   Courts that do not treat minorities as well as they treat whites

1   Serious problem
2   Somewhat of a problem
3   Minor problem
4   Not a problem at all
8   Don't know
9   Refused

C4   Courts that disregard defendants' rights

1   Serious problem
2   Somewhat of a problem
3   Minor problem
4   Not a problem at all
8   Don't know
9   Refused

C5   Courts that disregard the interests of crime victims

    1   Serious problem
    2   Somewhat of a problem
    3   Minor problem
    4   Not a problem at all
    8   Don't know
    9   Refused

C6   Courts in which six months pass from arrest to trial

    1   Serious problem
    2   Somewhat of a problem
    3   Minor problem
    4   Not a problem at all
    8   Don't know
    9   Refused

C7   Lawyers who are too expensive

    1   Serious problem
    2   Somewhat of a problem
    3   Minor problem
    4   Not a problem at all
    8   Don't know
    9   Refused

C8   Courts that are too expensive for the people who must use them

    1   Serious problem
    2   Somewhat of a problem
    3   Minor problem
    4   Not a problem at all
    8   Don't know
    9   Refused

C9   Courts that grant bail to persons previously convicted of crime

    1   Serious problem
    2   Somewhat of a problem
    3   Minor problem
    4   Not a problem at all
    8   Don't know
    9   Refused

C10   Courts that do not help decrease the amount of crime

    1   Serious problem
    2   Somewhat of a problem
    3   Minor problem
    4   Not a problem at all
    8   Don't know
    9   Refused

C11   Thinking now about the court cases you have personally followed, do they usually come out the way you think they should or not?

    1   Yes they do
    2   No they don't
    3   Not applicable
    8   Don't know
    9   Refused

C12   In general, do you think courts in this area deal too harshly, not harshly enough or about right with criminals?

    1   Too harshly
    2   About right
    3   Not harshly enough
    8   Don't know
    9   Refused

C13   Thinking now about drunk drivers, does the criminal justice system deal too harshly, not harshly enough or about right with drunk drivers?

    1   Too harshly
    2   Not harshly enough
    3   About right
    8   Don't know
    9   Refused

C14   In your opinion what is the most appropriate sentence for a person convicted more than once for drunk driving?
(read choices 1-5)

    1   License revoked
    2   A $ 1,000 fine
    3   Community service sentence
    4   One year in jail
    5   A prison term of more than one year
    8   Don't know
    9   Refused

C15   Persons accused of crimes often enter into negotiations with the prosecutor and judge and agree to plead guilty if the charges against them are reduced. Do you favor or oppose this process, referred to as "plea bargaining"?

1   Favor
2   Oppose
3   Neither favor nor oppose
8   Don't know
9   Refused

Next, people have said there are four purposes of criminal penalties. These are:
1. To discourage others from committing crimes.
2. To separate offenders from society.
3. To train, educate and counsel offenders.
4. To give offenders the punishment they deserve.

A1   Please tell me which of these four purposes do you think should be the **most** important in sentencing **adults**?
(may need to repeat the four purposes)

1   To discourage others from committing crimes
2   To separate offenders from society
3   To train, educate and counsel offenders
4   To give offenders the punishment they deserve
8   Don't know
9   Refused

A2   Which of these four purposes do you think should be the **most** important in sentencing **juveniles**?

1   To discourage others from committing crimes
2   To separate offenders from society
3   To train, educate and counsel offenders
4   To give offenders the punishment they deserve
8   Don't know
9   Refused

A3   In recent years, some legislatures have made imprisonment mandatory for convictions for some types of crimes. Do you think these mandatory sentences are a good idea, or should judges be able to decide who goes to prison and who doesn't?

1   Mandatory sentences are a good idea
2   Judges should be able to decide
3   Both
4   Neither
8   Don't know
9   Refused

A4   To lower the crime rate in the United States should money be spent on social and economic problems or on police, prisons and judges? Which comes closer to your view?

       1   Spend money on social and economic problems
       2   Spend money on police, prisons and judges
       3   Both
       4   Neither
       8   Don't know
       9   Refused

A5   In your opinion where does government need to make a greater effort these days: rehabilitate criminals who commit violent crimes or punish and put away criminals who commit violent crimes?

       1   Rehabilitate criminals
       2   Punish criminals
       3   Both
       4   Neither
       8   Don't know
       9   Refused

R1   Thinking of criminals who commit violent crimes do you think most, some, only a few, or none of them can be rehabilitated given early intervention with the right program?

       1   Most
       2   Some
       3   Only a few
       4   None of them
       8   Don't know
       9   Refused

       Next, please tell me whether you think each of the following proposals are good ideas or bad ideas.

R2   How about: Require prisoners to have a skill or to learn a trade to fit them for a job before they are released from prison.

       1   Good idea
       2   Bad idea
       3   Neither good nor bad
       8   Don't know
       9   Refused

R3   Require every prisoner to be able to read and write before he or she is released
from prison.

      1   Good idea
      2   Bad idea
      3   Neither good nor bad
      8   Don't know
      9   Refused

R4   Keep prisoners busy constructing buildings, making products or performing
services that the state would have to hire other people to do.

      1   Good idea
      2   Bad idea
      3   Neither good nor bad
      8   Don't know
      9   Refused

R5   Pay prisoners for their work, but require them to return two-thirds of this amount
to their victims or to the state for the cost of maintaining the prison.

      1   Good idea
      2   Bad idea
      3   Neither good nor bad
      8   Don't know
      9   Refused

R6   In some nations and in some states in the United States, in order to keep families
together, spouses are permitted to spend some weekends each year with their
husband or wife in special guest houses within the prison grounds.

      1   Good idea
      2   Bad idea
      3   Neither good nor bad
      8   Don't know
      9   Refused

R7   Refuse parole to any prisoner who has been paroled before for a serious crime.

      1   Good idea
      2   Bad idea
      3   Neither good nor bad
      8   Don't know
      9   Refused

R8   Appoint more judges in order to reduce the time between arrest and trial to a
      maximum of two months.

      1   Good idea
      2   Bad idea
      3   Neither good nor bad
      8   Don't know
      9   Refused

      Would you favor or oppose each of the following measures that have been
      suggested as ways to reduce prison overcrowding?

R9   How about: Shortening sentences?

      1   Favor
      2   Oppose
      3   Neither favor nor oppose
      8   Don't know
      9   Refused

R10   Allowing prisoners to earn early release through good behavior and
      participation in educational and work programs?

      1   Favor
      2   Oppose
      3   Neither favor nor oppose
      8   Don't know
      9   Refused

R11   Developing local programs to keep more nonviolent and first-time offenders
      active and working in the community?

      1   Favor
      2   Oppose
      3   Neither favor nor oppose
      8   Don't know
      9   Refused

R12   Giving the parole board more authority to release offenders early?

      1   Favor
      2   Oppose
      3   Neither favor nor oppose
      8   Don't know
      9   Refused

R13   Increasing taxes to build more prisons?

1   Favor
2   Oppose
3   Neither favor nor oppose
8   Don't know
9   Refused

CP1   In moving on to another topic, do you favor or oppose the death penalty for persons convicted of murder?

1   Favor
2   Oppose
3   Neither favor nor oppose
8   Don't know
9   Refused

I am going to read a list of items that affect some people's attitudes towards the death penalty. For each item please tell me if you would be more likely to favor the death penalty, more likely to oppose the death penalty or wouldn't matter. For example, if it is true that:

CP2   The death penalty is not a deterrent to murder.

1   More likely to favor
2   Wouldn't matter
3   More likely to oppose
8   Don't know
9   Refused

CP3   If it is true that: members of minority groups are more likely than others to receive the death penalty for the same crimes.

1   More likely to favor
2   Wouldn't matter
3   More likely to oppose
8   Don't know
9   Refused

CP4   If it is true that: some people who have been executed were actually innocent.

1   More likely to favor
2   Wouldn't matter
3   More likely to oppose
8   Don't know
9   Refused

CP5   If it is true that: poor people are more likely than others to receive the death penalty for the same crimes.

    1   More likely to favor
    2   Wouldn't matter
    3   More likely to oppose
    8   Don't know
    9   Refused

CP6   If it is true that: a life sentence, without any possibility of parole, was available.

    1   More likely to favor
    2   Wouldn't matter
    3   More likely to oppose
    8   Don't know
    9   Refused

CP7   If it is true that: keeping murderers in prison for life would cost less than the death penalty.

    1   More likely to favor
    2   Wouldn't matter
    3   More likely to oppose
    8   Don't know
    9   Refused

CP8   If it is true that: the murderer is a teenager under the age of 18.

    1   More likely to favor
    2   Wouldn't matter
    3   More likely to oppose
    8   Don't know
    9   Refused

CP9   If it is true that: the murderer is severely mentally retarded.

    1   More likely to favor
    2   Wouldn't matter
    3   More likely to oppose
    8   Don't know
    9   Refused

G1   In general, do you feel that the laws covering the sale of firearms should be made more strict, less strict, or kept as they are now?

    1   More strict
    2   Less strict
    3   Kept as they are now
    8   Don't know
    9   Refused

Please tell me for each of the following statements whether you strongly agree, agree, neither agree nor disagree, disagree or strongly disagree.

G2   Armed citizens are the best defense against criminals.

1   Strongly agree
2   Agree
3   Neither agree nor disagree
4   Disagree
5   Strongly disagree
8   Don't know
9   Refused

G3   Armed citizens are the best defense against government abuse of power.

1   Strongly agree
2   Agree
3   Neither agree nor disagree
4   Disagree
5   Strongly disagree
8   Don't know
9   Refused

G4   Parents should be charged with a crime if their children injure themselves or others with a gun kept in their household.

1   Strongly agree
2   Agree
3   Neither agree nor disagree
4   Disagree
5   Strongly disagree
8   Don't know
9   Refused

G5   It should be easier for law-abiding citizens to carry concealed handguns.

1   Strongly agree
2   Agree
3   Neither agree nor disagree
4   Disagree
5   Strongly disagree
8   Don't know
9   Refused

G6   Companies that manufacture guns with no hunting or sporting purpose should
      be held financially responsible when these guns injure or kill people.

      1   Strongly agree
      2   Agree
      3   Neither agree nor disagree
      4   Disagree
      5   Strongly disagree
      8   Don't know
      9   Refused

G7   In the last 5 years have you ever been a member of or contributed money to
      any organization, or contacted an elected official, or done anything else to
      express your views about gun control?

      1   Yes
      2   No
      8   Don't know
      9   Refused

S1   Changing topics, there has been a great deal of public debate about whether
      marijuana use should be legal. Which one of the following policies would you
      favor?
      (read choices 1-4)

      1   Using marijuana should be entirely legal
      2   It should be available by prescription for medical purposes
      3   It should be a minor violation like a parking ticket, but not a crime
      4   It should be a crime
      8   Don't know
      9   Refused

S2   If it were legal for people to use marijuana, should it also be legal to sell
      marijuana?

      1   Yes
      2   No
      8   Don't know
      9   Refused

S3   Which of the following do you think will do more to reduce the use of illegal
      drugs: punishing drug users or putting them into drug treatment programs?

      1   Punishing drug users
      2   Putting them into drug treatment programs
      3   Both
      4   Neither
      8   Don't know
      9   Refused

S4   Which of the following approaches to dealing with drug use in American society do you think would be most effective?
(read choices 1-4)

1   Military control to stop the shipping of drugs across American borders
2   Police efforts to get drugs off American streets
3   Educational programs to reduce the number of drug users in society
4   Drug treatment programs to reduce the number of drug users in society
8   Don't know
9   Refused

S5   Which approach do you think would be least effective?
(read if necessary)

1   Military control to stop the shipping of drugs across American borders
2   Police efforts to get drugs off American streets
3   Educational programs to reduce the number of drug users in society
4   Drug treatment programs to reduce the number of drug users in society
8   Don't know
9   Refused

S6   From what you can tell in your community, has the government's most recent war on drugs:
(read choices 1-3)

1   Reduced the amount of drug use
2   Increased the amount of drug use
3   Had no effect on the amount of drug use
8   Don't know
9   Refused

S7   Would you support legislation that prohibited the depiction of the use of **marijuana or other illicit drugs** in the movies, television or music videos?

1   Yes
2   No
8   Don't know
9   Refused

GA1   Next, how serious a problem are gangs in your community? Would you say they are: a serious problem, somewhat of a problem, a minor problem, or not a problem at all?

1   Serious problem
2   Somewhat of a problem
3   A minor problem
4   Not a problem at all
8   Don't know
9   Refused

GA2   in your opinion what is the **main** reason why young people in your community join gangs?
(do not read, select only one)

    1   For protection
    2   As a substitute for family
    3   It's part of their culture
    4   A lack of adult supervision
    5   A lack of employment opportunities for young people
    6   To commit crimes for the purpose of obtaining material goods
    7   Other, specify _____
    8   Don't know
    9   Refused

Please tell me for each of the following statements whether you strongly agree, agree, neither agree nor disagree, disagree or strongly disagree.

GA3   A juvenile charged with a **serious property crime** should be tried as an adult.

    1   Strongly agree
    2   Agree
    3   Neither agree nor disagree
    4   Disagree
    5   Strongly disagree
    8   Don't know
    9   Refused

GA4   A juvenile charged with **selling illegal drugs** should be tried as an adult.

    1   Strongly agree
    2   Agree
    3   Neither agree nor disagree
    4   Disagree
    5   Strongly disagree
    8   Don't know
    9   Refused

GA5   A juvenile charged with a **serious violent crime** should be tried as an adult.

    1   Strongly agree
    2   Agree
    3   Neither agree nor disagree
    4   Disagree
    5   Strongly disagree
    8   Don't know
    9   Refused

People have suggested a variety of measures that could be used to discourage youth gangs. Please tell me whether you strongly agree, agree, neither agree nor disagree, disagree or strongly disagree with each of the following.

GA6   To discourage youth gangs there should be stiffer sentences for juvenile offenders.

    1   Strongly agree
    2   Agree
    3   Neither agree nor disagree
    4   Disagree
    5   Strongly disagree
    8   Don't know
    9   Refused

GA7   To discourage youth gangs schools should improve security measures.

    1   Strongly agree
    2   Agree
    3   Neither agree nor disagree
    4   Disagree
    5   Strongly disagree
    8   Don't know
    9   Refused

GA8   To discourage youth gangs government should increase aid to youth centers.

    1   Strongly agree
    2   Agree
    3   Neither agree nor disagree
    4   Disagree
    5   Strongly disagree
    8   Don't know
    9   Refused

GA9   To discourage youth gangs there should be more employment opportunities for youth.

    1   Strongly agree
    2   Agree
    3   Neither agree nor disagree
    4   Disagree
    5   Strongly disagree
    8   Don't know
    9   Refused

GA10   To discourage youth gangs parents should be held legally responsible for their children's actions.

    1   Strongly agree
    2   Agree
    3   Neither agree nor disagree
    4   Disagree
    5   Strongly disagree
    8   Don't know
    9   Refused

GA11   In most places, there are juvenile justice programs that emphasize protecting and rehabilitating juveniles rather than punishing them. Do you think these programs have been given the necessary money and other support to be successful?

    1   Yes
    2   No
    8   Don't know
    9   Refused

GA12   Would you say these programs have been very successful, somewhat successful, not very successful or not at all successful at controlling juvenile crime?

    1   Very successful
    2   Somewhat successful
    3   Not very successful
    4   Not at all successful
    8   Don't know
    9   Refused

D1   Finally, I would like to ask you some questions about yourself. What is your current age?
(record exact number)

    _____

    98   Don't know
    99   Refused

D2   Which of the following best describes your racial or ethnic group?
(read list)

    1   White
    2   Hispanic
    3   African-American
    4   Other, specify _____
    8   Don't know
    9   Refused

D3   What was the last grade of school you completed?
       (do not read)

       1   Grade 0-4
       2   Grade 5-8
       3   Grade 9-11, some high school
       4   Grade 12, high school graduate
       5   Grade 13-15, some college, business or trade school
       6   Grade 16, college graduate
       7   Graduate work
       8   Don't know
       9   Refused

D4   Are you currently married, widowed, divorced, separated or have you never
       been married?

       1   Married
       2   Widowed
       3   Divorced
       4   Separated
       5   Never married
       8   Don't know
       9   Refused

D5   What is your zip code?
       (record exact numbers)

       __ __ __ __ __
       99999   Don't know/refused

D6   Generally speaking, do you usually think of yourself as a Republican, Democrat,
       Independent or other?

       1   Republican
       2   Democrat
       3   Independent
       4   Other, specify _____
       8   Don't know
       9   Refused

D7   Overall, do you consider yourself liberal, middle of the road or conservative?

       1   Liberal
       2   Middle of the road
       3   Conservative
       4   None
       8   Don't know
       9   Refused

D8   Which term best describes the community in which you live. Is it rural, a small town, a small city, a suburb or an urban area?

    1   Rural
    2   Small town
    3   Small city
    4   Suburb
    5   Urban
    8   Don't know
    9   Refused

D9   Which of the following best describes your current religious preferences: Protestant, Catholic, Jewish or something else?

    1   Protestant
    2   Catholic   (SKIP TO D11)
    3   Jewish   (SKIP TO D11)
    4   Other, specify _____   (SKIP TO D11)
    5   None   (SKIP TO D11)
    8   Don't know   (SKIP TO D11)
    9   Refused   (SKIP TO D11)

D10   Which denomination?
       (record exact response)

       _____

D11   Do you or anyone else in the household own any guns?

    1   Yes
    2   No   (SKIP TO D13)
    8   Don't know   (SKIP TO D13)
    9   Refused   (SKIP TO D13)

D12   Is the main reason for the gun sport or protection against crime?

    1   Sport
    2   Protection against crime
    3   Both
    4   Neither
    8   Don't know
    9   Refused

D13   How many people live in your household?
       (record exact number)

       _____

    88   Don't know
    99   Refused

D14   How many **different** telephone numbers are there in your household?
       (record exact number)

       _____

       1   Only one number for household
       8   Don't know
       9   Refused

D15   Please tell me your annual household income?
       (read list and record only one response)

       1   Less than $ 15,000
       2   Between $ 15,000 and $ 30,000
       3   Between $ 30,000 and $ 60,000
       4   Over $ 60,000
       8   Don't know
       9   Refused

       That completes the survey. Thank you for your cooperation!

D16   Record the sex of the respondent   **(do not read)**

       1   Male
       2   Female

References

ABC News/Washington Post. (1985). Drugs, alcohol trouble millions of families (Poll conducted May 8-15). *American Public Opinion Data* [Microfiche]. (Opinion Research Service)

Aberbach, J. D., & Walker, J. L. (1970). The attitudes of blacks and whites toward city services: Implications for public policy. In J. P. Crecine (Ed.), *Financing the metropolis: Public policy in urban economies* (pp. 519-538). Beverly Hills, CA: Sage.

Adams, M. (1990). Canadian attitudes toward crime and justice. *Forum on Corrections Research, 2*(1), 10-22.

Albrecht, S. L., & Green, M. (1977). Attitudes toward the police and the larger attitude complex: Implications for police-community relationships. *Criminology, 15*(1), 67-86.

Alderman, J. (1994). Leading the public: The media's focus on crime shaped sentiment. *The Public Perspective, 5,* 26-28.

American Correctional Association. (1995, June 14). *Americans overwhelmingly support a balanced approach to reducing crime* [Press release]. Laurel, MD: Author.

Antunes, G., & Hurley, P. (1977). The representation of criminal events in Houston's two daily newspapers. *Journalism Quarterly, 54,* 756-760.

Asher, H. (1988). *Polling and the public: What every citizen should know.* Washington, DC: Congressional Quarterly.

Barkan, S. E., & Cohn, S. F. (1994). Racial prejudice and support for the death penalty by whites. *Journal of Research in Crime and Delinquency, 31,* 202-209.

Bayley, D. H., & Skolnick, J. H. (1986). *The new blue line: Police innovation in six cities.* New York: Free Press.

Beckett, K. (1994). Setting the public agenda: "Street crime" and drug use in American politics. *Social Problems, 41,* 425-447.

Belyea, M. J., & Zingraff, M. T. (1988). Fear of crime and residential location. *Rural Sociology, 53,* 473-486.

Bennett, W. (1980). *Public opinion in American politics.* New York: Harcourt Brace Jovanovich.

Biderman, A. D., Johnson, L. A., McIntyre, J., & Weir, A. (1967). *Report on a pilot study in the District of Columbia on victimization and attitudes toward law enforcement* (President's

Commission on Law Enforcement and Administration of Justice). Washington, DC: Government Printing Office.

Bishop, G., & Klecka, W. (1978, March). *Victimization and fear of crime among the elderly living in high crime neighborhoods.* Paper presented at the annual meeting of the Academy of the Criminal Justice Sciences, New Orleans, LA.

Black, D. J. (1970). The production of crime rates. *American Sociological Review, 35,* 733-748.

Blotner, R., & Lilly, L. (1986). SPECDA: A comprehensive approach to the delivery of substance abuse prevention services in the New York City school system. *Journal of Drug Education, 16*(1), 83-89.

Blumstein, A. (1995). Prisons. In J. Q. Wilson & J. Petersilia (Eds.), *Crime* (pp. 387-420). San Francisco: ICS.

Blumstein, A., Cohen, J., & Rosenfeld, R. (1991, May). Trend and deviation in crime rates: A comparison of UCR and NCS data for burglary and robbery. *Criminology, 29,* 237-263.

Bohm, R. M. (1991). American death penalty opinion, 1936-1986: A critical examination of the Gallup polls. In R. M. Bohm (Ed.), *The death penalty in America: Current research* (pp. 113-145). Cincinnati, OH: Anderson.

Bohm, R. M., & Aveni, A. F. (1985, November). *Knowledge and attitudes about the death penalty: A test of the Marshall hypotheses.* Paper presented at the annual meeting of the American Society of Criminology, San Diego, CA.

Bonnie, R. J. (1992). America's drug policy: Time for another commission? *Journal of Research in Crime and Delinquency, 19,* 395-408.

Bordua, D. J. (1984). Gun control and opinion measurement: Adversary polling and the construction of social meaning. In D. B. Kates (Ed.), *Firearms and violence: Issues of public policy* (pp. 51-70). Cambridge, MA: Ballinger.

Bouma, D. H. (1973). Youth attitudes toward the police and law enforcement. In J. T. Curran, A. Fowler, & R. H. Ward (Eds.), *Police and law enforcement, 1972* (Vol. 1, pp. 219-238). New York: AMS.

Bradburn, N. M. (1992). Presidential address: A response to the nonresponse problem. *Public Opinion Quarterly, 56,* 391-397.

Bradburn, N. M., & Sudman, S. (1988). *Polls and surveys: Understanding what they tell us.* San Francisco: Jossey-Bass.

Brandl, S. G., & Horvath, F. (1991). Crime-victim evaluation of police investigative performance. *Journal of Criminal Justice, 19,* 109-121.

Brooks, L. W. (1993). Police discretionary behavior: A study of style. In R. G. Dunham & G. P. Alpert (Eds.), *Critical issues in policing: Contemporary readings* (2nd ed., pp. 140-164). Prospect Heights, IL: Waveland.

Brown, E. J., Flanagan, T. J., & McLeod, M. (Eds.). (1984). *Sourcebook of criminal justice statistics—1983.* Washington, DC: Government Printing Office.

Bureau of Justice Statistics. (1985). *Criminal victimization 1984.* Washington, DC: U.S. Department of Justice, National Institute of Justice, Office of Justice Programs.

Bureau of Justice Statistics. (1988). *Report to the nation on crime and justice.* Washington, DC: U.S. Department of Justice.

Caba, S. (1995, May 7). Justice hasn't ground to a halt, yet. *Houston Chronicle,* pp. 6A-7A.

Carter, D. L. (1985). Hispanic perception of police performance: An empirical assessment. *Journal of Criminal Justice, 13,* 487-500.

Center for Public Policy. (1988). *The Houston area survey.* Houston, TX: University of Houston, Center for Public Policy.

Center for Substance Abuse Research. (1995a, February 6). Are we getting our money's worth? New report looks at effectiveness of federal drug policy. *Cesar Fax, 4.*

Center for Substance Abuse Research. (1995b, April 17). 1995 survey of Americans' attitudes towards drug abuse and policy just released. *Cesar Fax, 4.*

Childs, H. L. (1965). *Public opinion: Nature, formation, and role.* Princeton, NJ: Van Nostrand.

Cohen, L. E., & Felson, M. (1979). Social change and crime rate trends: A routine activity approach. *American Sociological Review, 44,* 588-608.

Colasanto, D. (1990). Widespread public opposition to drug legalization. *Gallup Poll Monthly* (No. 292). Princeton, NJ: Gallup.

Combs, M. W., & Comer, J. C. (1982, December). Race and capital punishment: A longitudinal analysis. *Phylon, 43,* 350-359.

Converse, P. E. (1987). Changing conceptions of public opinion in the political process. *Public Opinion Quarterly, 51,* S12-S24.

Cook, P. J., & Moore, M. H. (1995). Gun control. In J. Q. Wilson & J. Petersilia (Eds.), *Crime* (pp. 267-294). San Francisco: ICS.

Cox, T. C., & White, M. F. (1988). Traffic citations and student attitudes toward the police: An examination of selected interaction dynamics. *Journal of Police Science and Administration, 16,* 105-121.

Crespi, I. (1989). *Public opinion, polls, and democracy.* Boulder, CO: Westview.

Cullen, F. T., Clark, G. A., & Wozniak, J. F. (1985). Explaining the get tough movement: Can the public be blamed? *Federal Probation, 49,* 16-24.

Cullen, F. T., Cullen, J. B., & Wozniak, J. F. (1988). Is rehabilitation dead? The myth of the punitive public. *Journal of Criminal Justice, 16,* 303-317.

Cullen, F. T., Golden, K. M., & Cullen, J. B. (1983). Is child saving dead? Attitudes toward juvenile rehabilitation in Illinois. *Journal of Criminal Justice, 11,* 1-13.

Cullen, F. T., Skovron, S. E., Scott, J. E., & Burton, V. S., Jr. (1990). Public support for correctional treatment: The tenacity of the rehabilitative ideology. *Criminal Justice and Behavior, 17,* 6-18.

Curtis, M. S. (1991). Attitudes toward the death penalty as it relates to political party affiliation, religious belief, and faith in people. *Free Inquiry in Creative Sociology, 19,* 205-212.

Danigelis, N. L., & Cutler, S. J. (1991). Cohort trends in attitudes about law and order: Who's leading the conservative wave? *Public Opinion Quarterly, 44,* 24-49.

Decker, S. H. (1985). The police and the public: Perceptions and policy recommendations. In R. J. Homant & D. B. Kennedy (Eds.), *Police and law enforcement, 1975-1981* (Vol. 3, pp. 89-105). New York: AMS.

Decker, S. H., Smith, R. L., & Uhlman, T. M. (1979). Does anything work? An evaluation of urban police innovations. In R. Baker & F. A. Meyer (Eds.), *Evaluating alternative law enforcement policies* (pp. 43-54). Lexington, MA: Lexington Books.

DiIulio, J. (1995, August). Crime in America: It's going to get worse. *Reader's Digest,* pp. 55-60.

Dillman, D. A. (1978). *Mail and telephone surveys: The total design method.* New York: John Wiley.

Dionne, E. J., Jr. (1992). The illusion of technique: The impact of polls on reporters and democracy. In T. E. Mann & G. R. Orren (Eds.), *Media polls in American politics* (pp. 150-167). Washington, DC: Brookings Institution.

Doble, J. (1987a, Winter). Interpreting public opinion: Five common fallacies. *Kettering Review,* pp. 7-17.

Doble, J. (1987b). *Crime and punishment: The public's view.* New York: Edna McConnell Clark Foundation.

Doble, J., & Klein, J. (1989). *Punishing criminals: The public's view. An Alabama survey.* New York: Edna McConnell Clark Foundation.

Dominick, J. R. (1978). Crime and law enforcement in the mass media. In C. Winick (Ed.), *Deviance and mass media* (pp. 105-130). Beverly Hills, CA: Sage.

Doob, A., & Roberts, J. V. (1982). *Crime and the official response to crime: The views of the Canadian public.* Ottawa: Department of Justice, Canada.

Drug use occupies emergency rooms, public opinion polls. (1994, July). *Public Health Reports, 109,* 586-587.

Drug use by youth continues to rise. (1995). *Substance Abuse Report, 26,* 1-2.

Duffee, D., & Ritti, R. R. (1977). Correctional policy and public values. *Criminology, 14,* 449-459.

Dunham, R. G., & Alpert, G. P. (1988). Neighborhood differences in attitudes toward policing: Evidence for a mixed-strategy model of policing in a multi-ethnic setting. *Journal of Criminal Law and Criminology, 79,* 504-523.

Durham, A. M., III. (1993). Public opinion regarding sentences for crime: Does it exist? *Journal of Criminal Justice, 21,* 1-11.

Ellsworth, P. C., & Gross, S. R. (1994). Hardening of attitudes: American's views on the death penalty. *Journal of Social Issues, 50,* 19-52.

Ellsworth, P. C., & Ross, L. (1983). Public opinion and capital punishment: A close examination of the views of abolitionists and retentionists. *Crime & Delinquency, 29,* 116-169.

Embree, B. G. (1993). Validity and reliability of self-reported drinking behavior: Dealing with the problem of response bias. *Journal of Studies on Alcohol, 54,* 334-344.

Erickson, R., Wright, G., & McIver, J. (1993). *Statehouse democracy.* New York: Cambridge University Press.

Erskine, H. (1974). The polls: Causes of crime. *Public Opinion Quarterly, 38,* 287-298.

Fagan, R. W. (1981). Public support for the courts: An examination of alternative explanations. *Journal of Criminal Justice, 9,* 403-418.

Falk, R., Siegal, H. A., & Forney, M. A. (1992, Fall). The validity of injection drug users' self-reported use of opiates and cocaine. *Journal of Drug Issues, 22,* 823-832.

Feagin, J. R. (1970). Home-defense and the police: Black and white perspectives. *American Behavioral Scientist, 13,* 795-814.

Ferraro, K. F., & LaGrange, R. L. (1987). The measurement of fear of crime. *Sociological Inquiry, 57,* 70-101.

Finckenauer, J. (1978). Crime as a national political issue: 1964-76. *Crime & Delinquency, 24,* 13-27.

Finlay, B. (1985). Right to life vs. the right to die: Some correlates of euthanasia attitudes. *Sociology and Social Research, 69,* 548-560.

Flanagan, T. J. (1987). Change and influence in popular criminology: Public attributions of crime causation. *Journal of Criminal Justice, 15,* 231-244.

Flanagan, T. J. (1989). Prison labor and industry. In L. Goodstein & D. MacKenzie (Eds.), *The American prison: Issues in research and policy* (pp. 135-161). New York: Plenum.

Flanagan, T. J. (1993, November). *Twenty years of public opinion on crime and criminal justice, 1973-93.* Paper presented at the annual meeting of the American Society of Criminology, Chicago.

Flanagan, T. J., & Caulfield, S. L. (1984). Public opinion and prison policy: A review. *Prison Journal, 64,* 39-59.

Flanagan, T. J., McGarrell, E. F., & Brown, E. (1985). Public perceptions of the criminal courts: The role of demographic and related attitudinal variables. *Journal of Research in Crime and Delinquency, 22,* 66-82.

Flanagan, T. J., & Vaughn, M. S. (1995). Public opinion about police abuse of force. In W. A. Geller & H. Toch (Eds.), *And justice for all: Understanding and controlling police abuse of force* (pp. 113-131). Washington, DC: Police Executive Research Forum.

Furman v. Georgia, 408 U.S. 238, 329 (1972).

Gallup, G. (1982, May). *The Gallup report* (No. 200). Princeton, NJ: Author.

Gallup, G. (1985, October). *The Gallup report* (No. 241). Princeton, NJ: Author.

Gallup, G. (1988). *The Gallup poll: Public opinion 1988.* Wilmington, DE: Scholarly Resources.

Gallup, G. (1991). *The Gallup poll: Public opinion 1991.* Wilmington, DE: Scholarly Resources.

Gallup, G. (1994a). *The Gallup poll: Public opinion 1994.* Wilmington, DE: Scholarly Resources.

Gallup, G. (1994b). Public wants crime bill. *Gallup Poll Monthly* (No. 347, pp. 11-15). Princeton, NJ: Author.

Gallup, G., & Newport, F. (1990). Americans now drinking less alcohol. *Gallup Poll Monthly* (No. 303). Princeton, NJ: Gallup.

Garofalo, J. (1977). *Public opinion about crime: The attitudes of victims and nonvictims in selected cities.* Washington, DC: Government Printing Office.

Garofalo, J. (1981a). Crime and the mass media: A selective review of research. *Journal of Research in Crime and Delinquency, 18,* 319-350.

Garofalo, J. (1981b). The fear of crime: Causes and consequences. *Journal of Criminal Law and Criminology, 82,* 839-857.

Gottfredson, S. D., & Taylor, R. B. (1984). Public policy and prison populations: Measuring opinions about reform. *Judicature, 68,* 191-205.

Gottfredson, S. D., & Taylor, R. B. (1985). Attitudes of correctional policymakers and the public. In S. D. Gottfredson & S. McConville (Eds.), *America's correctional crisis: Prison populations and public policy* (pp. 57-75). New York: Greenwood.

Goyder, J. (1987). *The silent minority: Nonrespondents on sample surveys.* Boulder, CO: Westview.

Graber, D. (1980). *Crime news and the public.* New York: Praeger.

Grandberg, D., & Grandberg, B. W. (1981). Pro-life versus pro-choice: Another look at the abortion controversy in the U.S. *Sociology and Social Research, 65,* 434-434.

Groves, R. M. (1987). Research on survey data quality. *Public Opinion Quarterly, 51,* S156-S172.

Hagan, J., & Albonetti, C. (1982). Race, class, and the perception of criminal injustice in America. *American Journal of Sociology, 88,* 329-355.

Hahn, H. (1971). Ghetto assessments of police protection and authority. *Law and Society Review, 6,* 183-194.

Handberg, R., & Unkovic, C. M. (1985). Public opinion, the death penalty, and the crime rate. *Free Inquiry in Creative Sociology, 13,* 141-144.

Harris, P. (1986). Oversimplification and error in public opinion surveys on capital punishment. *Justice Quarterly, 3,* 429-455.

Harrison, L. D. (1995). The validity of self-reported data on drug use. *Journal of Drug Issues, 25,* 91-111.

Harvey, O. J. (1986, December). Belief systems and attitudes toward the death penalty and other punishments. *Journal of Personality, 54,* 659-675.

Heath, L. (1984). Impact of newspaper crime reports on fear of crime: A multimethological investigation. *Journal of Personality and Social Psychology, 47,* 263-276.

Hengstler, G. A. (1993). The public perception of lawyers: ABA poll. *ABA Journal, 97,* 60-65.

Herbst, S. (1993). *Numbered voices: How opinion polling has shaped American politics.* Chicago: University of Chicago Press.

Himelfarb, A. (1990). Public opinion and public policy. *Forum on Corrections Research, 2,* 20-22.

Hindelang, M. J. (1974). Public opinion regarding crime, criminal justice, and related topics. *Journal of Research in Crime and Delinquency, 11,* 101-116.

Hindelang, M., Gottfredson, M., & Garofalo, J. (1978). *Victims of personal crime: An empirical foundation for a theory of personal victimization.* Cambridge, MA: Ballinger.

Innes, C. A. (1993). Recent public opinion in the United States toward punishment and corrections. *Prison Journal, 73,* 220-236.

Irwin, J., & Austin, J. (1994). *It's about time: America's imprisonment binge.* Belmont, CA: Wadsworth.

Jacob, H. (1971). Black and white perceptions of justice in the city. *Law and Society Review, 6,* 69-89.

Jamieson, K., & Flanagan, T. J. (1987). *Sourcebook of criminal justice statistics—1986.* Washington, DC: Government Printing Office.

Janofsky, M. (1994, December 13). Survey reports more drug use by teen-agers. *New York Times,* p. A1.

Jefferson, T. (1955). *The political writings of Thomas Jefferson: Representative selections* (E. Dumbauld, Ed.). New York: Liberal Arts Press.

Jeffords, C. R. (1983). The situational relationship between age and the fear of crime. *International Journal of Aging and Human Development, 17,* 103-111.

Jensen, E., Gerber, J., & Bebcock. G. M. (1991). The new war on drugs: Grass-roots movement or political construction? *Journal of Drug Issues, 3,* 651-667.

Johnston, L. D., O'Malley, P. M., & Bachman, J. G. (1991). *Drug use among American high school seniors, college students and young adults, 1975-1990: Vol. 1. High school seniors.* Rockville, MD: National Institute on Drug Abuse, U.S. Department of Health and Human Services.

Johnston, L. D., O'Malley, P. M., & Bachman, J. G. (1992). *Smoking, drinking, and illicit drug use among American secondary school students, college students and young adults, 1975-1991: Vol. 1. Secondary school students.* Rockville, MD: National Institute on Drug Abuse, U.S. Department of Health and Human Services.

Johnston, L. D., O'Malley, P. M., & Bachman, J. G. (1993). *National survey results on drug use from the Monitoring the Future study, 1975-1992: Vol. 1. Secondary school students.* Rockville, MD: National Institute on Drug Abuse, U.S. Department of Health and Human Services.

Jones, P. (1994). It's not what you ask, it's the way that you ask it: Question form and public opinion on the death penalty. *Prison Journal, 73,* 32-50.

Junger, M. (1987). Women's experiences of sexual harassment. *British Journal of Criminology, 22,* 358-383.

Karmen, A. (1984). *Crime victims: An introduction to victimology.* Pacific Grove, CA: Brooks/Cole.

Kelly, R. M. (1975). Generalizations from an OEO experiment in Washington, D.C. *Journal of Social Issues, 31*(1), 57-86.

Kennett, L., & Anderson, J. L. (1975). *The gun in America: The origins of a national dilemma.* Westport, CT: Greenwood.

Key, V. O., Jr. (1961). *Public opinion and American democracy.* New York: Knopf.

Kids and marijuana: The glamour is back. (1994, December 26). *U.S. News and World Report,* p. 12.

Kleck, G. (1991). *Point blank: Guns and violence in America.* New York: Aldine de Gruyter.

Knowles, J. (1984). *Ohio citizen attitudes concerning crime and criminal justice* (4th ed.). Columbus, OH: Governor's Office of Criminal Justice Services.

Koss, M. P. (1992). The underdetection of rape: Methodological choices influence incidence estimates. *Journal of Social Issues, 48,* 61-75.

Krisberg, B., & Austin, J. F. (1993). *Reinventing juvenile justice.* Newbury Park, CA: Sage.

LaGrange, R., & Ferraro, K. F. (1989). Assessing age and gender differences in perceived risk and fear of crime. *Criminology, 27,* 697-717.

LaGrange, R. L., Ferraro, K. F., & Supancic, M. (1992). Perceived risk and fear of crime: Role of social and physical incivilities. *Journal of Research in Crime and Delinquency, 29,* 311-334.

Langworthy, R. H., & Whitehead, J. T. (1986). Liberalism and fear as explanation of punitiveness. *Criminology, 24,* 575-591.

Lasley, J. R. (1994). The impact of the Rodney King incident on citizen attitudes toward police. *Policing and Society, 3,* 245-255.

Lavrakas, P. J. (1993). *Telephone survey methods: Sampling, selection and supervision* (2nd ed.). Newbury Park, CA: Sage.

Lawton, M. P., & Yaffe, S. (1980). Victimization and fear of crime in elderly public housing tenants. *Journal of Gerontology, 35,* 768-779.

Lee, G. R. (1982). Sex differences in fear of crime among older people. *Research on Aging, 4,* 284-298.

Lee, G. R. (1983). Social integration and fear of crime among older persons. *Journal of Gerontology, 38,* 745-750.

Levine, A. P. (1992). Looking for Mr. Goodlawyer. *ABA Journal, 76,* 60, 62.

Lippmann, W. (1965). *Public opinion.* New York: Free Press. (Original work published 1922)

Lipton, D., Martinson, R., & Wilks, J. (1975). *The effectiveness of correctional treatment.* New York: Praeger.

Liska, A., & Baccaglini, W. (1990). Feeling safe by comparison: Crime in the newspapers. *Social Problems, 37,* 360-374.

Liska, A. E., Sanchirico, A., & Reed, M. D. (1988). Fear of crime and constrained behavior: Specifying and estimating a reciprocal effect model. *Social Forces, 66,* 827-837.

Lizotte, A. J., & Bordua, D. J. (1980). Firearms ownership for sport and protection: Two divergent models. *American Sociological Review, 46,* 499-503.

Maguire, K., & Pastore, A. (1994). *Sourcebook of criminal justice statistics—1993.* Washington, DC: Government Printing Office.

Maguire, K., & Pastore, A. (1995). *Sourcebook of criminal justice statistics—1994.* Washington, DC: Government Printing Office.

Maguire, K., Pastore, A., & Flanagan, T. J. (1993). *Sourcebook of criminal justice statistics— 1992.* Washington, DC: Government Printing Office.

Martinson, R. (1974). What works? Questions and answers about prison reform. *Public Interest, 35,* 22-54.

Maxfield, M. (1987). *Explaining fear of crime: Evidence from the 1984 British crime survey* (Home Office Research and Planning Unit Paper No. 43). London: HMSO.

Maxfield, M. G. (1988). The London metropolitan police and their clients: Victim and suspect attitudes. *Journal of Research in Crime and Delinquency, 25,* 188-206.

McAneny, L. (1993). The Gallup poll on crime. *Gallup Poll Monthly* (No. 30, pp. 18-42). Princeton, NJ: Gallup.

McCorkle, R. C. (1993). Research note: Punish and rehabilitate? Public attitudes toward six common crimes. *Crime & Delinquency, 39,* 240-252.

McDonald, W. F. (Ed.). (1976). *Criminal justice and the victim.* Beverly Hills, CA: Sage.

McDowall, D., & Loftin, C. (1983). Collective security and the demand for legal handguns. *American Journal of Sociology, 88,* 1146-1161.

McGarrell, E., & Flanagan, T. J. (1985). *Sourcebook of criminal justice statistics—1984.* Washington, DC: Government Printing Office.

Miller, P. V., & Groves, R. M. (1981). Matching survey responses to official records: An exploration of validity in victimization reporting. *Public Opinion Quarterly, 49,* 366-380.

Mirande, A. (1981). The Chicano and the law: An analysis of community-police conflict in an urban barrio. *Pacific Sociological Review, 24*(1), 65-86.

Moore, D. W. (1992). *The superpollsters: How they measure and manipulate public opinion in America.* New York: Four Walls Eight Windows.

Moran, G., & Comfort, J. C. (1986, February). Neither "tentative" nor "fragmentary": Verdict preference of impaneled felony jurors as a function of attitude toward capital punishment. *Journal of Applied Psychology, 71,* 1146-1155.

Murty, K. S., Roebuck, J. B., & Smith, J. D. (1990). The image of the police in black Atlanta communities. *Journal of Police Science and Administration, 17,* 250-257.

Musto, D. (1987). *The American disease: Origins of narcotic control.* New York: Oxford University Press.

Nardulli, P. F., Eisenstein, J., & Flemming, R. B. (1988). *The tenor of justice.* Chicago: University of Illinois Press.

National Advisory Commission on Civil Disorders (Kerner Commission). (1968). *Report.* Washington, DC: Government Printing Office.

National Institute on Drug Abuse. (1990). *National Household Survey on Drug Abuse: Main findings* (DHHS Publication No. ADM 91-1788). Washington, DC: Department of Health and Human Services.

National Opinion Research Center. (1986). *General Social Surveys, 1972-1986: Cumulative codebook.* Chicago: Author.

Nejelski, P., & Wheeler, R. (1979). *Conference report* (Report of the Wingspread Conference on Contemporary and Future Issues in the Field of Court Management). Racine, WI: Institute for Court Management.

New Lexicon Webster's dictionary of the English language. (1989). New York: New Lexicon.

O'Brien, R. M. (1990). Comparing detrended UCR and NCS crime rates over time: 1973-1986. *Journal of Criminal Justice, 18,* 229-238.

Oldendick, R. W., & Link, M. W. (1994). The answering machine generation: Who are they and what problem do they pose for survey research? *Public Opinion Quarterly, 58,* 264-273.

Parker, K. (1993). Fear of crime and the likelihood of victimization: A bi-ethnic comparison. *Journal of Social Psychology, 133,* 723-732.

Parker, K. D., & Ray, M. C. (1990). Fear of crime: An assessment of related factors. *Sociological Spectrum, 10,* 29-40.

Peak, K., Bradshaw, R. V., & Glensor, R. W. (1992). Improving citizen perceptions of the police: Back to the basics with a community policing strategy. *Journal of Criminal Justice, 20*(1), 25-40.

Peek, C. W., Lowe, G. D., & Alston, J. P. (1981). Race and attitudes toward local police: Another look. *Journal of Black Studies, 11,* 361-374.

Pettinico, G. (1994, September/October). Crime and punishment: America changes its mind. *The Public Perspective, 5*(6), 29-32.

Piazza, T. (1993). Meeting the challenge of answering machines. *Public Opinion Quarterly,* *57,* 219-231.

Polling the nations [CD-ROM]. (1986-1993). Bethesda, MD: ORS.

Posner, R. A. (1995, September 1). The most punitive nation: A few modest proposals for lowering the U.S. crime rate. *Times Literary Supplement,* pp. 3-4.

President's Commission on Law Enforcement and Administration of Justice. (1967). *A national survey of police-community relations: Field surveys V.* Washington, DC: Government Printing Office.

Priyadarsini, S. (1984). Crime news in newspapers: A case study in Tamil Nadu, India. *Deviant Behavior, 5,* 313-326.

Pryor, D., & McGarrell, E. (1993). Public perceptions of youth gang crime. *Youth & Society, 24,* 399-418.

Rankin, J. (1979). Changing attitudes toward capital punishment. *Social Forces, 58,* 194-211.

Ratcliffe, R. G. (1995, August 27). Three million Texans say they'll get a gun permit. *Houston Chronicle,* pp. 1E, 4E.

Reiss, A. J. (1967). *Studies in crime and law enforcement in major metropolitan areas: Vol. 1* (President's Commission on Law Enforcement and Administration of Justice). Washington, DC: Government Printing Office.

Reiss, A. J. (1971). *The police and the public.* New Haven, CT: Yale University Press.

Rennie, Y. L. (1978). *The search for criminal man.* Boston: D. C. Heath.

Reno Police Department. (1992). *July 1992 telephone poll.* Reno: Author.

Riley, P. J., & Rose, V. M. (1980). Public vs. elite opinion on correctional reform: Implications for social policy. *Journal of Criminal Justice, 8,* 345-356.

Roberts, J. V. (1992). Public opinion, crime, and criminal justice. In M. Tonry (Ed.), *Crime and justice: A review of research* (Vol. 16, pp. 99-180). Chicago: University of Chicago Press.

Roll, C. W., & Cantril, A. H. (1972). *Polls: Their use and misuse in politics.* New York: Basic Books.

Rusinko, W. T., Johnson, K. W., & Hornung, C. A. (1978). The importance of police contacts in the formulation of youths' attitudes toward police. *Journal of Criminal Justice, 6*(1), 53-67.

Saad, L. (1994, June). Many Americans caught in emotional grip of O. J. Simpson affair. *Gallup Poll Monthly* (pp. 10-13). Princeton, NJ: Gallup.

Sarat, A. (1977). Studying American legal culture: An assessment of survey evidence. *Law and Society Review, 11,* 427-488.

Saris, W. E. (1991). *Computer-assisted interviewing.* Newbury Park, CA: Sage.

Sawyer, D. O. (1982). Public attitudes toward life and death. *Public Opinion Quarterly, 46,* 521-533.

Scaglion, R., & Condon, R. G. (1980). Determinants of attitudes toward city police. *Criminology, 17,* 485-494.

Schuman, H., & Presser, S. (1981a). The attitude-action connection and the issue of gun control. *Annals of the American Academy of Political and Social Science, 455,* 40-47.

Schuman, H., & Presser, S. (1981b). *Questions and answers in attitude surveys: Experiments on question form, wording, and context.* New York: Academic Press.

Schwartz, I. (1992). Juvenile crime-fighting policies: What the public really wants. In I. Schwartz (Ed.), *Juvenile justice and public policy* (pp. 214-248). New York: Lexington Books.

Schwartz, I. M., Abbey, J. M., & Barton, W. H. (1990). *The perception and reality of juvenile crime in Michigan.* Ann Arbor: University of Michigan, Center for the Study of Youth Policy.

Schwartz, I. M., Guo, S., & Kerbs, J. J. (1993). The impact of demographic variables on public opinion regarding juvenile justice: Implications for public policy. *Crime & Delinquency, 39,* 5-28.

Schwartz, I., Kerbs, J., Hogston, D., & Guillean, C. (1992). *Combating juvenile crime: What the public really wants.* Ann Arbor: University of Michigan, Center for the Study of Youth Policy.

Scott, M. (1992). Residual gains, reliability, and the UCR-NCS relationship: A comment on Blumstein, Cohen, and Rosenfeld (1991). *Criminology, 30,* 105-113.

Seltzer, R., & McCormick, J. P. (1987). The impact of crime victimization and fear of crime on attitudes toward death penalty defendants. *Violence and Victims, 2,* 99-114.

Sherman, R. (1994, April 18). Crime's toll on the U.S.: Fear, despair and guns. *National Law Journal,* pp. A1, A19-A20.

Shriver, J. (1989, June). Frustrated by criminal justice system, public demands harsher penalties. *Gallup Report, 284,* 23-31.

Singer, M. S., & Jonas, A. (1985). Attitudes toward actors in the justice system: Police and students in New Zealand: Part 1. Perceptions of police and university students: A New Zealand Study. *Police Studies, 8*(1), 51-53.

Skogan, W. G. (1990). The polls—A review. *Public Opinion Quarterly, 54,* 256-272.

Skogan, W. G. (1995). Reactions to crime and violence [Preface]. *Annals of the American Academy of Political and Social Science, 539,* 9.

Skogan, W., & Maxfield, M. G. (1981). *Coping with crime: Individual and neighborhood differences.* Beverly Hills, CA: Sage.

Skovron, S. E., Scott, J. E., & Cullen, F. T. (1988). Prison crowding: Public attitudes toward strategies of population control. *Journal of Research in Crime and Delinquency, 25,* 150-169.

Smith, D. A., & Uchida, C. D. (1988). The social organization of self-help. *American Sociological Review, 53,* 94-102.

Smith, L. N., & Hill, G. D. (1991). Victimization and fear of crime. *Criminal Justice and Behavior, 18,* 217-239.

Smith, M. R. (1994). Integrating community policing and the use of force: Public education, involvement, and accountability. *American Journal of Police, 13*(4), 1-21.

Smith, P. E., & Hawkins, R. O. (1973). Victimization, types of citizen-police contacts, and attitudes toward the police. *Law and Society Review, 8,* 135-152.

Smith, T. W. (1978). In search of "house effects": A comparison of responses to various questions by different survey organizations. *Public Opinion Quarterly, 42,* 443-463.

Smith, T. W. (1980). America's most important problem—A trend analysis, 1946-1976. *Public Opinion Quarterly, 44,* 164-180.

Snyder, J. R. (1993). A nation of cowards. *The Public Interest, 113,* 40-55.

Stafford, M. C., & Galle, O. R. (1984). Victimization rates, exposure to risk, and fear of crime. *Criminology, 22,* 173-185.

Steinhart, D. (1988). *N.C.C.D. focus—California opinion poll: Public attitudes on youth crime.* San Francisco: National Council of Crime and Delinquency.

Stinchcombe, A. L., Adams, R., Heimer, C. A., Scheppele, K. L., Smith, T. W., & Taylor, D. G. (1980). *Crime and punishment: Changing attitudes in America.* San Francisco: Jossey-Bass.

Sudman, S., & Bradburn, N. M. (1987). The organizational growth of public opinion research in the United States. *Public Opinion Quarterly, 51*, S67-S78.

Sullivan, P. S., Dunham, R. G., & Alpert, G. P. (1987). Attitude structures of different ethnic and age groups concerning police. *Journal of Criminal Law and Criminology, 78*, 177-196.

Surrette, R. (1992). *Media, crime and criminal justice.* Pacific Grove, CA: Brooks/Cole.

Takata, S., & Zevitz, R. (1987). Youth gangs in Racine: An examination of community perceptions. *Wisconsin Sociologist, 24*, 132-141.

Takata, S., & Zevitz, R. (1990). Divergent perceptions of group delinquency in a midwestern community: Racine's gang problem. *Youth & Society, 21*, 282-305.

Tanur, J. (1991). *Questions about questions: Inquiries into the cognitive bases.* New York: Russell Sage.

Taylor, D. G., Scheppele, K. L., & Stinchcombe, A. L. (1979). Salience of crime and support for harsher criminal sanctions. *Social Problems, 26*, 413-424.

Taylor, R. B., & Hale, M. (1986). Testing alternative models of fear of crime. *Journal of Criminal Law and Criminology, 77*, 151-189.

Thomas, C. W., & Hyman, J. M. (1977). Perceptions of crime, fear of victimization, and public perceptions of police performance. *Journal of Police Science and Administration, 5*, 305-317.

Traugott, M. (1992). The impact of media polls on the public. In T. Mann & G. Orren (Eds.), *Media polls in American politics* (pp. 125-149). Washington, DC: Brookings Institution.

Treaster, J. B. (1994, June 19). Study says anti-drug dollars are best spent on treatment. *New York Times*, sec. 1, p. 19.

Trojanowicz, R. C., & Banas, D. W. (1985). *The impact of foot patrol on black and white perceptions of policing.* Lansing, MI: National Neighborhood Foot Patrol Center.

Tyler, T. R., & Weber, R. (1982). Support for the death penalty: Instrumental response to crime, or symbolic attitude? *Law and Society Review, 17*, 21-45.

U.S. Bureau of the Census. (1990). *Census of population and housing.* Washington, DC: Government Printing Office.

U.S. Department of Justice. (1995). *The nations' correctional population tops 5 million* (No. NCJ-1564432) [Press release]. Washington, DC: Author.

Uslaner, E., & Weber, R. (1979). U.S. state legislator opinions and perceptions of constituency attitudes. *Legislative Studies Quarterly, 4*, 563-585.

Vidmar, N., & Ellsworth, P. (1974). Public opinion and the death penalty. *Stanford Law Review, 26*, 1245-1270.

Waddington, P. A. J., & Braddock, Q. (1991). Guardians or bullies? Perceptions of the police amongst adolescent black, white, and Asian boys. *Policing and Society, 2*, 31-45.

Walklate, S. (1992). Jack and Jill join up at Sun Hill: Public images of police officers. *Policing and Society, 2*, 219-232.

Warr, M. (1984). Fear of victimization: Why are women and elderly more afraid? *Social Science Quarterly, 65*, 681-702.

Warr, M. (1990). Dangerous situations: Social context and fear of victimization. *Social Forces, 68*, 891-907.

Warr, M. (1995). The polls—Poll trends: Public opinion on crime and punishment. *Public Opinion Quarterly, 59*, 296-310.

Warr, M., & Stafford, M. (1984). Public goals of punishment and support for the death penalty. *Journal of Research in Crime and Delinquency, 21*, 95-111.

White, M. F., & Menke, B. A. (1978). A critical analysis of surveys on public opinions toward police agencies. *Journal of Police Science and Administration, 6*, 204-218.

Wilkins, L. T. (1974). Directions for corrections. *Proceedings of the American Philosophical Society, 118*, 235-247.

Wilkins, L. T. (1984). *Consumerist criminology*. New York: Barnes & Noble.

Will, J. A., & McGrath, J. H. (1995). Crime, neighborhood perceptions, and the underclass: The relationship between fear of crime and class position. *Journal of Criminal Justice, 23*, 163-176.

Williams, F. P., Longmire, D. R., & Gulick, D. B. (1988). The public and the death penalty: Opinion as an artifact of question type. *Criminal Justice Research Bulletin, 3*, 1-5.

Williams, J. S., Thomas, C. W., & Singh, B. K. (1983). Situational use of police force: Public relations. *American Journal of Police, 3*(1), 37-50.

Williams, P. (1993). Fear of crime: Read all about it? The relationship between newspaper crime reporting and fear of crime. *British Journal of Criminology, 33*, 33-56.

Wiltz, C. J. (1982). Fear of crime, criminal victimization and elderly blacks. *Phylon, 43*, 283-294.

Winfree, L. T., & Griffiths, C. T. (1977). Adolescents attitudes toward the police: A survey of high school students. In T. N. Ferdinand (Ed.), *Juvenile delinquency: Little brother grows up* (pp. 79-99). Beverly Hills, CA: Sage.

Wood, F. W. (Ed.). (1990). *An American profile—Opinions and behavior, 1972-1989*. Detroit, New York, London: Gale Research.

Wright, J. D. (1984). The ownership of firearms for reasons of self-defense. In D. B. Kates (Ed.), *Firearms and violence: Issues of public policy* (pp. 301-327). Cambridge, MA: Ballinger.

Xu, M., Bates, B. J., & Schweitzer, J. C. (1993). The impact of messages on survey participation in answering machine households. *Public Opinion Quarterly, 57*, 232-237.

Yankelovich, Skelly, and White, Inc. (1978). Highlights of a national survey of the general public, judges, lawyers, and community leaders. In T. J. Fetter (Ed.), *State courts: A blueprint for the future* (pp. 5-69). Williamsburg, VA: National Center for State Courts.

Yarmey, D. A. (1991). Retrospective perceptions of policing following victimization. *Canadian Police College Journal, 15*, 137-143.

Yeric, J. L., & Todd, J. R. (1983). *Public opinion: The visible politics*. Itasca, IL: F. E. Peacock.

Yin, P. (1980). Fear of crime among the elderly: Some issues and suggestions. *Social Problems, 27*, 492-504.

Young, R. L. (1991). Race, conceptions of crime and justice, and support for the death penalty. *Social Psychology Quarterly, 54*(1), 67-75.

Young, R. L. (1992). Religious orientation, race and support for the death penalty. *Journal for the Scientific Study of Religion, 31*(1), 76-87.

Zamble, E., & Annesley, P. (1987). Some determinants of public attitudes toward the police. *Journal of Police Science and Administration, 15*, 285-290.

Zevitz, R. G., & Rettammel, R. J. (1990). Elderly attitudes about police service. *American Journal of Police, 9*, 25-39.

About the Editors

Timothy J. Flanagan, Ph.D., is Professor of Criminal Justice and Dean of the College of Criminal Justice at Sam Houston State University, where he is also Director of the university's Criminal Justice Center. Flanagan directed the project that produced the *Sourcebook of Criminal Justice Statistics* on behalf of the U.S. Department of Justice from 1977 to 1991 and has published scores of journal articles, reviews, edited books, and research reports. His research focuses on the effectiveness of correctional programs, criminal justice statistics, public opinion on justice issues, and criminal justice higher education. His most recent work, *Long-Term Imprisonment: Issues of Science, Policy and Correctional Practice,* was published by Sage Publications in April 1995.

Dennis R. Longmire is Professor of Criminal Justice and Director of the Survey Research Program at Sam Houston State University's College of Criminal Justice. He received his Ph.D. from the University of Maryland's Institute of Criminal Justice and Criminology in 1979. His current research interests include public attitude studies about crime, criminals and the administration of justice, and the use of popular literature in criminal justice education.

About the Contributors

Kenneth Adams is Associate Professor and Assistant Dean of Graduate Studies in the College of Criminal Justice at Sam Houston State University. He received his Ph.D. in criminal justice from the State University of New York at Albany. He currently is directing an NIJ-sponsored evaluation of gun purchase background checks in Florida.

Myrna Cintrón is Assistant Professor of Criminal Justice at Sam Houston State University. She received her Ph.D. in criminology from Florida State University in 1991. Her primary research interests include the abuse and control of drugs and ethnic issues in criminal justice.

James A. Dyer is Associate Professor in the Department of Political Science and Senior Study Director in the Public Policy Research Institute at Texas A&M University. He received his Ph.D. from the University of Minnesota. He has conducted numerous surveys on criminal justice, health, race relations, substance abuse, and other social issues and is the coauthor of *An Introduction to Political Science Methods*.

Simone Engelhardt-Greer is pursuing her M.A. degree in criminal justice at Sam Houston State University. She received her B.S. degree in criminal justice and criminology from East Tennessee State University in 1994. Her areas of interest include research, theory, juvenile delinquency, victimology, and crime prevention.

Jurg Gerber is Assistant Dean for Undergraduate Studies and Associate Professor, College of Criminal Justice, Sam Houston State University. He received his Ph.D. in sociology from Washington State University in 1988. His primary research interests involve corporate crime, drugs, and drug control policy. Recent publications have appeared in *Social Justice* and the *Journal of Offender Rehabilitation.*

Bahram Haghighi is Associate Professor of Criminal Justice at the University of Texas–Pan American. He received his Ph.D. in criminal justice from Sam Houston State University in 1985. His research interests include parole release, correctional industries, and victimology.

W. S. Wilson Huang is Assistant Professor in the Department of Criminal Justice at Georgia State University. He received his Ph.D. in criminal justice and criminology in 1990 from the University of Maryland, College Park. His research interests include international crime statistics, inequality and violence, and computer mapping.

W. Wesley Johnson is Assistant Professor of Criminal Justice at Sam Houston State University. He received his Ph.D. from Florida State University in 1992. His research interests include substance abuse and control, corrections, and social control.

Laura B. Myers is Assistant Professor of Criminal Justice at Sam Houston State University. She received her Ph.D. in criminology from Florida State University in 1990. Her research areas include criminal justice ethics, criminal justice education, cultural diversity, and criminal courts. Recent publications include an article on sentencing disparity and county context in the *Journal of Criminal Justice* and an article on computer use in criminal justice academic programs in the *Journal of Criminal Justice Education.*

Barbara Sims is a doctoral student in criminal justice at Sam Houston State University, where she serves as Coordinator of the Criminal Justice Center's Survey Research Program. Her research and teaching interests include public opinion research on crime and criminal justice, the development and evaluation of criminological theory, issues of punishment in the American criminal justice system, and the relationship of race/ethnicity, gender, and socioeconomic status to crime.

Jon Sorensen is Associate Professor of Criminal Justice at the University of Texas–Pan American. He received his Ph.D. in criminal justice from Sam Houston State University in 1990. His research interests include capital punishment and homicide.

Ruth Triplett is Assistant Professor at Sam Houston State University. She received her Ph.D. in criminology from the University of Maryland, College Park in 1990. Her research interests include labeling theory, symbolic interaction, and gender in criminological theory.

Michael S. Vaughn is Assistant Professor in the Department of Criminal Justice at Georgia State University. He received his Ph.D. in criminal justice from Sam Houston State University in 1993. His research interests include legal issues in criminal justice and cross-cultural crime.